Robert le Diable
The Ballet of the Nuns

Robert le Diable
The Ballet of the Nuns

BALLET BY

FILIPPO TAGLIONI
NOTATED BY AUGUST BOURNONVILLE

MUSIC BY

GIACOMO MEYERBEER

RECONSTRUCTED BY

KNUD ARNE JÜRGENSEN

LABANOTATION AND PERFORMANCE NOTES BY

ANN HUTCHINSON GUEST

THE NOVERRE PRESS

First published in 1997

This edition published in 2016 by
The Noverre Press
Southwold House
Isington Road
Binsted
Hampshire
GU34 4PH

Copyright © 2016 by Ann Hutchinson Guest and Knud Arne Jürgensen.

ISBN 978-1-906830-76-2

Permission for public performance must be obtained in writing from Knud Arne Jürgensen and Ann Hutchinson Guest, Language of Dance Centre, 17 Holland Park, London W11 3TD, United Kingdom.

No part of this book may be reproduced or utilized in any form or by any means, electronic or mechanical, including photocopying and recording, or by any information storage or retrieval system, without permission in writing from the publishers. Printed in India

Permissions for illustrations and photographs given by:
Bibliothèque des Arts Décoratifs, Paris (front cover, page 9)
Bibliothèque Historique de la Ville, Paris (page 22)
Bibliothèque Nationale de France, Paris (pages 7, 20, 21)
Dance Collection, The New York Public Library for the Performing Arts, Astor, Lenox and Tilden Foundation (page 9)
Nic Espinosa (page 16)
Museo Teatrale alla Scala, Milan (page 4)
The Royal Library of Copenhagen (pages x, 11, 12, 14, 170, 171, 172)
S. Thorbek (page x)
The Vaganova School, St. Petersburg (page 19)
Count Arvid Wachtmeister (page 9)

Peter Teigen for moments in the ballet located in the dance score (pages 67, 69, 73, 85, 92, 97, 103, 109, 113, 120, 123, 126, 134, 139, 141, 145, 146, 151, 155, 157, 159, 163)

Cover Photo: Statuette by Ambroise René Maréchal of Louise Fitzjames as the Abbess Héléna in Act III of *Robert le Diable* (Paris 1841).

In recognition of his life-long dedication to notate
and to preserve the ballets of his own time
this volume is dedicated to the memory of

AUGUST BOURNONVILLE

CONTENTS

Introduction to the Series ix

Foreword xi

Acknowledgements xiii

Introduction 1

Historical Background 5
    The Task of Reconstruction 15

Augmenting the Dance Heritage 17

Production Notes 20
    Historical 20
    Contemporary 28

The Plot 29

Study and Performance Notes 31

Labanotation Glossary 55

The Choreographic Score of *Robert le Diable - The Ballet of the Nuns* 59
    Bacchanale 61
    Allegro Vivace 96
    1er Air de Ballet 113
    2me Air de Ballet 130
    3me Air de Ballet 144

Appendix A - The Sources 165

Appendix B - Giacomo Meyerbeer's Notes in his Musical Drafts 169

Appendix C - Examples of Bournonville's Dance Notations 170

Appendix D - August Bournonville's and Emil Hansen's Production Notes . . . 173

Appendix E - The Original Danish and French Texts 187

Appendix F - Notes on Adjustments Made for the Reconstruction 190

Appendix G - The Piano Score 191

INTRODUCTION TO THE SERIES

The *Language of Dance Series* aims to expand the literature of dance through publication of key works that cover a range of dance styles and dance periods.

A language is spoken, written and read. Those intimately involved in the study and performance of dance will have experienced the language of dance in its 'spoken' form, i.e. when it is danced. During the years spent in mastering dance, the component parts are discovered and become part of one's dance language. Through its written form these component parts, the 'building blocks' common to all forms of dance become clear, as well as how these blocks are used. The study of the Language of Dance incorporates these basic elements and the way they are put together to produce choreographic sentences. How the movement sequences are performed, the manner of 'uttering' them, rests on the individual's interpretation.

Through careful selection of appropriate movement description, these gems of dance heritage have been translated into Labanotation, the highly developed method of analyzing and recording movement.

In the *Language of Dance Series* understanding of the material is enriched through study and performance notes, which provide an aid in exploring the movement sequences and bringing the choreography to life. Whenever possible there is included historical background to place the work in context, as well as additional information of value to researchers and dance scholars.

Dr. Ann Hutchinson Guest, Editor

Dr. Knud Arne Jürgensen at work in the Royal Library, Copenhagen.

Excerpt with A. Bournonville's notation in the *répétiteur's* copy for the third solo variation of the abbess Héléna in Act III of *Robert af Normandiet* (Copenhagen 1873).

FOREWORD

Here, in these pages, a precious segment from balletic history, long thought to be irretrievably lost, is brought out of oblivion and presented, for the first time, for scholarly study and performance.

The Ballet of the Nuns from Meyerbeer's grand opera, *Robert le Diable*, which made theatrical history in its time and is today recognized as one of the seminal works of the Romantic ballet, was long believed to have been lost, in the sense that its choreography had been forgotten, apparently beyond recall. But happily, lying unsuspected in the Royal Library, Copenhagen, until the Danish dance historian, Knud Arne Jürgensen, rediscovered it, a record did exist - in the form of notes on Filippo Taglioni's choreography for the Ballet of the Nuns, made by the ballet-master, August Bournonville, when visiting Paris in 1841.

Bournonville's manuscript, in his own choreographic shorthand, is sufficiently specific to be deciphered with some accuracy by a specialist in the Bournonville style of the period. There can be no one better qualified for this task than Knud Arne Jürgensen, who is known for his magistral works on the Bournonville school and repertory. Not content with just publishing these notes verbatim, Jürgensen decided to put them to the practical test of working them out on dancers - an essential process in any historical reconstruction. To record his reading of the text he sought the collaboration of Ann Hutchinson Guest, the foremost authority on dance notation, to translate it into Labanotation in the most careful detail. Accompanied by an account of the ballet's creation at the Paris Opéra in 1831 based on Knud Arne Jürgensen's meticulous research, and by detailed analytical performance notes supplied by Ann Hutchinson Guest, this dance score enables us to recapture some of the magic that Romanticism brought to the art of ballet more than a century and a half ago.

Knud Arne Jürgensen and Ann Hutchinson Guest have once again put those who treasure the traditions of ballet in their debt.

Ivor Guest

Portrait of August Bournonville (1842)
by Emilius Bærentzen.
(Courtesy of Knud Arne Jürgensen, Copenhagen)

ACKNOWLEDGEMENTS

First we must recognize our indebtedness to August Bournonville for his painstaking recording in his dance notation method the Ballet of the Nuns from *Robert le Diable* which he had seen in Paris in 1841 and 1847. Without his notations we would have no knowledge of the content of that historic ballet, and our dance heritage would be the poorer.

In working out the solo dances for the Abbess, Héléna, we were fortunate to secure the interest and cooperation of Royal Danish Ballet dancer and present Deputy Director of that company, Benedikte Paaske. Through her artistry the choreography came to life and we could appreciate how delightful these solos are.

For the *corps de ballet* section we are grateful to the late Bridget Espinosa who so kindly made seventeen advanced students available to us for a week at the London Studio Centre. These rehearsals provided the opportunity to get this section notated and for Jean Johnson Jones to gain experience in notating during a rehearsal situation. Our thanks go to Jean for pulling together the first pencil draft of the score. It was at this time we were fortunate enough to be awarded a grant from the Radcliffe Trust for the notating of the ballet and organization of the material. Jürgensen's experience and success in producing this ballet in Italy and Russia indicated the importance of making this heritage available for study.

For the many beautiful photographs by Peter Teigen, illustrating the ballet, we are indebted to Harold King, Artistic Director of London City Ballet, to his staff and to the dancers of that company who provided the opportunity to record the many significant moments in the choreography. Particular mention should be made of Virginnia Viney and Marius Els who at short notice took on the parts of Héléna and Robert.

We are indebted to Ivor Guest for the translations of the French texts for inclusion in the book and also for his advice on iconography and verification of historical facts. The music on each page of the Labanotation score was engraved by Tim Crawford.

The meticulous checking of the book, in particular the Labanotation score, by Ray Cook will facilitate future study and revival of the ballet - our appreciation goes to him for the hours he spent on this task.

Our thanks go also to Roma Dispirito who has had the major responsibility in producing the score on CALABAN (the Computer Aided Labanotation system developed by Andy Adamson at Birmingham University, UK) and also in producing the camera-ready copy of the book, the special appendices and, in particular, her careful handling of the Danish text, so unfamiliar to her. We appreciate the rôle which Jane Dulieu played as Roma's mentor, her careful checking and proofreading of the book.

Ann Hutchinson Guest, Knud Arne Jürgensen
November 1996

INTRODUCTION

by Ivor Guest

In the triumph of Romanticism on the French stage two productions shine out like beacons to highlight the infectious new movement that was carrying all before it when Charles X, last of the Bourbon kings, fled into exile in 1830. The first of these was Victor Hugo's drama, *Ernani*, which won the battle - and a battle it was, with champions of the old and the new literally at each other's throats - at the Comédie-Française in 1830; and the other, Meyerbeer's grand opera, *Robert le Diable*, which one year later no less decisively established Romanticism on the stage of a newly invigorated Paris Opéra.

The juxtaposition of these two occasions might suggest a change of revolutionary character, but they were only events in a gradually changing aesthetic, for Romanticism had been insinuating itself in literature, music and art for ten years and more in a gradually evolving process. Indeed its roots could be traced further back still, for an aesthetic movement does not burst forth out of nothing, but is gestated gradually as new ideas shape themselves alongside those long established to fuse into the spirit of a new age. So it was with Romanticism, which was basically a movement of revolt, pitted by a younger generation against what they saw as the over-formalised precepts and attitudes of their elders.

In the field of ballet the neo-classical works of Gardel that had for long dominated the Opéra began to lose their appeal in the 1820s, as a public in which the senior and more conservative element was increasingly giving way to a younger generation that was yearning for more stimulating, more expressive approaches. Already there were indications of rejuvenation in the ballet. In 1827 the Opéra had engaged Marie Taglioni, a young ballerina with a style that was excitingly and refreshingly free of academic conventions and held promise of a more poetic approach to her art, while in the commercial theatres such as the Porte-Saint-Martin new talent was emerging - a brilliant young dancer called Perrot, and the choreographer, Jean Coralli.

The newly appointed Director of the Opéra, Louis Véron, made some important changes in the ballet. He gave Taglioni, previously merely one of six *premières danseuses*, a new contract which acknowledged her supremacy; he terminated the contract of the former ballet-master, Jean Aumer, and engaged Coralli in his place; and he acceded to Taglioni's wish that her father should choreograph the ballets in which she would dance. These moves preceded the production of *Robert le Diable*, in which, as was obligatory at the Opéra, an important ballet scene would be featured, and would be produced, not by Coralli, but by Filippo Taglioni.

This scene, the Ballet of the Nuns, would break new ground in the manner in which it was wedded to the opera's plot. Far from being a conventional *divertissement* inserted as an interlude while the action was suspended, it crystallised a decisive moment in the drama in a manner that singing could never have so effectively achieved. The Mephistopholean figure of Bertram has brought Robert to a ruined cloister to steal a magic branch from the reclining statue of a saint that will give him the power to gain the object of his desire. First, Bertram enters alone to invoke the spirits of long-dead nuns who in their life-time had broken their vows. At his bidding the spectral figures appear in their white habits, which are cast off to reveal the simple dance costumes they are wearing underneath. There then follows a long bacchanalian scene in which, encouraged by their abbess, Héléna, they give rein to their depravity. At the moment when Bertram brings in Robert, they conceal themselves. At the sight of the magic talisman, Robert is filled with trepidation. Thinking he recognises his mother's angry expression in the features of the statue, he is on the point of leaving when the nuns reappear. Then follows the ballet itself, as the abbess exerts her charms to tempt him to seize the branch. Finally she leads him to the tomb, allowing him to steal a kiss as she points to the talisman that is his for the taking. Once he has it in his hand, life seems to ebb away from the nuns who return to the tombs from whence they came.

The triumph of the Ballet of the Nuns was all the more exceptional in its time for being achieved by a collaboration of remarkable distinction: Taglioni and his daughter, the choreographer and his muse, who revealed themselves as the most potent partnership; the producer, Henri Duponchel, to whom was due the conception of the cloister scene (replacing the pallid classical setting that was originally planned), and Pierre-Luc Charles Cicéri, the most celebrated designer of his time: and of course Meyerbeer himself and his experienced librettists, Eugène Scribe and Germain Delavigne. All these talents miraculously came together in a collective process of creation that prefigured the artistic collaborations that were to distinguish the Diaghilev Ballet eighty years later.

The Ballet of the Nuns that resulted was to be acknowledged as the precursor of the *ballets blancs* that would be such a feature of the new type of ballet that was to capture the imagination of the public for generations to come. It could truly be said that it marked the birth of the Romantic Ballet. The white-clad spirits that flitted in a mysterious glow achieved by the newly-invented gas-lighting presented a vision in which the dancers themselves appeared insubstantial and their movements unearthly - a weightless, skimming flight that for many achieved a poetic exaltation.

Thus, it seems, was born the costume that became the basic model for sylphides, wilis, peris, naiads, dryads and other elemental spirits that populated the ballet stage of the nineteenth century. The absence of a costume design for *La Sylphide* has long intrigued dance historians. The sleep-walking costume worn by Pauline Montessu in *La Somnambule* (1827) certainly foreshadows the *ballet blanc*, but that of the nuns in *Robert le Diable* was an even more obvious precursor. It leads one to wonder whether, when the white habits had been cast aside, the dancers appeared merely in the plain white costume they normally wore for class and rehearsal, such as that in which Fanny Elssler was drawn to by her friend, Mrs Grote[1] - a costume that could boast of no designer.

Strangely, however, Marie Taglioni seems to have had little enthusiasm for her rôle as the abbess. After the first three performances she withdrew, pleading injury to her foot, and her understudy, Amélie Legallois, took over. Meyerbeer believed she wanted to give up the part, and lodged an objection, asserting his contractual right that none of the major characters was to be played by an understudy during the first six performances. The ballerina graciously did the right thing, and in December resumed the part of the abbess; but after playing it just three times more to fulfil her obligations, she then relinquished it, never to dance it in Paris again.

Meyerbeer may have guessed correctly that she was distracted by the preparations that had already begun for *La Sylphide*, the ballet that was to become synonymous with her name and seal her reputation as the most celebrated ballerina of her age, but her withdrawal from *Robert le Diable* seems so final that it is hard not to suspect some distaste for the rôle of the temptress Héléna. At the end of her first rehearsal with Adolphe Nourrit, the tenor who played Robert, she had wept from nervous exhaustion, and it is possible that this scene continued to drain her emotional energies to such an extent as to become a trial from which she longed to be released. Obviously much more comfortable with the sentimental rôle of the sylphide which she was then beginning to learn, she may well have found the conflict between the two personalities too much to bear and grasped at the opportunity to divest herself in the one that was uncongenial.

The idea of presenting on stage a bevy of lapsed nuns revelling in their mortal sins and tempting Robert to commit an act of sacrilege might have appeared shocking to the more devout, but to a public accustomed to the melodramas of the boulevard theatres, and familiar with the popular translations of English "gothic" horror novels, it appears to have been found generally unobjectionable.

In the event *Robert le Diable* immediately became one of the most popular operas in the French repertory,[2] being given more than 750 times before it was finally dropped in 1893. Arthur Saint-Léon revised the choreography in 1870, but seemingly retained the general flavour of the original, for Théophile Gautier was still able to wax enthusiastic over the mysterious entrance of the nuns - despite a sudden flood of electric light at the moment when Robert is being tempted. Degas too was entranced, and in the 1870's painted two canvasses showing, from the second or third row of the orchestra stalls, the entrance of the nuns before casting off their habits.

A revival of *Robert le Diable* was presented at the Paris Opéra in 1985, but the truncated ballet scene was a sad parody which deserves no more than to be passed over in silence. The opera itself was received with enthusiasm, and in the present climate, with Meyerbeer being recognised as the major figure of French Romantic grand opera, a revival is surely overdue. Let us hope that when that comes about, the opera will be staged with proper respect for the lyric, choreographic and scenic components which, between them, make up the entirety of a work born of an exceptional artistic collaboration.

Notes

1. Reproduced in Ivor Guest, *Fanny Elssler* (London, 1970).

2. In the course of more than three centuries only four operas have been more frequently performed at the Paris Opéra: Meyerbeer's *Les Huguenots*, Gounod's *Faust*, Saint-Saëns' *Samson et Dalila*, and Verdi's *Rigoletto*.

Portrait of Giacomo Meyerbeer (1830s).

Portrait of Filippo Taglioni (1830s).
(Courtesy of Museo Teatrale alla Scala, Milan)

HISTORICAL BACKGROUND

by Knud Arne Jürgensen

"The first white ballet".

This is the term generally used to describe Filippo Taglioni's Act III ballet *divertissement* in Giacomo Meyerbeer's five-act grand opera *Robert le Diable* (premièred at the Paris Opéra on November 21, 1831).[1]

Certainly, this divertissement had an exceptionally important influence on the course of ballet history. Not only was it created for one of the greatest ballerinas of all time, Marie Taglioni, but it also portrayed a completely new and richer vision of a subterranean world of fantasy in which the religious and the profane were depicted with an audacity never before seen on stage. With its setting in a moonlit cloister and its theme of lapsed nuns being summoned from their tombs to dance a ghostly *Bacchanale*, it was the precursor of the *ballets blancs* that were such a feature of ballet in the Romantic period, in particular *La Sylphide* (premièred only four months later on March 12, 1832), and *Giselle* (1841).

The choreography of this ghostly scene shows how the erotic and the demonic - often tightly interwoven - were essential features in the artistic physiognomy of the period. In the third act of *Robert le Diable*, the hero goes to find a magic charm which can only be obtained through the intercession of a band of dead nuns. Diabolically benevolent, the nuns, having forsaken their religious vows, can communicate with the forces of evil to obtain the needed talisman.

Much has been written and said about this divertissement and its significance in ballet history, but until recently little has been known about its actual choreography and the dance style of this epoch-making ballet. The hesitation of leading scholars to deal in depth with the aesthetics and the dramaturgical aspects of this ballet is beyond doubt based on the fact that, until now, no truly reliable historical sources have come to light that allow for a study of this ballet in terms of its actual steps and movements on the stage. Moreover, only very few written sources have been preserved which can tell in depth about the genesis and the creative process of The Ballet of the Nuns.

In his book *The Romantic Ballet in Paris*[2] Ivor Guest reconstructs the story of the creation of the ballet and its first performance. From there we learn that the sections for the *corps de ballet* were mounted in six weeks, while the ballerina's part (the abbess Héléna) was created in less than three weeks.

One of the most important primary sources for the study of the original contents and the genesis of the work is Meyerbeer's autographed music sketch for this scene[3]. There the composer inserted a great number of production notes concerning the ballet's *mise-en-scène*. These notes are mingled with other indications expressing his wishes for the contents and the exact nature of both the choreography and the pantomime. Through these notes it becomes clear that the scene in *Robert le Diable* where the hero finds the talisman that will win him the love of the Princess Isabelle, was originally conceived in a rather conventional mythological manner. Thus, in Meyerbeer's notes the character of the abbess Héléna is named "Lea" (or "Leà") which beyond doubt is a reminder of the original wish of the Paris Opéra director, Louis

Véron, to insert a more conventional mythological dance scene in Act III of *Robert le Diable*. That project, however, was changed at an early stage into the moonlit cloister scene of St. Rosalie as a result of the intervention of Henri Duponchel (the then head of the scenery and costume department of the Opéra) who vivaciously protested against Véron's original mythological theme for this ballet[4].

From Filippo Taglioni's 1831 diary[5] we know that the first rehearsal of the ballet was held on October 6th 1831. Meyerbeer's notes in the music drafts can consequently be dated to shortly before this date. They not only provide many precious details about the pantomime performed by the nuns during the *recitatives* of Robert, but they also reveal how closely Meyerbeer collaborated with the choreographer when composing this ballet. An example of this is evidenced in his note inserted in the drafts underneath a section of twelve bars that originally constituted the end of what later became the first solo-variation of the abbess Héléna. It reads as follows:

"If Mr. Taglioni finds this piece too long, one can always omit what is between the two asterisques."

This clear sensitivity on the composer's part of achieving the closest degree of affinity between music and choreography certainly constituted one of the main reasons for the extraordinary success of this ballet. Only rarely did a ballet *divertissement* created within a large operatic context receive so much attention and care from its music composer as is the case with this work. This refined interaction between music and choreography is also revealed in the words of the reviewer of *Journal des Débats,* who reported about the ballet on 16.12.1831:

The scene changes, to show the cloister with its deep and sombre vaults and the burial place of the nuns of St. Rosalie. The musical accompaniment changes too; trombones and bassoons are heard in unison, their solemn, funereal strains announcing the arrival of Bertram; and the cellos and bassoons in concert add their sad, severe harmony to the obligatory recitative sung by that spirit of darkness. This invocation is one of great beauty:

> For just an hour, leave your funerary bier,
> Oh nuns, arise!

And the nuns, obeying the discretionary power of their overload, rise up and, little by little, resume an ephemeral existence, and - since the Devil has not restored their faculty of speech, fearing they might have the whim to tell us about their lives - they remain silent, leaving it to the orchestra to depict their feelings and to add a second interpretation to their gestures by inviting their expressive pantomime. Only the singing of the instruments strikes the ear during this long and beautiful scene, whose charm, picturesque imagery, varied colours and details that are full of spirit and strength of sentiment, creates a profound impression on the soul. The grandeur of the music heightens in immense progression the splendour of the scenery and the seductive quality of the pantomime.

As the nuns rise up, the bassoons alone play a passage with a rising melody that follows the movement of the statues as they slowly describe a quarter-circle to arrive at a perpendicular position. Double basses playing *pizzicato* and muted trombones follow in the mysterious course indicated by the bassoons. Gradually the orchestra comes to life with all the instruments successively joining in, and the minor key, which has dominated throughout this electrifying and fantastic operation, suddenly gives way to a resounding ensemble in C major, and the restoration of E natural indicates to less intelligent listeners that the ladies are coming to life and announce that they have once again become women of the world. The nuns are aware that they only have 59 minutes grace; they are none the sadder for that, and hasten to make the most of the time Master Lucifer has kindly granted them. These merry sisters begin by casting off their veils and their long habits, revealing only their light ballet skirts. Each of them drinks deeply of Cyprus wine or Val de Pegnas to refresh her mouth in which spiders have perhaps been spinning their webs; this gives them the courage to dance, and here they are spinning like tops, dancing rounds and the farandole, and disporting themselves like women possessed. This rousing gallop, to a 6/8 melody in D minor with triangle accompaniment, and all the merry making necessarily takes place in a sepulchral gloom. (*See* Appendix E)

HISTORICAL BACKGROUND 7

Lithograph of the original décor for Act III in *Robert le Diable* (Paris 1831). This scene is of The Procession of the Nuns which procedes the actual ballet.

Costume drawing by G. Lepaulle for the Nuns in Act III of *Robert le Diable* (Paris 1831).
(Cliché Bibliothèque Nationale de France, Paris)

Another important source for the study of the original *mise en scène* of Filippo Taglioni's ballet is a contemporary manuscript, a staging manual for *Robert le Diable* (now in Bibliothèque Historique de la Ville, Paris). It holds a detailed description of the general stage movements throughout the entire Act III finale that reveals many important details not found elsewhere (*see* Production Notes, pp. 22-23). Filippo Taglioni himself, however, is rather sparse in his comments about the creation of this ballet. In his diary only three encounters with Meyerbeer are listed. They are followed by four rehearsals of the ballet, and a description of its first performance reading as follows:

7.8.1831: "I have been to Mayer Beer's to hear the music he has composed for Robert the Devil."
20.8: "On the 20th I went to Mayer Beer's, he played me the music of the seduction scene of the nuns from Robert the Devil destined for my daughter, this music is charming."
6.10: "The 6th. 1st rehearsal of the scene of the nuns."
15.10: "The 15th. I presented Mayer Beer to my daughter."
22.10: "Rehearsal of the scene of the nuns with costumes. It did not go as I would have wished. I began the entrance of Robert (Nourrit)."
31.10: "Began the seduction scene with my daughter."
6.11: "6th Rehearsal of the nuns with Nourrit. Marie wept because the rehearsal had over-tired her."
21.11: "21 November. First performance of Robert the Devil [...] In the scene change from the grotto to the cloister, the cloud curtain which rises while the scenery is being changed, the ropes which held up this curtain, being hitched up cross-wise, broke, and the whole cloth fell on the tomb where my daughter was lying, who happily was saved." (*See* Appendix E)

Robert le Diable became an instant success in Paris and was soon after also mounted all over Europe; it received more than four-hundred-and-seventy performances in Paris alone during Meyerbeer's lifetime. The essential part played by the ballet in this extraordinary success of the opera becomes evident from a letter written on December 2, 1831 by the composer to Véron only a fortnight after the Paris première. Having learned from the poster on that day that Marie Taglioni was no longer announced in the rôle of the abbess Héléna he somewhat angrily, but politely, wrote:

"I venture, Monsieur, to rely on your spirit of justice and the interest you show in the authors that as from Monday you will no longer give "Robert" without Mlle Taglioni. As I am personally convinced that Mlle Taglioni is indispensable for the complete success of this work, I care about this with all my heart and soul and insist on it, particularly since the regulations and my contact formally entitle me to it." (*See* Appendix E)

The rôle of the abbess was danced by Taglioni only six times, after which it was taken over by the French ballerina, Louise Fitzjames, who danced it 232 times. The reason for this change of cast may perhaps have been caused by Taglioni having already begun rehearsing her father's new ballet *La Sylphide* in this same period. Or it may have resulted from the fact, that what this ballerina probably lacked most in the rôle, was the kind of bizarre erotic charisma needed for this strange 'religious' female devil. Perhaps Taglioni also felt that the rôle of the malevolent abbess was too much in contrast with that of the benevolent *Sylphide*, the creation of which completely absorbed her energies during this period. Subsequently she may herself have asked to be released from this part in *Robert le Diable*. Whatever the case, her successor clearly seem to have possessed the kind of erotic charisma needed for the rôle of the abbess since Louise Fitzjames was to perform this strange supernatural part more than two-hundred times during the following years. For the 1832 production of *Robert der Teufel* in Berlin, Meyerbeer provided additional music for Taglioni who again danced the rôle of the abbess.

Pastel miniature by Erik Ruuth of Marie Taglioni as the abbess Héléna in *Robert af Normanndie* at Stockholm's Royal Theater (Operahuset), September 20, 1841. The fine details of the original costume can be seen here. It is part of a series of five miniatures showing scenes from Taglioni's guest appearances in the summer of 1841. It was first reproduced in Mary Skeaping and Anna Greta Ståhle, *Balett på Stockholmsoperan* (P. A. Norstedt & Söners Förlag, Stockholm, 1979). The original is now preserved at the Christineholm manor house, Sörmland, Sweden.

(Count Arvid Wachtmeister)

(New York Public Library)

Eugénie Lecomte, who danced Héléna in the New York production of *Robert le Diable* in 1837. This print by E. W. Clay, was an early example of a titillating publicity stunt; she did not actually dance bare-breasted.

Statuette by Ambroise René Maréchal showing Louise Fitzjames as the abbess Héléna in Act III of *Robert le Diable* (Paris 1841).
(Reproduced by permission of Bibliothèque des Arts Décoratifs, Paris)

Scene with Marie Taglioni and A. Nourrit in Act III of *Robert le Diable* (Paris 1831). This moment reflects meas. 222 - 224, page 129.

(Ivor Guest collection)

(Private collection, Copenhagen)

This lithograph is drawn by Schoeller and lithographed by Andreas Geiger in Vienna, 1833. It shows the final scene of the Act III ballet in the 1832 Vienna production of *Robert der Teufel* and was first published in Adolph Bäuerle's *Wiener Theaterzeitung* as part of a series named "Gallerie interessanter und drolliger Scenen".

In the spring of 1841, the Danish choreographer and ballet-master, August Bournonville, visited Paris and saw (according to his travel-diary) Fitzjames performing as the abbess Héléna three times at the Paris Opéra. During a later visit to the French capital in 1847 he again attended several performances of this work.

Once back in Denmark Bournonville notated the choreography of Fitzjames' performance in a Danish *répétiteur's* music copy of Meyerbeer's opera. This volume (which dates from the first 1833 Danish performance of Meyerbeer's opera, mounted with choreography by Pierre Larcher) is now in Copenhagen's Royal Library (*see* Appendix A). It was used for all later restagings of Meyerbeer's opera in Copenhagen between 1833 and 1863.

In his notes in this volume Bournonville clearly indicates Louise Fitzjames' Paris performances as his choreographic source with the inscription "dansé par L: F. James -". These notes, which most probably were written in preparation for Bournonville's first complete staging of Meyerbeer's opera in Copenhagen on January 18, 1848 (in Denmark the opera was given with the title *Robert af Normandiet*), seem later to have been supplemented with another description of the ballet, written as preparation for his staging of the Act III ballet in *Robert der Teufel* at Vienna's Kärnthnerthor Theatre on July 23, 1855. Moreover, the entire ballet was re-notated by him when he mounted the opera for the last time in Copenhagen on January 19, 1873.

Finally, for the last restaging of Meyerbeer's opera in Copenhagen on February 28, 1893, Bournonville's successor, Emil Hansen, made a complete transcription of the 1873 production notes to which he added his own further explanatory details.

What strikes one at first when comparing these four descriptions of the same ballet (*see* Appendices C and D) spanning a period of more than a half century, is their extraordinary similarity of content. Although some minor differences in individual steps occur, each phrase seems as a whole to have been faithfully reproduced during this period. The Copenhagen notes for *Robert le Diable* are therefore an excellent example of the reliability of Bournonville's production notes in reflecting what actually took place on stage. Moreover, taken together these notations represent, so far as is known, the only extensive record of a dance that was originally choreographed by Filippo Taglioni.

Excerpt with August Bournonville's notations in the répétiteur's copy
for the second solo variation of the abbess Héléna in Act III
of *Robert af Normandiet* (Copenhagen 1873).

What, therefore, remains to be answered is the extent to which Bournonville's and Hansen's notes can confidently be claimed to reflect the original 1831 Paris version of Taglioni.

In order to seek answers to this question we can turn to the few surviving written sources for Taglioni's Paris version and compare these with Bournonville's and Hansen's notes. The main differences between the two versions relate, perhaps not very surprisingly, to the actual number of nuns performing the ballet. At Copenhagen's then much smaller theatre, Bournonville's staging included (according to his choreographic notes) a *corps de ballet* of only sixteen nuns, while Taglioni's original 1831 Paris version seems to have counted well over thirty women (excluding the several supernumeraries who also took part in the so-called *"Procession des Nonnes"* which precedes the actual ballet).

This rather limited number of dancers seems to have led to Bournonville's decision, in 1848, to omit six music sections in the *Bacchanale* (of 16, 4, 40, 31, 16, and 10 measures respectively) and making a minor cut of 19 measures in Héléna's first variation, the so-called *"Séduction par l'ivresse"* (*see* Appendices D and G).

Moreover, the smaller stage in Copenhagen probably also caused Bournonville to arrange the groupings and placement of the nuns on stage differently from those in Taglioni's version. However, the fact that according to Palianti's manuscript stage manual and Bournonville's choreographic notes (*see* Appendix D) the *corps de ballet* forms the same half-circle grouping during their first entrance gives a clear indication that both versions probably were very similar with regard to the general choreographic evolution and movements on stage.

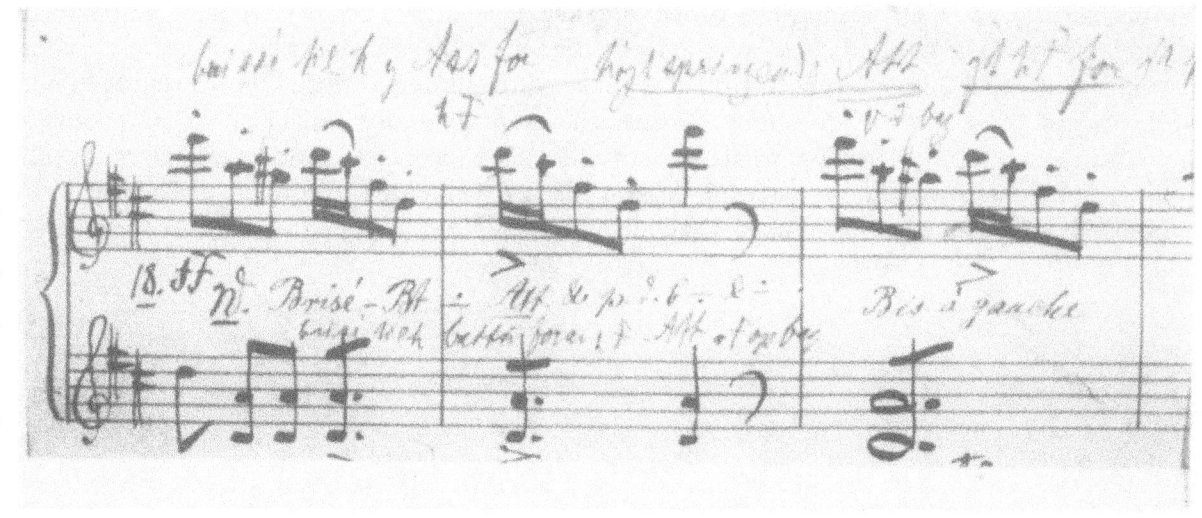

Excerpt with Emil Hansen's notations in the répétiteur's copy for the
solo variation of the abbess Héléna in the Act III *Bacchanale* of
Robert af Normandiet (Copenhagen 1873).

This degree of similarity also seems to have extended to the actual steps. Thus, in Héléna's second solo-variation (named *"Séduction du jeu"*) the ballerina performs a step sequence three times while travelling backwards on a diagonal toward the upstage right corner. This section (meas. 249 - 254 in the Labanotation score) holds a striking similarity with a similar passage in the second solo variation danced by the Sylph in the Act II *divertissement* of Bournonville's version of *La Sylphide*. Moreover, in Bournonville's technical manuscripts that sequence is often named as *"Pas de Taglioni"* which clearly refers to its original interpreter. Marie Taglioni may, therefore, perhaps originally have performed these steps in *Robert le Diable* in 1831 and later also included them in her father's *La Sylphide* premièred only three months after Meyerbeer's opera. The facts are here only circumstantial, but convincing.

Another indication that supports the theory of the Copenhagen version being a choreographic 'replica' (although somewhat *en miniature*) is the circumstance that before the 1873 staging of Meyerbeer's opera Bournonville did not receive any credit for mounting this ballet in Copenhagen. Knowing his keen interest in always obtaining the correct credits for those works he considered as truly his own, it is therefore noteworthy that the 1848 Copenhagen staging of the ballet in *Robert le Diable* was never officially credited to anyone on the posters, in spite of the fact that he clearly was solely responsible for this production. Subsequently, it seems that Bournonville from the very outset considered this ballet as a work for which he should be given no explicit credit as choreographer. His 1848 staging is described in his diary as follows:

30.12.1847, 4.1, 5.1., and 6.1.1848: "Rehearsal of Robert"
7.1: "Rehearsal of Robert from 10 to 2 $^1/_2$"
17.1: "Rehearsal session on Robert"
18.1: "Dances in Robert. The opera was performed extremely well." (*See* Appendix E)

The 1848 production of *Robert le Diable* was given thirteen times, the last time on September 29, 1864 (with Act III being given separately one time on January 12, 1849).

About his later staging of the ballet at Vienna's Kärnthnerthor Theatre on July 23, 1855 Bournonville stated:

2.7.1855: "Visit to the director, cordial reception everywhere. Decided immediately that Juliette [Price] shall make her début as Héléna in *Robert le Diable* on July 12."
4.7: "Rehearsal of Robert [...] Composed the dance for Juliette."
19.7: "Rehearsal at the Burgtheater, 8 o'clock Robert, which was excellently performed."
20.7: "Rehearsal at the B[urg]Theater, 8 o'clock. It went very well."
21.7: "8-11. General rehearsal of *Robert le Diable*. Juliette performed the rôle of Héléna, it went very well and many people expressed their satisfaction with her."
23.7: "Robert of Normandiet [i.e. *Robert le Diable*]. Juliette's first début. She performed very well, but enjoyed only a cool reception. Of course it saddened us, but we soon gained courage when we learned that the coolness was caused not by her performance rather than by the surprise effect of her dance style which they are not accustomed to here. We hope for more luck in the future. The girl [i.e. Juliette Price] proved on this occasion to possess a fine character of personality." (*See* Appendix E)

Juliette Price performed the part of the abbess seven times in Vienna, the last time on March 9, 1856. According to his diary, Bournonville later also taught this rôle to the Italian ballerina, Pia Ricci, on October 24, 1855. She however, did not perform the part before October 29, 1856, well after Bournonville had left the Habsburg capital.

About his last staging of Meyerbeer's opera in Copenhagen on January 19, 1873 he noted:

2.10.1872: "wrote and studied the dance for Robert [le Diable]."
3.10: "Composing the dance for Robert."
7.10: "Rehearsal of [...] Robert."
10.10: "Teaching the dances for Robert."
1.11: "Meeting about the costumes in Robert."
10.12: "Rehearsal of Robert."
13.12: "Afternoon rehearsal of Act I and III of Robert."
14.12: "Rehearsal of the dances in [...] Robert."
15.12 and 16.12: "Stage instruction for Robert."
17.12: "Rehearsal of Act III of Robert [...] written, read and composed."
18.12: "Meetings about the *régie* [...] stage instruction for Act IV and V in Robert."
19.12: *"Mise en scène* for Act I and II of Robert."
20.12: "Rehearsal of the *mise en scène* for Act III and IV (my scene with the tombs went very well)."
30.12: "Rehearsal of the scene of the tombs in Robert."
2.1.1873: "Rehearsal of the first two acts of Robert [...] written and composed."
3.1: "Rehearsal of Robert, Act III and IV with orchestra [...] composed."
4.1: "Composed and held an evening rehearsal of Robert."
5.1: "Wrote and composed."
8.1: "Brief rehearsal with [Maria] Westberg."
9.1: "Rehearsal of Robert, Acts I, II and IV."
10.1: "Rehearsal of Act III and V of Robert."
13.1: "Rehearsal of the whole of Robert (Westberg danced extraordinarily well)."
15.1: "Rehearsal of the whole of Robert."
17.1: "General rehearsal of Robert of Normandie [i.e. *Robert le Diable*] which went very well for a full house (Westberg performed her rôle excellently)."
21.1: "Attended the 2nd performance of Robert which went well for a full house, but sleepy audience." (*See* Appendix E)

(The Royal Library, Copenhagen)

Maria Westberg who performed the rôle of the abbess Héléna in *Robert af Normandiet* (Copenhagen 1873). Photograph taken by the firm Hansen, Schou & Weller (Copenhagen, c. 1877-1885).

The 1873 production received five performances during Bournonville's lifetime (the last given on March 6, 1873). E. Hansen's later restaging of the ballet on February 28, 1893 was given five times (the last on April 13, 1893) after which the opera definitively went out of the Copenhagen repertory.

Notes

1. According to André Levinson (*Marie-Taglioni*, Paris 1929 pages 37, 38) the opening scene of the Ballet of the Nuns was *reglée* by Jean Coralli. This statement for which no proof has yet been found may indicate that Coralli actually arranged the so-called *Procession des Nonnes* which precedes the actual ballet.

2. Second, revised edition (London 1980, pp. 110-112).

3. The Musical sketch for this scene is today held by the Paris Opéra Library, *see* Appendix B.

4. cf. Guest, p. 110.

5. This diary is now in the Paris Opéra Library, call no. Fonds Taglioni R 25.

The Task of Reconstruction

When facing the task of reconstructing an opera-ballet like that in *Robert le Diable*, one which is so interwoven with the opera's general context, two questions have to be answered:

(1) Is the reconstruction aimed primarily at showing the choreographic and stylistic characteristics of this epoch-making ballet as a work in its own right?
(2) Is it aimed primarily at revealing the ballet's rôle in the general scheme of the opera?

Furthermore, presenting a reconstruction suitable for performances on its own, must in both cases deal with the basic question of whether or not to include the character of Robert.

If the reconstruction aims at focusing on the choreography itself by presenting the ballet as a pure dance *divertissement* out of the operatic context, then no immediate need for including Robert on the stage arises. On the other hand, if the reconstruction aims at showing the choreography in a broader dramaturgical context Robert's presence is mandatory to give meaning to particular gestures of Héléna and the nuns.

In the reconstruction I have chosen a compromise between the two possibilities. By following closely Bournonville's musical cuts and by omitting Robert's recitative «*Voici ce lieu, témoin d'un terrible mystère!*» (originally sung between the *Bacchanale* and Héléna's first solo variation) the reconstruction allows for a study of the choreography in its own right, but is here presented together with the most essential mime scenes performed by Robert, the abbess, and the *corps de ballet*. Only one mime scene (that in which the nuns play dice) has not been reconstructed because sufficient notes do not exist to create a truly reliable historical reconstruction of this section. Instead, the original stage indications published in the printed score have here been included together with the accompanying music (*see* meas. 215-225 in the Labanotation score). By including these indications for the dramatic action with the accompanying music, I hope to have illustrated fully those parts of the ballet, for which no (or insufficient) notes prohibits a historical reconstruction.

Finally, by reprinting Meyerbeer's complete music for the entire Act III finale (as published in the piano score which was used for Bournonville's 1873 Copenhagen staging of the opera) the broader context of the ballet within the opera will be available for the reader, in this way facilitating comparative studies of this extraordinary work of theatrical dance.

Having reconstructed and mounted this ballet on three occasions (London Studio Centre, March 1985, The Vaganova School, St. Petersburg 1986 and Teatro San Carlo, Naples, 1988), I have personally been surprised by the high technical demands and artistic quality required for this work. Judging, for instance, from the notes of the *divertissement's* final *Pas seul d'Héléne*, I believe we must revise our ideas about the technical capacity of the leading ballerinas of the last century. The individual steps, the length of the solo variations, and the technical demands revealed by these notes all seem to indicate that Marie Taglioni and her many successors in the rôle must have possessed an extraordinary range of technical ability paired with also considerable stamina. Perhaps this rare blend of demanding technique and spirit in dance constitutes the true secret of why this ballet fascinated the audiences so much and spearheaded a change in the whole course of dance history.

Knud Arne Jürgensen working on the reconstruction of the choreography of *Robert le Diable* with one of the students of the London Studio Centre while Ann Hutchinson Guest and Jean Johnson Jones record the sequence in Labanotation (London, March 1985).

AUGMENTING THE DANCE HERITAGE

THE FIRST WHITE BALLET
THE RECONSTRUCTION STORY

by Ann Hutchinson Guest

Would dance enthusiasts, reading of the beginning of the Romantic period, ever have thought that it might be possible to revive the first 'white ballet', the Ballet of the Nuns, the dance of the abbess Héléna, and the lapsed nuns to be enjoyed by performers and audiences now and in the future? But exactly this has taken place through the careful research of Knud Arne Jürgensen, dance historian affiliated with the Royal Library in Copenhagen.

How did all this come about? Jürgensen became acquainted with the Bournonville School while playing for ballet classes during his student days at the Royal Academy of Music in Copenhagen. His interest led him to take classes so that he could gain greater knowledge and understanding of the Bournonville style and repertory. This dance background proved invaluable when as assistant librarian he found a cache of Bournonville's notes on ballets in the Royal Library. Studying every source for information on Bournonville's terminology, he soon discovered he could bring together the pieces of information into a coherent whole, his first revivals in bringing the movements to life were realized through working on the solos with members of the Royal Danish Ballet.

Jürgensen discovered that the archives also contained Bournonville's notes on ballets other than his own. Amongst them were the dances from Act III of Meyerbeer's opera *Robert le Diable*, which Bournonville had seen in Paris in 1841, and later recorded in preparation for producing the ballet in Copenhagen. After Jürgensen initially revived the three solo dances for Héléna, the abbess, with Royal Danish Ballet dancer, Benedikte Paaske in 1985, he needed a group of dancers with which to create the formations and sequences for the 16 nuns. Hence the link with the London Studio Centre, made through Ann Hutchinson Guest, his 'partner' in this particular project. The results of the revival were then recorded in Labanotation in preparation for the publication of this book, the aim being to present the ballet in its historical setting, together with the scholarly information [needed] on the period, its importance in the development of ballet choreography, the dance sequences themselves, and the finalized Labanotation score. The aim has been to provide both material for research and study as well as the information needed for mounting the work for professional performance.

Knud Arne Jürgensen is not the first to have delved into the Danish archives to study Bournonville's notes; Niels Bjørn Larsen, the late Allan Fridericia and his wife Elsa Marianne von Rosen, and others have made use of these sources, but mainly in relation to the existing Bournonville repertory. Jürgensen, on the other hand, has made a deep study of Bournonville's notes from the earliest period in his career through to his later notations and so has gained a valuable insight into the exact meaning of Bournonville's terms and shorthand devices. A general study of the ballet terminology of the period also added to Jürgensen's knowledge. In some cases, as with the ballet for *Robert le Diable*, the same dance was recorded more than once, thus providing many additional clues. The link with Labanotation came when he first met Ann Hutchinson at the 1979 Bournonville centenary in Copenhagen and found that her enthusiasm over and interest in Bournonville's notes matched his own. Capturing the results of his labor in Labanotation for future generations to read was a logical step, and has so far produced the re-creation of 24 unknown Bournonville dances entitled *The Bournonville Heritage* and published by Dance Books (London) in 1987.

Work on the material from *Robert le Diable* was made possible initially through a grant from the Radcliffe Trust. The first trial working together came when Jürgensen visited the College of the Royal Academy of Dancing in 1984 and taught one of Héléna's solos to the third year students. On this occasion it was evident that Jürgensen had not only an intellectual understanding of the material, but could also demonstrate the steps physically, illustrating the style clearly in his own body through expressive arm, head and torso gestures.

Knud Arne Jürgensen's first public presentation of his work came in 1981 when a Danish television program, entitled "Bournonville Forgotten but also Preserved" featured a general introduction to the Bournonville sources and the possible different approaches to making use of this material. This was illustrated by Jürgensen's and Dinna Bjørn's revival of the *Pas de trois* from Bournonville's first original ballet *Soldier and Peasant*, choreographed in 1829. In this first revival Jürgensen and Bjørn had adopted a mixture of 'interpretive' and 'authentic' attitudes in bringing the material to life. An explanation of the difference in these two approaches is now in order: Because the Bournonville heritage, both the ballets and the school of training, have been handed down generation to generation, there are many dancers who have a clear physical sense of this style and who feel that the immediate physical reaction to the music is the key; the notes which Bournonville left on paper being primarily a memory aid, a "springing-off point" in providing ideas of what the sequences should be. Thus, in this 'interpretive' approach, there is a desire to have freedom in interpretation not only in the subtle nuances of how the described movements may be performed, but also leeway in arranging the material itself. On the other hand the 'authentic' attitude takes the point of view that the script should be respected, i.e. given Cavalier treatment and the dance expression found within the defined sequences. As John Barton, director of the Royal Shakespeare Company in England said:

"Shakespeare is his text. So if you want to do him justice you have to look for and follow the clues he offers. If an actor does that he will find that Shakespeare himself starts to direct him".

Dance, of course, is not identical to drama, but a sensitive artist can find the meaning in the prescribed movements - if he or she has the time needed. At a "Bournonville Day" held by the Society of Dance Research in London in 1986, Peter Schaufuss, in describing his experiences in mounting Bournonville ballets for other companies, stated at the start that time is indeed the greatest problem. It is a common occurrence that because of time constraints dancers do not perfect difficult movements, but change them to something which comes more easily to their bodies. The challenge of making something unfamiliar 'sing', of finding the inner expression must to often be bypassed.

Jürgensen likes to make the point that in any revival it is the dancers who bring the work to life, and should receive credit for this, particularly when there has been a serious effort made to conform to the written sequences. Patience and understanding is also needed when the written record is incomplete or unclear; at such times research is needed in trying out the various possibilities of interpreting the instructions. Jürgensen is not against a more flexible use of the Bournonville notation, he and others feel that much of interest can be achieved through experimentation, but let such versions be so labelled and stated as adaptations as they are in music. A good case in point is his 1983 revival of the *Cracovienne* as danced by Fanny Elssler. Some people have found the choreographic material to be 'dull' and repetitious and in need of 'updating', yet Lis Jeppesen's and Yolanda Seyfried's performances of this work are totally enchanting. Elssler's *Cachucha*, revived by Ann Hutchinson Guest, has also be criticized as too simple and repetitious, yet ballerinas do not learn it with ease and face the challenge of finding their own way of presenting it with all the charm, the flirtatious warmth and sparkle which critics of the time found in Elssler's performances. To achieve this result the dancer must have not only a strong stage personality but also a subtle sense of where variation in presentation can be introduced without altering the actual steps. Nowhere is that more evident than in the Ballet of the Nuns from *Robert le Diable*.

Lena Kozjakova and students of the Vaganova School in St. Petersburg rehearsing Knud Arne Jürgensen's reconstruction of the choreography of *Robert le Diable* (St. Petersburg, October 1986).

PRODUCTION NOTES

Historical

The Scenery (Paris, 1831)

In planning the décor for the opera *Robert le Diable* Pierre-Luc Charles Cicéri was no doubt influenced by cloisters he had seen, for example the Sainte-Trophine in Arles with its vast collonades or the one in Montfort-l'Amaury. One of his sketches for the original production with its overpowering tombs and sepulchres as well as dominating, heavy arches provides an appropriate atmosphere.

Sketch by Pierre-Luc-Charles Cicéri of the scenery for Act III in
Robert le Diable (Paris 1831).
(*See* also page 7).

Maquette by Pierre-Luc-Charles Cicéri of the scenery for Act III in *Robert le Diable* (Paris 1831).

The Scenery (Copenhagen, 1833)

Two excerpts taken from Thomas Overskou's Danish manuscript *mise-en-scène* for *Robert af Normandiet* (i.e. *Robert le Diable*), 1833 read as follows:

(p. 52):   "A wilderness with ruins or an old temple, where the colonnade stretches into the distance."

(p. 78):   "From the end of the terzet darkness has fallen, now the mists fade and a pale moonlight falls over the long colonnade of the ruins, which end in the distance in a collapsed arch."

The Mise-en-scène (Paris, 1831)

There are three sources for the original Paris Opéra *mise-en-scène*: 1) L. Palianti's manuscript; 2) Meyerbeer's notes in his autographed musical drafts; 3) annotations in the printed piano score.

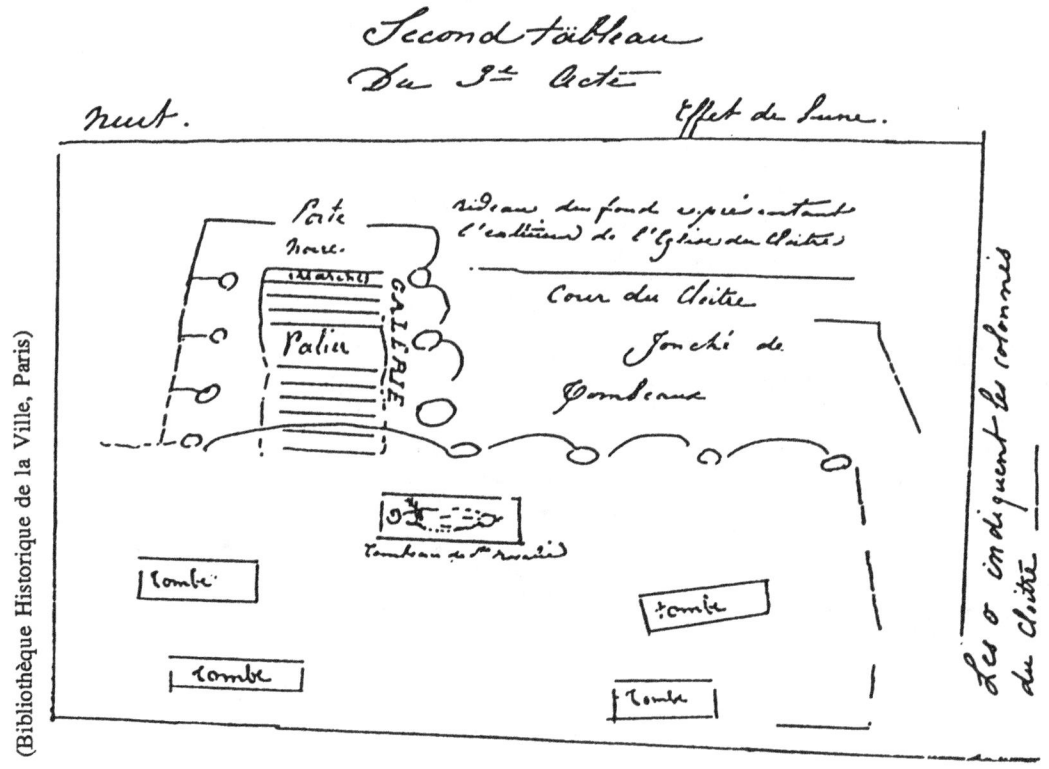

(Bibliothèque Historique de la Ville, Paris)

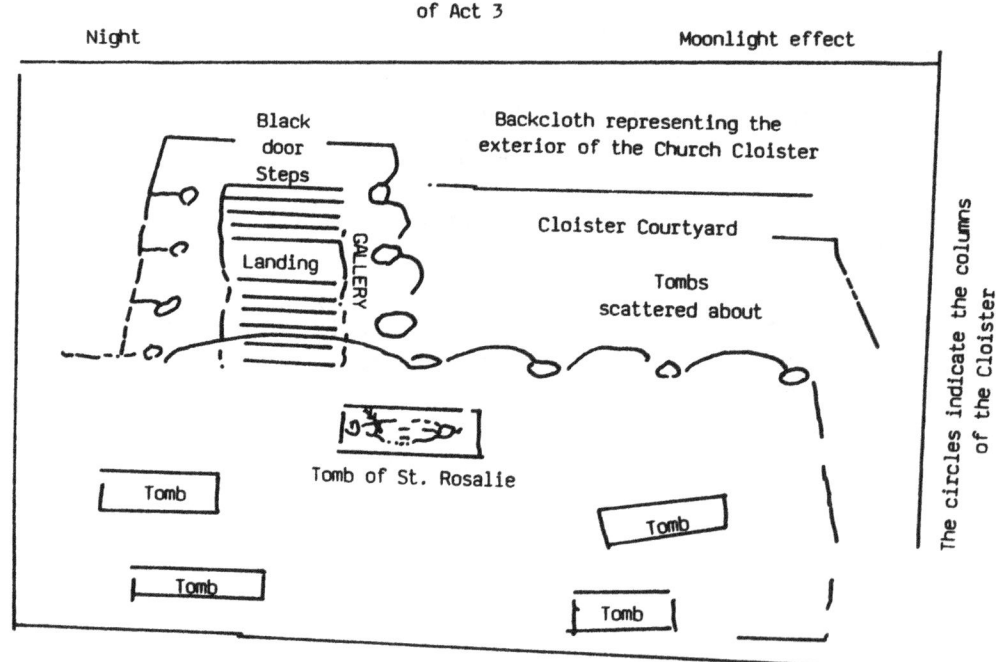

PRODUCTION NOTES - HISTORICAL

Pages 22 and 23 present extracts from L. Palianti's manuscript copy of a publication by Maison Duverger describing the staging of the ballet in Act III of Meyerbeer's *Robert le Diable* (Paris Opéra, November 21, 1831; now in Bibliothèque historique de la Ville, Paris). The *mise-en-scène* for Act III as included in the printed piano score is given on page 24; the *Bacchanale* would have taken place in the area between the four tombs.

"...The nuns have entered silently, with very small steps; several groups even slide in on wing-traps and in this way enter the stage from all sides of the cloister; those who were lying on the tombs also descend from them and form a ring around Bertram whose commands they await, and he withdraws.

They then retire into the wings and in a flash divest themselves of their habits, and appear in simple skirts and bodices of muslin, their legs and arms covered with flesh-coloured tights, and their hair hanging loose and long; they give themselves up to their gaming and their profane passions. But they hear Robert approaching and hide behind the columns and tombs. Robert enters from the back and is unable to restrain a feeling of horror; he makes his way across this silent space, arrives at the tomb of St. Rosalie, wishes to flee, and is suddenly surrounded by a band of women, gazing admiringly at him, and intent on ensnaring him. They all set a trap for him, two of them and the Abbess seeking to entice him, moving voluptuously around him; he flees from them, for they disgust him; others drag him close to the first tomb, on the audience's right, inviting him to play dice with them; the Abbess grasps hold of him, she speaks to him of love and its pleasures, and shows him his mother's tomb and the green branch, and after many enticements sinks down voluptuously; he allows himself be drawn away, he kisses her forehead, and moves forward to seize the branch.

At once an infernal din breaks out; flames course through the monastery; there is a clanging of heavy chains, the women dance in a circle around him, they then rush through the gallery, holding one another by the hand; he makes his escape at the back.

For a moment the nuns give themselves over to new follies. But the infernal din is heard again, together with the sound of exorcisms. Demons appear, several nuns being seized by them as they brandish their flaming torches, and all immediately fall lifeless.

During this last action an infernal chorus has been heard, and devils have invaded the most remote parts of the monument...."

The original *mise-en-scène* as recorded in Meyerbeer's autographed notes in his musical drafts are given in Appendix B (the 1831 Paris version).

Text in the Printed Piano Score

The text in the printed piano score (*see* Appendix G) is as follows:

No. 15. Finale, Section A - Scene and Evocation. [Bertram, the Mephistopholean figure's recitative is as follows:] «Here then are the ruins of the ancient monastery, dedicated by St. Rosalie to the cult of the Lord! These daughters of the altars whose faithless ardour, burning for other deities a shameless incense where virtue once reigned, made pleasure reign!»

«Oh Nuns who lie beneath this cold stone, do you hear me! Leave your funerary bed! Arise! Have no fear of an immortal saint, have no fear of a terrible anger! King of the Underworld, it is I who calls. King of the Underworld, it is I who calls, it is I, it is I, it is I, I who am damned like you, like you! Oh Nuns, do you hear me? Nuns, arise!» [The will o' the wisps fly over the tombs].

The tombs open. The Nuns emerge from them, covered with their shrouds and silently move forward in procession to the front of the stage.

Meas. 124: «Once daughters of Heaven, today of Hell, listen to my supreme command: here there comes to you a knight of whom I am fond, he is to pluck this green branch! But if his heart hesitates and evades my will, let him be seduced by your charms, force him to fulfil his important promise by concealing from him the trap into which he has been led by my hand!» [The *Bacchanale* follows.]

Section B - *Bacchanale*: Bertram's will has given these formerly inanimate bodies the instinct of passions. The Nuns, having recognized one another, express their pleasure at seeing him again. Héléna, the Abbess, invites them to profit from the moments and give themselves up to pleasure; this command is fulfilled. The Nuns bring out from the tombs the objects of their profane passions: amphoras, goblets and dice appear. Some make offerings to an idol, while others tie up their long robes and decorate their heads with wreaths of cypress to enable them to dance more lightly. Soon they are listening only to the call of pleasure, and the dancing becomes an ardent bacchanal.

Meas. 412: The Nuns see Robert from afar, and abruptly interrupt their dancing and hide.
Meas. 426: Robert: «This is the place, the scene of a terrible mystery! It fills me with an indefinable horror! These Cloisters, these tombs, fill my heart with a foreboding from the distant past. Now I see that branch - the talisman, the dreaded talisman that is to endow me with both power and immortality! What is there to fear? Take courage!» *[he moves forward to grasp the branch but recoils in terror.]* «Great God! In a vision of my angry mother, yes, I clearly saw her features! But the deed is done, let us away, for I can do no more!» *[At the moment Robert wishes to leave he finds himself suddenly surrounded by all the nuns.]*

Section D - 1er Air de Ballet: The Nuns offer cups to Robert while dancing around him, and themselves drink in long draughts.

Meas. 504: Robert refuses to drink. Héléna, chiding the Nuns for their reiqué manners, approaches Robert and seeks to seduce him with graceful poses.

Meas. 522: Robert admiringly gazes at Héléna.

Meas. 528: Robert accepts the cup which Héléna offers him, and drinks.

Meas. 537: Dancing, the Nuns surround Robert. Héléna gently leads him toward the branch.

Meas. 548: Robert moves slowly toward the branch. Seeing him take the branch the Nuns laugh aside amongst themselves.

Meas. 554: Robert backs away, appalled.

Meas. 559: The Nuns confer among themselves.

Section E - 2me Air de Ballet: Héléna and the Nuns again try to arouse Robert's passion.

Meas. 572: Dancing, they lead him to the place where is the gold and the dice.

Meas. 614: The Nuns gamble greedily.

Meas. 628: Robert, who was taking part in the gaming, becomes disgusted at the Nuns' greed.

Meas. 636: Observing him, Héléna leads him back to the gaming and herself plays dice but with decency and grace.

Meas. 654: Héléna gently leads Robert toward the branch, the Nuns laugh secretly.

Meas. 660: Robert backs away in terror.

Meas. 665: The Nuns confer among themselves.

Section F - 3me Air de Ballet: Seduction by love. Solo by Héléna.

Meas. 691: Dance of the other Nuns.

Meas. 697-702: Héléna and the other Nuns alternately.

Meas. 727: Héléna allows Robert to steal a kiss as she points out the branch which he must pluck.

Meas. 741: At the moment when Robert plucks the branch, thunder breaks out, the Nuns change into spectres, and demons rise from the depths of the earth, all forming themselves into a group around him, dancing in a disorderly chain. He makes his way through these spectres, brandishing his branch. The chorus sings: «He is ours, everyone come hither, yes, we are triumphant! Yes, we are triumphant, spectres, demons, come hither....» etc.

The Mise-en-scène (Copenhagen, 1833)

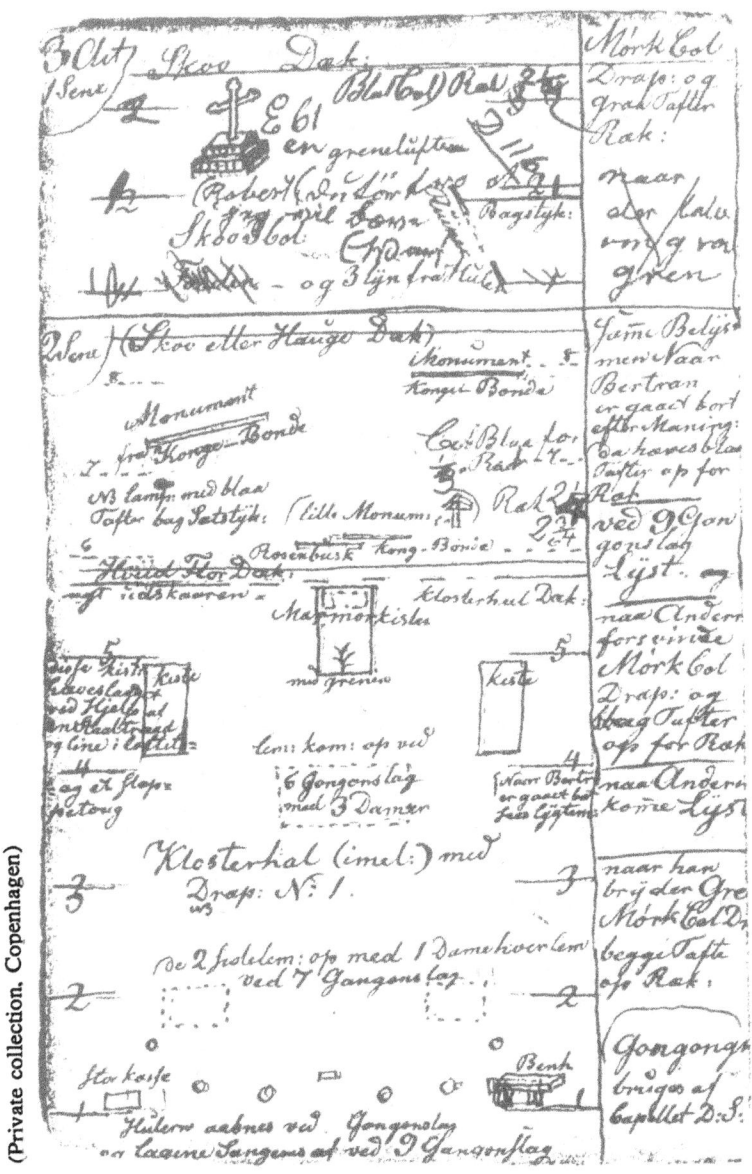

The stage director's record of the scenery
in Act III of *Robert af Normandiet*
(Copenhagen 1833).

For the contents of Thomas Overskou's Danish *mise-en-scène* for the 1833 Copenhagen première of *Robert af Normandiet, see* Appendices A and E.

Costumes

According to Palianti's manuscript staging manual for *Robert le Diable* the costumes of the nuns in the 1831 Paris production were as follows:

"They retire into the wings, in an instant removing their habits, and appear in simple muslin skirts and bodices, their legs and arms covered with skin-coloured fleshings and their hair dishevelled and loose."[1]

The costume of Héléna in the 1833 Copenhagen version is described in the tailor's record (now in DKKkt, call no. G 11, p. 108) as follows:

"A corsage of chamois, a skirt of French merino's, and a shirt with black ribbons of velvet attached to it, and with a similar belt."

The Props

According to Palianti's manuscript staging manual the props for *The Ballet of the Nuns* in the 1831 Paris production were as follows:

Golden goblets and cups.
A green branch on the tomb of St. Rosalie.
A golden statue [i.e. St. Rosalie].
Torches [for the démons].

According to the stage director's lists of props ("Requisitbog/No. 33", pp. 84-85, now in a private collection, Copenhagen) the props in the 1833 Copenhagen version were as follows:

The Abbess: 1 golden goblet, 1 golden cup
16 Nuns: 2 golden goblets, 2 dices
The Statue of St. Rosalie: 1 branch of pine tree
The Démons: 10 torches
The Ladies: 8 scarves

---

[1] Knud Arne Jürgensen states about the hair style of the nuns: '...I believe that 'the dishevelled and loose hair' is only true for the final chorus in Act III after the actual ballet. During the ballet itself I believe that the nuns all had their hair collected tightly, but in such a way that they could easily loosen it when the final chorus began (after the ballet) and the demons appeared to chase the frightened nuns into the same trap doors from where they had originally arrived.'

PRODUCTION NOTES

Contemporary

The Scenery

The effect of a cloister needs to be established by appropriate drops and backcloth. The tombs can be open at the back if the effect of the nuns rising from these tombs needs to be established. This is the case if meas. 1-148 with the so-called *Procession des Nonnes* is performed as a prologue to the actual ballet.

Much of the appropriate atmosphere will be achieved through the lighting.

Costumes

The ballet costume should be the standard classical long tutu. The effect of their having been nuns can be achieved through use of black ribbons crossing from one shoulder, across the waist over to the other side to the bottom of the skirt.

Front view   Back view

The Props

Goblets are needed as drinking cups for the nuns near Robert who encourage him to drink.

An evergreen branch (in different sources palm, cypress or olive are suggested). The size should be an arm's length.

For future productions of this ballet the historical production notes provide the basis for decisions and choices that need to be made. Thus each producer should consider these historical notes in the task of mounting this ballet, depending on the chosen context of the production.

THE PLOT

The Action of the Opera Leading to the Act III Ballet

The opera is set in the early eleventh century. The principal rôle, Robert the Devil, is the offspring of Berte, Duchess of Normandy, and a mysterious emissary of hell, who, in human form, had seduced her.

Because of Robert's evil behaviour his subjects have driven him out of Normandy, and on his arrival in Sicily he meets the Princess Isabelle with whom he falls in love. Consumed by his passion, Robert attempts to abduct Isabelle, but is prevented by the knights of her father's court. They are on the brink of tearing him to pieces, but are held back by the sudden arrival of a mysterious knight. He bears the name Bertram, but is really Robert's satanic father. Unaware of this, Robert acknowledges Bertram as his rescuer and companion, while Bertram hopes to take possession of Robert's soul by luring him to eternal damnation.

In the Finale of Act III the scene represents the cloister and tomb of St. Rosalie. Bertram summons from their graves a band of lapsed nuns, who, in life, had proved unfaithful to their religious vows. The ghostly nuns rise from their graves and are suddenly seized by their sinful passions. Headed by the abbess, Héléna, their dancing becomes increasingly orgiastic in a long bacchanale. This scene is suddenly interrupted by the arrival of Robert, whom Bertram has sent to the nunnery so that he can fetch a talisman that will help him win a tournament and Isabelle's heart on the following day.

At his arrival the nuns hide, and Robert, who imagines that he sees his mother, Berte, in the features of the marble statue of St. Rosalie, tries to escape. But out of nowhere the nuns enter again and surround him. Urged by Héléna, they lure him on with drink, revelry, and sexual temptation. With his senses completely overwhelmed Robert is led to the talisman, an evergreen branch placed in the hands of the statue of St. Rosalie.

At the very moment when he plucks it, thunder rolls and lightning flashes, and from the trap-doors emerge a group of hideous phantoms by which the entire cloister changes into a scene of hell. An infernal chorus exults over Robert's apparent damnation while accompanying the final scene in which the phantoms seize the lifeless nuns and carry them back again to their resting place.

The Ballet Itself

The ballet begins with the entrance of the nuns for the *Bacchanale*. They question why they are there and recall that they once had a pulse, a mind and a heart. They embrace one another and then begin to dance, but pause to remember the graves from which they rose. Dismissing such thoughts from their minds they resume their dance, launching into the Bacchanale which proceeds with many changes in formation and steps. The abbess, Héléna, then joins them and dances a solo section during which the nuns surround her and then open out into a half circle. Robert enters. He is at first uncertain but then advances and is led by Héléna to sit on a tomb downstage. The nuns arrange themselves into groups to observe Héléna's first solo variation.

In this she is joined at first by two of the nuns who soon leave her to kneel on either side of Robert, and then by four other nuns before coming forward to dance alone. At the end of this solo she takes a goblet from the upstage left group and offers it to Robert, who accepts it and returns to his seat, admiring the goblet. As Héléna's second solo continues Robert is lured by the downstage left nuns to join them. Héléna ends by running toward Robert, and then beckons him to follow her toward the branch, located in the upstage right corner on the tomb of St. Rosalie. Robert withdraws in horror, thinking he sees his mother's face in the statue of St. Rosalie. He returns to his seat and his attention is then drawn to Héléna, who dances for him and then beckons to him to follow her. He approaches her but the four nuns who were sitting by his side restrain him and draw him back again to the tomb where he had been sitting. Héléna withdraws to the three upstage right nuns who surround her. She then gestures to them to open up and let her through so that she can dance the third solo variation for Robert. At the conclusion of this solo four of the upstage left nuns join her. Robert rises and walks toward them. All the nuns run to form a long diagonal line, facing St. Rosalie's tomb and the branch. Héléna blows Robert a kiss and indicates the branch. Robert responds by blowing a kiss and then moves toward the branch, passing Héléna. He picks up the branch and, turning toward Héléna, flourishes it triumphantly above his head. At this moment Héléna, facing away from him, sinks to her knee with a deep backbend, her arms outstretched in abandon.

STUDY AND PERFORMANCE NOTES

The *Bacchanale*

Identification of the dancers:
The corps de ballet dancers who enter stage left are identified as A1-6. Those entering stage right are B1-6. At times the four C girls are more featured than the others. They enter last, following the other girls: C1, C2 entering stage left; C3, C4 entering stage right. The notes given here are usually for those who are on stage left at the beginning. Unless noted otherwise, the stage right (St.R) dancers move symmetrically to those on stage left (St.L).

St.L: (St.R≝) [1-2] Led by A1, as though answering a call, the eight girls enter with swift, light 'running' steps for 8 counts, circling around the stage left area. During this run the right arm performs a slow, low *port de bras*.

St.L: (St.R≝) [3-5] Each takes a step forward on the right foot into a *temps levé* in 1st *arabesque* (counts 1, 2), the right arm raised forward high. This *temps levé* acts as an impetus to continue the circular run to their finishing positions. During this run the arms lower to *demi-seconde*.

St.L: (St.R≝) [6] Now that all are in place in a large semi-circle with the four C girls center upstage, the dancers perform a *soutenu* turn *en dedans* with full *port de bras* to 5th, continuing with *bourrées* to complete two more turns in place.

St.L: (St.R≝) [7-8] Settling down quietly, they come to rest on the right leg, the left leg *pointe tendue croisée derrière*. The arms lower with an outside guidance, then, with a slight, lifted 'breath', they change to an inside guidance, ending by bringing the arms down and across in front of the chest, palms 'upward', elbows slightly away from the body. The dancers at the side of the stage turn the upper body slightly toward the audience. This ends the first phrase.

The next section is a mime sequence, the gestures express the thoughts of the nuns. For this a brief change in identification of the dancers is needed. Starting with A1, then A2, the dancers are lettered 'a' and 'b' alternately, all around the semi-circle. The 'b' girls perform the lateral symmetry of what is written here for the 'a' girls. All face the center of the circle (the focal point). The words giving the meaning of the mime gestures are written next to the movements.

'a': ('b'≝) [9] First the right arm opens out sequentially in an overcurve to the right diagonal, the head and chest inclining slightly away from the gesture. The same gesture is then performed with the left arm, the thought expressed being: "Here, and here".

'a': ('b'≝) [10] Now leaning diagonally forward to the left and turning the chest to the right, each 'a' girl makes a larger, more sweeping gesture with both arms opening diagonally, the right arm starting before the left, but both ending together. As she does so, she looks to the 'b' girl at her right.

'a': ('b'≝) [11] Leaning forward, with her left arm extended forward low, each 'a' girl now feels her left pulse with the tips of her right index and middle fingers. Her eyes focus on her left wrist. Next she touches her temples, head inclined forward.

'a': ('b' ≝) [12] Lastly, with head upright, she touches her left breast with both hands, indicating 'heart'. This is followed by a breath in and then out as she nods her head emphatically, saying "yes!" while looking at center stage.

'a': ('b' ≝) [13] Now each 'a' and 'b' pair (having adjusted the supporting foot if necessary), facing in toward each other takes a step toward each other, as, with gathering arm movements they gently embrace one another, 'a' embracing 'b's waist, while 'b' embraces 'a' around the shoulders. Next each 'gives a kiss', offering her cheek (a shift of her head) so that left cheeks are nearly touching. The same is performed to the other side, the right cheeks nearly touching.

'a': ('b' ≝) [14] The dancers then turn toward the girl on the other side and perform the same embrace and 'kissing' of cheeks. Only the end girls, A1 and B1 who have no partner stand quietly facing the center, arms side low, looking at each other.

St.L: A, C1, C2; (St.R: B, C3, C4 ≝) [15-16] Next the dancers form trios, A1-3, and A4-6; the C girls form two duos, stage right dancers follow suit. The center girls in the trio (A2, A5) stand still, while during five slow counts the outer girls take a slow undercurve step toward her. (Note: all adjust the step as needed to get into the required position.) All A girls are now facing stage right. With a soft upward curve all carry the arms diagonally low to take the hands of the others. A1 and A3 grasp inside hands in front of A2, their outside hands grasping A2's hands. C1 and C2 turn to face downstage right, and with the same slow undercurve step and the same arm gesture as the others, they take each others' hands. C3 and C4 perform the same to the other side, facing downstage left. However, just before the next traveling pattern they need to adjust by turning to face upstage left.

ALL: [17-19] The trios now cross the stage with fast 'running' steps, the A trios passing downstage of their counterpart B trios. The paths should have a slight curve toward downstage. On arriving at the other side each trio wheels around with the center girls (A2, A5) as the pivot. The B girls move symmetrically. The pairs of C girls curve clockwise, each pair circling around each other before arriving at their places in a line upstage.

St.R: A, C1, C2: (St.L: B, C3, C4 ≝) [20] All A dancers perform a *soutenu* turn *en dedans* to the right, arms up in 5th, they then release hands. In each trio the outside girls lean in toward the center girl as they turn. The C1 and C2 girls lean to the right, then lower their arms as they come to rest, torso upright, The A and B girls lower their arms as in [7-8] but more swiftly, arriving with their arms crossed by the end of [20].

Mime Section

C1, C2: (C3, C4 ≝) [21-22] Facing front, the C girls now mime "We - there - slept". For "we" each touches near the center of her chest with the 4th and little fingers. For "there" they turn and step to stage right, pointing offstage, past the upstage right corner with an upward curved gesture with the right arm, the left arm lowering unobtrusively. Turning to face front, they express "slept" by sinking into a *fondu* on the right leg as the left foot slides out to the side, the torso leaning to the right (toward the wings) as the hands come together near the right shoulder, the head inclining and resting on the right upper arm. They then hold [23-24].

St.R: A3, A2: (St.L: B3, B2 ≝) [23-24]. The two downstage A and B pairs now mime "From these graves we arose." With a low step forward on the upstage foot, they lean forward and gesture with the downstage arm toward the floor some distance in front of them ("From these graves"). Coming up nearly upright, they gesture to themselves, the 4th and little fingers touching the front of chest ("we"). For "arose" they come upright and, taking an undercurve step backward, the arms rise upward, rotated inward and led by the fingertips as preparation for bringing them down to side low with a succession on a straight path, led by the wrists (heels of the hands). On this gesture the chest stretches and arches slightly backward as the head inclines and turns away from the audience.

During the next eight measures [25-32] the mime passage expresses "We, here and here, these graves renounce (defy)". The C dancers begin the sequence slightly ahead of the others. The series of gestures are almost identical; where the C girls point toward the wings when referring to the 'graves', A and B point to the floor toward center stage.

C1, C2: (C3, C4 ≝) [25-28] Facing front, they take a step forward with the left foot, arms side low, as preparation for the gesture "we" (fingers to chest), followed by opening gestures, first to the left and then to the right, expressing "here and here". Turning to face stage right, they step and gesture toward the upstage right corner, turning the upper body and gesturing upward, pointing and looking in that direction ("these graves"). Returning to face front, they step forward, again with the "we" gesture, and then, turning the chest slightly to the right and the head even more to the right, they push away toward the left forward diagonal with two accents, the heel of hand leading, to express "renounce".

St.R: A (St.L: B ≝) [25-28] Making the "we" gesture at the same time as the C dancers, the A group takes a step forward as (without pointing finger) they gesture "There", the left arms opening toward the left high diagonal direction, as, looking up into that direction, the head inclined slightly to the right. This same gesture is then taken to the other side with the right arm ("and There"). Bringing the right arm down, the left opens up from near the chest as the chest twists to the left, the torso leaning forward as a *fondu* takes place on the left supporting leg, the right leg sliding backward as a result of lowering. At the same time the left arm gestures with an overcurve to forward low, the index finger pointing toward the floor at center stage ("these graves"). With this gesture they look toward center stage and nod the head twice. Next they step backward and again gesture "we" before taking an undercurve step backward with the same "renouncing" (pushing away) gesture as performed by C1, C2, as though saying "We defy!".

A, C1, C2: (B, C3, C4, ≝) [29-32] This next mime phrase expresses "Here, we, will dance." First the C girls gesture "here", pointing as before to the floor. On [30] as they gesture "we", the A girls mime more swiftly the same "Here" and "We" then, on [31] all take a slow backward undercurve step, the free leg closing to *pointe tendue croisé derrière*. At the same time the arms rise up overhead, the hands circling one another in the classical rendering of the message 'to dance,' the arms opening slightly at the end, as the head looks up.

ALL: [33-35] Just before the three transition measures, all turn left so that the center of the stage is on their right. They now run clockwise into a circular formation.

ALL: [36-37] Moving in unison, all step on the right foot, into a *temps levé* in low *arabesque*, the arms in 3rd *arabesque*, slightly to the right of the body, led by the outer surface of the arm, the head inclined and turned to the left away from the arms. As they begin to repeat this pattern to the other side, the arms, lower slightly before rising again to 3rd arabesque. During these arm gestures the upper body (shoulder section) follows passively. Turning to face out (backs to the center of the circle) all do three swift *glissades* to the right side, closing twice in front, the third one behind, the arms lowering via side to *bras bas*. With a spring onto the right foot they turn slightly toward the line of the circle, the arms coming up into 4th, the right arm forward, the left out to the side, both with palms down.

ALL: [38-39] Each dancer now circles clockwise around herself with a sliding forward step on the left foot followed by three slow hops in place, the free leg in a low *attitude*. During the step and on each hop the arms lower slightly with a soft succession, rising again while in the air. After the last hop, a quick upbeat hop with an unfolding leg gesture with the right leg leads into a repeat of the previous three-count phrase, traveling again in the line of the circle.

ALL: [40-41] The dancers now repeat the *temps levé* steps of [36-37] with a different ending after the third *glissade*. By the third *glissade* all should have returned to the place on stage where they were at [32]. In closing this last *glissade*, the dancers turn slightly to the left in preparation for a *pas de basque sauté* with straight legs (a little hitch kick) during which the arms open in a low 'presentation' gesture, the upper body inclining diagonally left and the head turning slightly to the left.

A, B: [42-43] After landing from the *pas de basque* they take a very low step forward on the left foot [42] facing away from the center of the circle, the right leg bent, toe touching, the torso inclined forward as the arms make a *port de bras* down, forward and up to 5th to prepare for the rise on the left *pointe* into *attitude* [43]. The B girls make a quick *coupé* under into *attitude relevé* on the other side.

C1, C2: (C3, C4≛) [42-43] After the *pas de basque sauté* the two C girls perform a 1 and a half *soutenu* turn *en dedans* to the right with a full *port de bras*, ending facing downstage left. On [43] they step forward onto the outside foot, placing the free leg *croisé derrière*, arms crossed loosely in front of the chest.

The floor plan is a help in understanding the next patterns. The movement phrase starts in the middle of the measure.

C1, C2: (C3, C4≛) [43½-45] The C girls start a slight zig-zag step, repeated three times, during which they cross on a curved path, exchanging places with C3 and C4, C1 slightly in the lead as she and C2 cross behind C3 and C4. The pattern starts with a diagonal *piqué* step to the left, the right leg unfolds sequentially across into the same diagonal direction, the torso leans forward slightly, the chest twisting to the right as it inclines to the left. The arms are in opposition, the left arm unfolds forward low (as though over the right leg) while the right arm unfolds diagonally backward as a balance. The focus is on the left hand. On the two quick forward transition steps the arms move to a low 1st in preparation for the repeat to the other side. The pattern alternates for a total of three times [44], producing a slight zigzag path which results in an overall straight path before they curve counterclockwise into place. At the start of [45], the tempo of the foot pattern moves to half-time, the *pique* with the free leg unfolding is slower and is followed by four *chassé-coupé* steps curving on a three-quarter spiral around to the left, the left arm rising to 5th on the first *chassé*, the chest leaning to the left, toward the center of the circling. The last forward *chassé* step is at the start of [47].

A: (B≒) [43½-49] All A group (stage right) turn to have the center of the circle on their right and, with A4 as the leader, they promenade across the center of the stage, each passing in front of a B person, to take their places facing outward in a curved line in the general area where the B group had been. Each fairly slow *promenade* step is followed by a *petit battement* behind and then in front of the ankle. The arms are held side low. After four such steps, at [45 ½] the dancers break into faster walking steps to complete their path, fanning out as they arrive in place at the beginning of [49].

C1, C2: (C3, C4≒) [47-49] The last forward *chassé* step on the left foot is followed by a slower backward undercurve step during which the torso inclines forward while the arms perform a gathering *port de bras* ending up in 5th [47]. Closing into 5th front, [48], they *(sissonne)* forward, the right leg backward. On this movement the left arm, led by the heel of the hand, extends forward with a body inclusion, ending with the palm down, the gesture "move away" being toward the 'wing girls', those at the end of the line. Next they perform a full *soutenu* turn *en dehors*, arms in 5th, followed by a full *bourrée* turn in place, concluding with a step forward toward downstage right. This step occurs after the A and B groups have concluded their run.

A: (B≒) [49½-53] With their backs to the center of the circle the dancers take a small step backward on the right foot, the arms moving in opposition, the head inclined and turned slightly to the right. Each step is followed by a *petit battement* beating in front then behind before the next step. Four such step patterns, zig-zagging slightly, are performed before they take a slow forward sliding undercurve step on the right foot [51½], the arms moving up and out in a slow full *port de bras* [52-53].

C1, C2: (C3, C4≒) [49½-53] Wheeling around a half circle to the left, the two girls repeat the forward *piqué developpé* step of [43½] starting on the right foot, the arms in opposition. Two quick steps lead into a repeat on the other side. This step is performed four times in all, the last time ends with C1 taking a single step on the right foot while C2 with three steps does a half turn to the left to face C1. Holding left hands, arms forward high and rounded, they continue another half circle around each other with three slow forward *chassé coupé* steps, the chest and head inclined to the right. At the end of [52] both take two quick steps, C2 making a half turn to the left to join C1 in facing downstage right.

In the next section circling paths dissolve into three horizontal lines across stage, the C girls in the front, the B girls in the middle, the A girls in the back.

A: (B ≝) [53½-55] Circling clockwise, led by A3, the A girls perform the same quick *piqué développé* step followed by the two quick transition steps, arms in opposition (as the C girls did before), alternating four times, circling clockwise.

A, B: [55½-61] The dancers continue circling clockwise but now with a series of four slow *chassé-coupé* steps, the right arm in 5th, the chest leaning in toward the center of the circle. After four such 'gallop' steps A3 has reached her original position downstage as in [53]. On [57½] they begin to 'run', A3 still the leader. She continues on a large circular path, then, reaching upstage right she travels straight across to the upstage left area. Just before [57½] the B group does a quick half turn to the right and, led by B4, circles clockwise. As B4 reaches the center of stage right, she breaks the circle to establish the line straight across the center of the stage, to stage left. On [60½] A and B all *bourrée* a full turn in place, those on stage right ending facing stage left, those on stage left performing an extra half turn to end facing stage right.

C1, C2: (C3, C4 ≝) [53½-55] Facing center stage, the C girls now perform four times the backward step followed by the *petit battement*, as performed earlier [49½-51] by A and B.

C1, C2: (C3, C4 ≝) [55½-61] With an undercurve forward step to *pointe tendue*, the dancers start a slow full *port de bras*, closing into 5th as the arms arrive out into 2nd. On [57½] all C girls are alike as they 'run' clockwise around the stage, led by C2. As she arrives downstage she runs straight across toward stage right to form the front line. While in their line [61] they *bourrée* in place turning clockwise. The stage left girls complete one turn to end facing stage right; the stage right girls do a half turn to end facing stage left. By [61½] all of the lines are slightly 'staggered' to allow the dancers to cross with the next phrase.

St.R: (St.L. ≝) [61½-64] Each group now crosses the stage, using four alternating step *temps levés* in low *arabesque*, the arms moving with an undercurve from 1st to diagonally across toward the supporting leg, the head inclining and turning toward the direction of the arms. A quick light *glissade* closing into 5th, turning to face upstage right, prepares for a low *grand jeté en tournant* ending in a low *attitude*, arms up in 5th. Three *pas de bourrées* on *pointe* in place with a full turn to the left end this phrase [64½], the last step into 5th being at the start of [65]. The dancers who had been on stage right end stage left, facing downstage right, and vice versa.

ALL: [65-68] The dancers now divide into three groups (shown on the floor plans of [65-67]). The five stage left girls move first, the five stage right girls move second, and last are the center six girls. The movement performed in canon is a kneel onto the downstage leg, facing in, (stage right for the first group). The arms cross the chest as they kneel and then move forward low and up into 3rd *arabesque,* the upstage arm being higher; the kneel takes place on count 2 of [65]. The second group kneels on count 2 of [66]. On [67] the center six girls sink into a *fondu*, the downstage leg *pointe tendue en arrière*, torso tilted toward the supporting leg, arms crossed near the chest, those on stage right move symmetrically to those on stage left.

C: [67½-68½] The C girls move in canon, C4 starting. Standing in fondue, each does a quick *pointe tendue croisé*, the arms moving across the body led by the heels of the hands as though pushing something away. C4 faces downstage left, C1 is next, facing downstage right. Then, moving in unison, C2 and C3 take the *croisé* position [68½]. A transition is needed for C3, C4 into the next pattern [68½]. Turning to face downstage right they close the right foot 5th behind. From here on all C girls move in unison. All take a quick upbeat step on the left foot, arms in a low 1st. Because of the *fermata* in the music the movements are not as quick as they appear on paper. The arms open, rounded, and slightly forward of sideward low.

St.L: A4-A6, B1-B3: (St.R: A1-A3, B4-B6 ≒) [69-72] The girls now on stage left rise and, led by A6, 'run' downstage circling clockwise ending in a line at stage left. The six stage right girls led by A1 perform the same to the other side. This change of formation ends at the start of [72]. They end in the 'rest' position on the downstage leg, the arms side high. They hold until [83] watching the C girls.

C: [69-74] The C girls now move forward to greet the audience. Two forward *emboîté* steps on *pointe* toward downstage right are followed by a step on count 3 and a *ballonné sauté* landing on count 1, the foot ending *cou de pied devant* in preparation for a *jeté* forward into *attitude croisé* landing on count 3, the arms open in a low greeting gesture, the torso inclining slightly forward. This pose is held briefly before three quick *glissades* in a small quarter circle to the right, the arms slowly moving to *bras bas*. A *jeté* over with a quarter turn right onto the right foot to face upstage left, leads into four slow *pas de bourrée piqué* steps in 5th, turning a quarter right to face downstage left. Facing downstage left the C group now performs a repeat of the first part of the sequence beginning with the same *emboîté* steps, the *ballonné sauté* and *jeté into attitude* but without the *glissades*.

C: [75-78] (A, B hold) With the arms in low 1st, the C girls take five quick *bourrée* steps backward. After the fifth step the free leg unfolds forward low while the arms softly unfold to a low 3rd, the head inclined away from the gesturing leg, the eyes focused on the right foot. This pose is suspended until a quick *coupé* over on *fondu* prepares for a repeat of this short *bourrée* sequence. At the end of the repeat instead of the *coupé* over, the pose is sustained. On [77] the right foot closes into 5th before a slow three-quarter *soutenu* turn *en dedans* to the left, ending facing downstage right, the arms slowly rising to 5th. This four-measure phrase ends with a *cabriole croisé derrière,* the arms in *arabesque croisé,* the head inclined and turned to the left. The pattern of [75-78] is then repeated to the other side.

St.L: A4-6, B1-3: (St.R ≒) [83-86] The six girls on stage left turn to face upstage and, led by B1, curve around with swift steps to up-stage center, into a flattened semi-circle, ending on [86]. As they travel the right arm opens up, rising into the diagonal. They end facing in toward center stage in a high 5th position on *pointe,* left foot front. Arms raised side high, each lightly grasp her neighbours' hands. Staying where they are, the A and B girls

C3, C4: (C1, C2 ≒) [83-86] Just before [83] C1 and C2 turn on the left foot to face downstage right; C3 and C4 still face downstage left, thus the pairs are facing in toward each other. With a quick backward *croisé* undercurve step to *pointe tendue,* C1 and C2 raise their right index finger to their lips (mouth), saying "Silence" to each other. With a *petit battement* front and back, they turn to face the other corner and repeat the step and the finger to the lips on the other divide up into 'a' and 'b', A1 being 'a', A2 being 'b' and so on. As seen in the next floor plan, they turn in toward each other and then away, at which point they are facing in toward the next individual.

'a': ('b'≙) [87-88] In these two measures, the girls acknowledge each other, first to one side, then the other. Facing diagonally in toward her first 'b' partner, each 'a' girl takes a slow low diagonal step toward her, the free right foot ending in a low *retiré derrière;* her arms moving to a low 1st position as the upper body turns to the left, her head inclines to the right while turning left to look at her partner. On counts 3 and 4 the arms open to low second as each takes a step and close on *pointe* turning a quarter away from this partner to repeat the same pattern to the right. Each 'b' girl performs the same slow step pattern to the right, relating to the 'a' girl on her right and then, on the repeat, to the 'a' girl on her left. The two down-stage girls, A1 and A6 have no 'partner' down-stage of them and so face directly toward center on the repeat of the step. During [87-88] their arms remain in a side low position.

St.L: A4-A6, B1-B3 (St.R≙) [89-92] The 'a' and 'b' girls now return to being stage left and stage right. Pausing in 5th on *pointe* for four counts [89], the girls then 'run' clockwise led by B1 into a line across the stage in the center area [90-91]. The stage right group is led by B6 and curves anti-clockwise into a line across the upstage. As soon as they have arrived at their new places, (about [92]) they all join the C girls in *bourrées* on the spot, circling clockwise, the arms opening out sideward and then, with a reverse *port de bras* coming via 5th into the familiar position crossed in front of the chest.

side. The pattern is performed twice more but instead of the last *petit battement*, as a preparation for the next section, the pairs of C girls turn so that C1 and C2 are facing each other, as are C3 and C4.

C1, C3: (C2, C4≙) [87-88] The C girls perform a similar but slightly more elaborate pattern in relating to each other. Facing downstage right, C1 and C3 take an overcurve step diagonally forward, ending in a *fondu* with the free foot in a low *retiré derrière*. As they step the left arm moves to a low 1st position while they raise their right arm forward high, to take their 'partner's' left hand. The head inclines left, they look under their right arm at the partner. Turning a quarter away from this partner with two *bourrée* steps in 5th, they then *piqué* toward downstage left and *fondu* in a high *attitude*, torso inclining diagonally forward over the supporting leg, arms in *attitude grecque*. At this point the two center girls, C2 and C3, face each other; the end girls face outward.

C1, C3: (C2, C4≙) [89-92] Starting as though moving into a *soutenu* turn *en dedans* to the left, C1 and C3 walk three steps on half-toe in an individual seven-eighths circle counterclockwise around themselves ending facing front, their arms moving to low 1st position. On [90] they *bourrée* forward toward the audience, the torso at first inclined slightly forward, the arms drawing in and then opening out into the 'greeting' position with an overcurve gesture. They then *bourrée* on the spot, circling twice clockwise [91, 92] while they bring their arms with a reverse port de bras to end crossed in front of the chest.

ALL: [93-96] Unison movement follows. Facing downstage right, all take three forward *emboîté* steps, the third step melting into a forward undercurve step on the left foot, the right ending *pointe tendue derrière* as the arms open into a low greeting position. The three quick *glissade* steps that follow in [94] continue travelling in the same direction but with the dancers facing front. As the left leg makes a low *rond de jambe en dehors,* the torso tilts to the right and the left arm makes a full *port de bras* opening diagonally back as though echoing the leg gesture. The face looks toward downstage left, and the right arm opens to the side. A quick sprung *coupé* leads into a 'Danish' *contretemps* toward downstage right as the arm comes full circle up to 5th again. The *contretemps (coupé chassé, temps levé* on the right foot as the left beats behind before passing forward into a low *chassé)* leads into fast high forward steps with feet parallel. A step on the right foot leads into a *jeté* over turning to the right, this is accompanied by an upward curved gesture of the left arm opening diagonally toward the audience, the chest leaning into that direction on the *jeté*. The turning continues with two *piqué pas de bourrées* ending in 5th on *pointe*, right foot front, facing downstage left, the right arm having moved into the typical period gesture of being rounded in front and slightly across the chest, the lower arm rotated inward so that the palm faces outwards.

ALL: [97-100] This four-measure phrase which starts with the *emboîté* steps is then repeated to the other side.

ALL: [101-104] Keeping their formation in three horizontal lines, the dancers all face stage right and perform two *posés, temps levés* in low *arabesque* the arms in a nearly parallel 3rd *arabesque* line, the *temps levé* is first on the right foot, then on the left, the arms lowering slightly in between [101]. They 'turn the corner' with a step on the right foot and a *jeté* over landing on count 3, ending with a *petite jeté* over to face stage left the arms coming to *bras bas,* [102]. These two measures are then repeated to the other side [103,104].

ALL: [105-106] Now facing front, two slow *glissade jeté* over to right and left are performed. On the *jeté* the body leans toward the working leg, the same arm making a low gracious upward curved gesture diagonally forward, the head inclined and turned in that direction.

ALL: [107-109] With C4 as the leader, the dancers begin to 'run', 'snaking' across the stage (see floor plan) to end with all sixteen in a diagonal line from upstage right to downstage left, finishing in 5th left foot front on *pointe.*

ALL: [110-112] In rapid canon, starting with C4, after the 5th position, each in turn swivels quickly to face upstage right, arms in 5th, and then immediately drops to kneel backward on her right knee, arms across her chest just before unfolding them to a 3rd *arabesque* line toward where Héléna is about to enter.

Allegro Vivace

H: [112-116] Running in swiftly from upstage right with much authority and energy, Héléna lands on [113] with an *assemblé en avant,* her left arm forward, her right arm sideward as she flies through the air. The music has now changed to a moderate 6/8 which is best counted by marking all six beats. Her landing from her entrance *assemblé* is the take off for a *sissonne* in *attitude croisé,* during which she looks toward the audience. Again she springs up into a *petite jeté* traveling toward upstage before a similar *jeté* traveling downstage, the left foot ending *cou* *de pied derrière*. On the first *jeté* her left arm opens to the side, and her gaze is diagonally forward low to the left. On the second *jeté* both arms end in *bras bas* and her gaze is diagonally forward low to the right. Turning with a rise to face downstage right, a *chassé* step on the left foot leads into a fast *bourrée* forward on half-toe, closing on count 4 into 5th in *plié*. From here a quick unfolding *sissonne fermé* to the right leads into a quick *glissade* turning to the right, this is the preparation for a half turn *grande jeté en avant* toward downstage left, her arms opening out into the greeting gesture, the torso inclined diagonally toward the audience. Immediately there is a *coupé* under on the left foot to spring into the air into an *assemblé*.

H: [117-120] Héléna now repeats her opening *assemblé* but this time her arms are in 1st *arabesque* on the landing. This is followed by the *sissonne* to *attitude* as in [113, 114] but, after the *jeté* diagonally forward, she does a *jeté* over turning to the right, landing on the left foot, immediately rising to continue the turn in a low attitude croise to end facing downstage left. On landing from the *jeté* her chest inclines to the left; during the turn it makes a *renversé* as the right arm performs an inward *port de bras* (diagonally backward high, overhead to 1st position) in opposition to the left arm which meets the right in 1st (a windmill like action). Near the end of this turn the right leg has a space hold, ending in a low *attitude devant* before, a sprung *coupé* over onto the right foot, the chest now inclined to the right. A *coupé* under with the left foot starts a *grand pas de basque* turning to face downstage right, each leg extending forward in the air (as in a hitch kick) the landing being followed by a step forward on the left foot. At the end of this step the arms perform the 'greeting' *port de bras* [120].

H: [121-124] A mime passage now follows in which Héléna expresses, "You, and you, here, dance". Facing downstage right she makes a curved unfolding gesture towards the girls in the upstage right area, turning her upper body and looking toward them [121]. She then performs the same gesture to the other side, addressing the downstage left girls, [122]. With an upward curving gesture to forward low with her right arm, she points to the floor with her right index finger, indicating "Here." This is followed by three small steps backward as she performs with both arms the mime action for 'dancing', the hands circling each other overhead, the arms ending opening out sidewards.

Group: [124] As Héléna performs the 'dancing' gesture all the girls rise and step forward on the left leg, the arms coming to a low 1st position.

H: [125-128] With an accented rise on the right foot to a low *retiré* position on count 1, she lowers with a *fondu* to 4th, as the left foot is placed backwards on count 4 (of 6/8 meter). A double *attitude pirouette en dedans* on *pointe* follows [126]. As she lowers facing downstage right her arms open sideward and then sweep down and into the position crossed in front of the chest as she takes a step forward on the left foot, her chest inclining to the right while turning to the left [128 count 1]. The end of [128] is the start of her solo, a *coupé*

Group: [125-130] In a rapid canon all follow B6 who 'runs' counterclockwise into a large circle, her left arm forward 'leading the way'. On count 6 of [126] all start a *posé temps levé* in low 1st *arabesque*, landing on count 1 of [127], followed by a forward step on count 2. This three-beat pattern is repeated twice more before all run into the formation of a half circle facing in, looking toward Héléna. All finish on [130] in *5th* on *pointe*, right foot front, arms up sideward, hands touching.

under on the right foot being the preparation for an open *brisé* (similar to a beaten *glissade*) traveling toward stage right.

Group: [130-136] Hold this position during Héléna's solo.

Héléna's Solo

H: [129-132] The open *brisé,* performed with the usual upper body inclination and arms, lands on count 6 of [128], the *chassé* step across on count 1 leads into an *assemblé* over, the arms opening out to 2nd, before coming to low 1st. A *sissonne* into *attitude* with the upper body inclined to the right, lands on the right leg (count 6) and is followed by a quick *jeté* over turning to the right, the right arm rising to 5th, as the left arms opens to 2nd, the body now inclining to the left. Turning continues during the *pas de bourrée* under on *pointe*, and ends facing downstage left on count 4, both arms in 5th. The end of the *pas de bourrée* on count 4 is also the start of the repeat of the open *brisé* sequence to the other side [131, 132] which ends on the left foot facing downstage right.

H: [133-136] Two small *sauts de basque* to the right with full *port de bras* landing on counts 3 and 6, traveling slightly upstage right, are followed by stepping backward into 4th facing downstage right for a slow preparation for a double (two and three-eighths) *pirouette en dedans* to the left [135] ending facing stage left. On the preparation the left arm sweeps via diagonally backward and downward into 1st, the gesture taking most of [134]. After the *pirouette* she lowers into *arabesque fondu,* her arms in 3rd *arabesque,* and, as her torso inclines diagonally forward left and opens (rotates) toward the audience, she places her left hand under her left ear as though listening, her right hand being near her left elbow. Her head turned to the right, remains upright.

H: [137-140] Bringing her arms to low 1st, she turns to face downstage left and, with a low unfolding forward gesture, steps on her right foot into a slow one and three-quarter *attitude* turn *(promenade) en dehors* [138-139], her upper body inclined to the right, her head slightly turned, her eyes focused at first start at the audience. At the conclusion of the *promenade* [140] she is facing downstage right. With a slow *fondu*, she extends her left leg diagonally backward as her torso inclines diagonally forward, chest arched slightly backward, arms on a sideward high to low line, the left arm up, palms facing 'down', her head turned to the left and looking upward to the left. At the end of [140] she recovers from this position in preparation for what follows.

Group: [137-140] The girls are now again identified as 'a' and 'b', alternately with B6 (downstage right) as 'a'; C4 (downstage left) being 'b'. Still touching hands and working in pairs, each girl moves toward her partner with a high *balancé*-like step, relating to her and then does the same to the other side, as follows:

'b': ('a' ≜) Each 'b' takes a very small step on *pointe* to the right toward her partner, the left leg coming to a *cou de pied derrière*, the head and upper body incline to the left as she looks at her partner. The end girls lower their free arm to side low. On count 4 each takes a very small step to the left on half-toe and then closes the right foot in front on count 6, before repeating the pattern alternately for a total of four times. At the end they let go of hands.

Group: [141-154] At the start of [141] all lower to the left leg, the right placed *pointe tendue croisé derrière*, the arms crossed in front of the chest. They wait here, watching Héléna until [155].

H: [141-152] The music in 6/8 is counted by the basic eighth-note beat. Facing front and starting with the left foot she performs a quick *pas de bourreé* under (counts 1,2), the arms rising directly to side high, palms 'down', and then a *ballonné* under with the right foot, turning to face downstage right (count 3), the arms lowering to 3rd, right arm front, and then to *bras bas* on the quick *glissade en arrière* closing on count 4. This leads into a *jeté battu* over (count 5) onto the right foot facing front. A *coupé* under on the left foot (count 6) frees the right leg to perform a little *rond de jambe en dehors* which is the start of the repeat of this whole measure to the other side [142]. At the end the *coupé* under leads into an *assemblé* under turning to face downstage left on count 1 of [143]. Next a *sissonne simple*, the right foot *cou de pied derrière* (count 2), followed by a *jeté battu* over (count 3). The arms remain *bras bas* until the three-quarter *soutenu turn en dehors* (counts 4,5) which follows, during this they rise to 5th. Ending facing downstage right, a *fondu* on the right prepares for an *assemblé en avant*. During this *assemblé* the arms move with an undercurve from a rather closed-in 1st position to arabesque line, right arm front, palms down on count 1 of [144]. This whole measure is then repeated to the other side [144], but the *soutenu* turn (counts 4,5) ends facing front. There is again a *fondu* on the right leg as a preparation for a slightly slower *glissade en arrière*, (counts 1,2) [145]. The arms which had finished the *port de bras* in 2nd, rise slightly on the glissade before lowering to *bras bas* during the *entrechat trois* which follows. The slower *glissade* is repeated again on counts 5 and 6, closing on count 1 of [146]. The *entrechat trois* repeats landing on count 3. The left leg then extends backward before a *coupé* under leading into a little turning *pas de basque sauté* onto the right foot, the arms opening to the low greeting position. A full *soutenu* turn *en dedans* to the right follows immediately [147] during which the arms move to *bras bas*. This pattern - *coupé pas de basque, soutenu* turn - repeats ending facing front on count 4 [148]. A *fondu* on the right leg (count 6) frees the left leg to begin a rapid six count *bourreé en arrière* at the start of which the torso leans slightly forward as the arms make a *port de bras* through the greeting gesture to 2nd [149]. There should be little traveling on this *bourreé* as she still has to remain more or less center stage. [150] is a quick preparation in 2nd and then a double *pirouette* to the right [150], followed by a simple step backward to *pointe tendue croisé*, facing downstage right. With her left arm she makes a sweeping gesture toward Robert [151], who, holding his mantel with his right hand at his left shoulder, has just entered from the downstage left wing [152]. She makes a similar gesture to her right as though inviting him in.

H: [153-155] She motions toward the stage right girls and turning to face front makes a sweeping gesture as though to usher them out. Turning to face downstage left, she runs forward quickly. She stops in front of Robert and stepping forward on the left foot, sinks on a fondu into a small *revèrence*.

R: [153-155] He reacts to Héléna by stepping backward and leaning slightly away from her (to his left) while looking at her [153]. He then walks forward toward her [154] before stopping [155].

H, R: [156-162] Gesturing to Robert with her right hand, she takes his right hand in hers and takes three steps backward, he following her. At [158] she pulls him into a fast walk in a half circle counterclockwise around her, at the end of which she lets go his hand, stands facing upstage right and performs a full *port de bras* which ends with open 'welcoming' arms as she does a slight curtsey to Robert. He stands, facing her, right hand above left shoulder. He acknowledges her with a gesture of his left arm toward her before he turns and walks swiftly to the downstage right corner where he sits on the tombstone facing center stage [161]. On [160½] Héléna performs a *temps levé* in low *arabesque* and 'runs' in a small counterclockwise half circle to end facing downstage right, her left foot *pointe tendue derrière*, her arms across her chest. There is a pause [162] before she begins her solo.

A, B, C: [155] With a *temps levé* in 1st *arabesque* on the right foot leading into a run, B6 leads the group in a counter-clockwise circle, each dancer entering the canon to perform the same movement two fast counts after the previous one. They circle the stage to end in groups in the upstage corner areas: B6 and six other dancers end in the upstage right corner [160]; seven other dancers led by B2 form a similar group in the upstage left corner. The last to get into place are C3 and C4 who end in front of the upstage left group. As the corps arrive at their places [end 159] the four back girls in each group perform a half *soutenu* turn ending facing toward center stage, the outside leg *pointe tendue effacé derrière*; (B5 and B6 ≒ of A3, B4), arms rounded side high, linking with (but not grasping) their neighbour's wrist. The three girls in front C1, C2, A6, face the corner and drop to their left knee as they lunge forward, arms side low, grasping each other's hands. C3 and C4 follow Héléna and just have time to get into place, turn to face downstage right in the 'repose' position, arms across the chest [161]. All look at Héléna; the girls facing back have their heads turned to the right and look toward Héléna over their shoulders.

C3, C4: [163-165] Hold before joining Héléna on [166].

R, Group: [163-174] Hold.

H: [163-167] Facing downstage right, Héléna performs an opening gesture with her right arm toward C3 [163 count 4, 164 count 1]. She then gestures similarly to her left toward C4, as though inviting them to join her. Héléna, C3 and C4 then perform a *soutenu* turn *en dedans* to the right with a gathering *port de bras* up to 5th [166]. They pause in 5th before stepping forward on the right foot, closing the arms across the chest, as they look at Robert [166].

1er Air de Ballet - *Séduction par l'ivresse*

H, C3, C4: [168-172]. They take two slow steps forward; on the first step on the left foot, still looking at Robert, their arms move horizontally across to the left, the right arm being led by the thumb edge of the wrist; this is then repeated to the other side. A step into an *assemblé battu* follows, the legs beating forward low ending in 5th, left foot front, arms in low 1st position. Next they *relevé* on the right foot, the left leg passing backward into a long *attitude* as the chest inclines and turns to the left. The leg then extends to *arabesque* as the arms, turning inward, then press outward against the air with the 'heel' of the hand, as though parting the air in front of them [169]. This two-measure pattern, with the two slow steps and the arm gesture, is repeated identically [170, 171]. During these four measures Héléna, C3 and C4 have been advancing toward Robert. With arms raised sideward all three take a quick step on the left foot into a quick *glissade* as preparation for a *piqué step* into a low forward *développé* with the left leg, the upper body inclining slightly backward, the left arm rising overhead to 4th. All *tombé* forward [start of 173].

H: [173-175] On the *tombé* she leans forward and her left arm lowers to address Robert [173]. She pauses and then [174] 'runs' around clockwise toward the upstage right group. As she passes near them she beckons to them (gathering motion) with her left arm. She ends in front of them facing downstage left.

C3, C4: [173-175] The *tombé* leads into a repeat of [172] but ends with a quick step forward on the left foot. An *en dehors relevé* turn ends with a low *développé* leading into a clockwise 'run' [174] to end near Robert, C3 on his right, C4 on his left. Arriving in place they do a *soutenu* turn toward Robert, ending in a 4th position kneel on their inside knee, facing center stage.

R: [174] As the three dancers (H, C3,4) curve around in front of him he gestures toward Héléna with his left arm, then returns his hand to rest on his right leg.

A3, B4-B6: [175] Walk through the three front girls (B1, A1,2) and stand right foot *pointe tendue*, arms crossed in front of the chest.

B1, A1, A2: [175] Still facing upstage right, they rise and walk through the four girls and, after a half *soutenu* turn, take a pose facing slightly toward the center girl, with the leg *pointe tendue effacé derrière* away from the center girl, A2, who has her foot in repose. All have arms crossed in front of the chest.

R, C3, C4; B1, A1, A2 and UL Group: [176-183] Hold.

H, A3, B4-B6: [176-179] All five now repeat the four-measure pattern of [168-171] starting on the other side.

H, A3, B4-B6: [180-182] The quick step and *glissade* pattern of [172] is repeated on the other side. On the *tombé* Héléna gestures with her left arm toward the upstage left group. The four girls repeat the *glissade, piqué, tombé,* followed by the *en dehors* turn into a run curving around to the left led by B6. On [182] Héléna runs curving to the left, ending in front of the upstage left group, facing downstage right toward Robert, at start of [183].

H: [183] As she lowers onto her right leg into a low 4th position lunge she performs a full circular *port de bras* to the left with torso inclusion, ending with her body upright and her arms in 2nd, her weight having been taken in an undercurve step backward on her left foot. A *fermata* in the music provides the extra time needed for a full movement.

A3, B4-B6: [183] Having run into place [183] the girls do a *soutenu* turn to the left into their pose on the right knee, facing upstage right, arms sideward, holding hands (or appearing to) behind their backs.

C3, C4: [183] On [183] they get up, do a *soutenu* turn in toward Robert and return to their kneeling position.

R, A3, B4-6: [184-330] Hold. (Note: some dancers are involved in the mime section.)

H: [184-201] There are two fermatas in the music here. Stepping forward on her right leg she rises in low *arabesque* as a preparation for the *coupé chassé demi contretemps* which follows on [185], the left arm sweeping down, forward and up in a sagittal circle. A step on the left foot leads into an *assemblé battu* ending to facing front, during which the arms rise to side high but close *bras bas* on the landing [start of 186]. With a rebound spring, arms raised slightly side high, she beats the legs before landing in a long *attitude*, the torso inclined to the right, as she looks upward to the left. The arms undulate with a soft downward deviation a quick sprung *coupé* at the end of [186] leads to a repeat of [185, 186] (the *chassé demi contretemps* toward downstage right etc.) The landing in *attitude* is now followed by a quick *coupé* under into a fast light *glissade derrière* followed by a fast *glissade* over finishing in 5th, the traveling being diagonally forward to lead into a circular path [189, count 2]. A *posé* step forward on the right foot is accompanied by inclining and turning her chest to the left as her head inclines and looks toward Robert. The arms have opened forward and out to the sides, the left arm higher. Stepping across with the left foot, she repeats the two *glissades* and the *posé* step as she continues to circle [190]. The two *glissades* in the next measure are open *glissades*, the second one ending as a *chassé* through on the left foot. During these *glissades* her arms slowly rise to side high, as she continues to circle clockwise retaining a focus on Robert. The last *glissade* is a preparation for a quarter *piqué attitude* turn to the right, performed with the torso tilted forward, the arms in 3rd, the right arm in front [192]. The turn ends on a *fondu* facing downstage left, the right arm inturned across the body, the hand sideward, palm forward, the left palm facing backward. A *coupé* under into a low *rond de jambe en dehors* with the right foot [end of 192] leads into a repeat of [185-188] on the other side, now traveling toward downstage left [193-196]. [197-199] is a repeat of [189-191] on the other side, curving now around to the left. At the end of [198] she takes a goblet from C1 in her left hand. The *attitude* turn that follows ends facing front. As she does the *fondu* she changes the goblet to her right hand. During [200] the swift *glissade* into 5th on count 3 is followed by a swift *relevé* on *pointe*, the right leg raised to a low 2nd, the arms opening to a low greeting position, count 4 of [200]. She then closes in 5th *plié* before a repeat on the other side of the swift *glissade* and *relevé* to 2nd [201].

H: [202-206] Closing into 5th *plié* at the start of [202], she turns to face downstage right and walks swiftly toward Robert, grasping the goblet in both hands. She ends these steps in a low lunge on the right foot, her torso leaning forward as her arms gesture forward and up to 5th, presenting the goblet for all to see. This is followed by an undercurve step backward, her torso inclining to the right on the way to coming upright. After a pause she takes an undercurve step forward, her arms curving downward on the way to a rounded 3rd *arabesque*, the goblet now only in her left hand. At this point Robert, who has risen and approached her, takes the goblet from her in both hands [205]. A quick *soutenu* turn on *pointe* to the left, during which her arms open out and close in again across her chest, is followed by a brief pause and then a repeat of the *soutenu* turn [206]. Robert returns to near the tomb.

H: [207-210] With a step forward on the left foot she begins an identical repeat of [168-171] advancing toward Robert.

R, Group: [207-215] Robert admires the goblet. The downstage left group invites him to join them. He moves quickly downstage left into their midst. They make a place for him to sit on the coffin. They form a new group around him. On [211] C3 sits and C4 rises to a standing position. On [215] A3 and B4 sit while B5 and B6 stand on the left leg, the right *pointe tendue effacé*.

H: [211-215] With arms raised sidewards, she takes a small quick step forward on the left foot into a swift *glissade*. The arms return to *bras bas* as the foot closes in 5th. A low unfolding gesture with the left leg leads into a step forward as the arms open to a rounded 'greeting' gesture, the torso turned and inclined to the left, the head vertically upright and turned to the right addressing Robert [211]. This same pattern is repeated, the right foot closing into 5th back before starting the swift *glissade*. On the step forward her right arm opens to the side as the chest turns in that direction, her left arm gesturing toward Robert [212]. She then turns to run a five-eighths circle clockwise, toward the end of which she runs straight toward the downstage left corner group, following Robert, ending with a forward step, right foot *pointe tendue derrière* [214]. On the last part of the run her arms move into the low crossed diagonals directions before opening side low. She pauses [215] facing downstage left.

H, R: [216-224] She beckons with both arms to Robert to follow her. He rises and moves toward her. She takes his hands and, walking backward, leads him to the branch. Letting go his hands, she steps aside [219], he runs quickly to St. Rosalie's tomb. Arriving close he stops abruptly [221] and recoils, retreating with horror [222, 223] as he thinks he sees his mother's face in the effigy. He turns and runs to the downstage left tomb [224]. Héléna appears to follow after him but stops short [225].

Group: [216-224] The nuns laugh among themselves, seeing that Robert wants to pick up the branch. The upstage right group move away from the tomb. When Robert recoils the nuns who are standing change to supporting on the other foot.

2ᵐᵉ Air de Ballet - *Séduction du jeu*

H: [225 count 3-236] With three long slow backward undercurve steps starting on the left foot, each ending in *pointe tendue* and with flowing arm gestures from side to side Héléna moves away from Robert while looking at him all the time. On [229] after a slow *coupé* over on *fondu* the leg straightens as the left leg slides out to *pointe tendue derrière* while the arms move from down to up passing close to the body in 1st and, ending in 2nd [230]. Moving across the body, with an undercurve, the right arm opens diagonally out. This gesture is then repeated with the left arm [231, 232], an introduction into her next solo. At the end of [232], a *fondu* on her right leg, the left coming to *cou de pied derrière*, the right arm rising overhead and the chest tilting to the right, are preparation for her next solo. This starts with a *coupé* under leading into a *temps levé* with a *rond de jambe en dehors* accompanied by a low *port de bras*. A *petit jeté devant* onto the right foot and another *derrière* lead into a *jeté en avant*, the arms performing a greeting *port de bras*. This is immediately followed by a *cabriole en arrière* as the arms open wide with wrists inturned and flexed backward (thumb edge forward). The *coupé, rond de jambe*, etc. [233] are repeated, performed circling on the spot, the *jeté en avant* concluding the turning to face downstage left [234]. The *cabriole* at the end is replaced by a *relevé* on the right foot in *arabesque*, the greeting arm position being now with rounded arms and palms down [236].

H: [237-248] Still facing downstage left and traveling backward, she steps on her left foot into a *ballonné sauté* under, her right arm unfolding as it opens diagonally outward. A *jeté battu* over, the right arm coming to a low 1st, ends this pattern [237], which is then repeated [238]. A step backward on half-toe and a quick *développé à la seconde* into 2nd position *plié*, is the preparation for a single *pirouette* to the right, the right foot *sur le cou de pied* [239]. On the *piqué* forward into *attitude* which follows, the head is inclined to the left and turned to the right to look under the raised right arm (looking at the downstage right group) [240]. A *fondu* on the right leg at the end of this measure leads into a repeat of the eight-measure phrase, the *coupé* under, *rond de jambe* sequence [233-240], the *piqué* in *arabesque* looking under the arm [248] again ending facing downstage left.

H: [249-254] This next step produces a zig-zag floor pattern traveling toward stage right. As before there is a *fondu* after the *arabesque*, easing into a step backward on the left foot and two *jetés battus* over ending on the left foot. Facing front, Héléna then makes almost a full *piqué* turn on the right foot in *attitude* to end facing downstage left. During the turn her right arm moves to the charming period gesture across the body, somewhat bent, the hand turned inward, palm forward, the little finger edge up [250]. The *fondu* that follows prepares for these two measures [249, 250] to be repeated identically twice more [251-254].

H: [255-272] The last *fondu* in [254] leads into a quick *glissade en arrière* with the left foot, as preparation for the *cabriole en arrière*, the arms in *epaulé arabesque* line, the body facing *croisé* [255]. Her arms come in across her chest as her left leg closes behind in 5th into a half *soutenu* turn *en dehors* [256]. With a *fondu* on her right leg she turns to face downstage right, inclining her chest to the left as her left leg extends forward before taking a step into a *'glissade' battu* traveling forward toward downstage right, her arms in 3rd, right arm low in front. A step forward on her left foot links with the step on the right foot into a *grand jeté* forward onto the left, her torso slightly forward, her arms opening into the greeting position addressing C3 and C4 [258]. A linking step on the right leg leads to the forward undercurve step on the left foot ending in *pointe tendu*, her chest forward as her arms move in a full *port de bras* down, forward, and then into 4th, her right arm up as the body arches backward. As the movement ends her head is turned to the left (looking towards Robert) [259]. An undercurve step backward starts at the end of [259] and into [260] as she changes her arms into 4th, left arm up. During [260] she performs a half turn to the right then a step forward on the left foot turning to face downstage left to start the repeat of [257-260] on the other side [261-264]. She looks at Robert as she opens her right arm, gesturing toward him. Again she does a half turn, now to the left, and a step forward on the right foot, turning to face downstage right.

H: [265-268] With a quick *fondu* as preparation her right foot *cou de pied devant* she starts the *ballonné* under, *jeté battu* sequence of [245], but now the arms are held *bras bas*. The *en dehors soutenu* turn which follows [266] is a full turn to the left during which her arms come in across her chest. At the end of this measure she starts an undercurve step forward, torso inclining forward, her left arm up in 4th, her head turned to the left, looking under her arm at Robert [267]. On [268] she concludes a backward undercurve step, during which she changes her arms, her torso now inclined backward and slightly arched diagonally backward left.

H: [269-272] On [269] she lowers her arms to *bras bas*, closes her left foot into 5th behind as she starts a repeat of [265] an *entrechat trois*, ending with the left foot *cou de pied derrière* before a *jeté* over. This is followed by a slow three-quarter *soutenu turn en dehors* with a *port de bras* up to 5th, ending facing downstage left toward Robert [270]. Two slow undercurve steps backward follow, the first with the arms coming in close to the body before moving out to a pose with palms forward (as though pushing the air forward, perhaps discouraging Robert), her arms rounded forward, the left higher than the right, looking at Robert as she inclines her upper body slightly to the right [271]. On the second backward step both arms are forward high, normal palm facing, as she inclines the body to the left [272].

R: [273-278] Robert rises, gesturing toward Héléna, pauses, then walks rapidly toward her, his right arm raised forward high. He waits [274], as Héléna moves backward with undercurve steps, he slowly walks backward [275, 276] and sits down again [277].

H: [273-278] A quick *fondu*, her arms drawing in towards the body, leads into a swift *bourrée* backward [273], her head inclining to the right as her arms unfold forward with an undercurve, led by the heel of the hand, as though pushing Robert away. Her arms draw in again as this pushing gesture is repeated [274]. The two backward undercurve steps are repeated as before [275, 276], but on the second one her arms open to the side slightly above shoulder level, palms down. On the *bourrée* backward [277] she gathers her arms over forward into the crossed position in front of her chest, this gesture being addressed to the nuns. She ends in 5th on *pointe*, right foot front [278], facing front but looking at Robert.

A3, B4,5,6: [273-278] The four downstage left girls see Robert move toward Héléna and run forward to stop him, surrounding him, putting a hand on his shoulder to restrain him as they stand on *pointe* in 5th [274]. They *bourrée* backward, guiding him back to the downstage left corner [275, 276]. As he sits on the tomb they resume their previous poses.

A1, A2, B1: [278] Taking hands as if to form a ring around her, the three upstage right girls surround Héléna as if trying to include her (catch her) into their group. The center girl, A1, stands with her left foot *pointe tendue* in 2nd, each outer girl is on her inside knee, her free leg extended to the side.

There is here a music cut of 52 bars (the scene in which the nuns play with the dice). What appears to be a fermata in the music here is a silent measure of music [279].

A1, A2, B1: [279] Move back into previous position.

H: [279-291] Taking a low step diagonally across with her right foot, and leaning to the right diagonal, during the silence, she looks and gestures to the left, performing a "move aside and stay there" instruction to the nuns in the downstage left area, the two accented 'patting' motions being on the music notes at the start on [280]. Turning to downstage right, she performs the same general movement to the other side, addressing the nuns to her right [281]. Then facing downstage left, she takes a step forward as she performs an opening, spreading gesture as though saying "Please leave the space open for me" [282]. Lowering her arms to rounded *demi-bras* she takes five slow steps forward on *pointe*, then, with legs parallel, a fast *couru*. This speeding up is free in timing; it does not have to be exact [284-286]. Stepping into a low lunge with her right foot, she gestures to Robert with an undercurve forward movement as though beckoning to him, turning her head to the right and looking at the audience [286]. With her arms in 4th *en avant*, she does a quick preparation into a slow three-eighths piqué turn in low *arabesque*, her left arm up overhead [287]. This leads into a 'run' traveling half of a circle counterclockwise, ending facing downstage right, her left foot *pointe tendue* forward [288, 289]. During this 'run', which slows down to two steps before the *tendue*, her arms lower sideways before moving into a low 1st with the *tendue*, as she turns her head to the left to look at Robert. She then opens her arms sideward as if with a breath [290] before crossing them in low level as preparation for an opening gesture out to the side, 'spreading the air', the arms inturned, led by the heel of the hands. At the start of this gesture she lunges forward on her left foot, her torso inclined forward as she looks again at Robert [291].

3ᵐᵉ Air de Ballet - *Séduction de l'amour - Pas Seul d'Héléna*

H: [292-307] The music now changes to an adagio-like 4/4. On the upbeat note at the end of [291] she brings her left arm across to the right to start a *grand port de bras*, her arms circling around counterclockwise as her body bends to accommodate the large circle [292, 293]. The end of this *port de bras* leads at once into a double *pirouette* on *demi-pointe* in *attitude* ending facing stage left [294], the arms coming at the start to 1st and remaining there during the turn until the heel is lowered when inclining to the right, she opens her left arm, the right moving up to 5th as her head turns and inclines to the right to look at the audience [295]. Lowering her arms to a low 1st she makes a full slow turn to the right (still in *attitude*), ending facing stage left, her arms rising to 1st *arabesque* toward the end of the turn when her leg extends into *arabesque* [296]. With a little preparatory 'breath' lift of the wrist (and sequential hand movement) she then performs a *penché*, her left arm lowering toward the floor and returning to 1st *arabesque* as she comes up [297, 298]. With a quick *fondu* on her left foot she turns to face downstage left and closes into 5th on *pointe*, right foot behind, her arms side high, palms down [299]. Looking diagonally left, head inclined to the right, she makes a beckoning gesture with her left hand to the nuns at her left, and repeats the same gesture with her right hand to those at her right [300]. Coming off *pointe* she takes an undercurve step backward as her arms lower to *demi-bras* in preparation for a *port de bras* into *attitude* arms as the right leg moves through *passé* into *attitude* [301]. Turning quickly to face downstage right, she closes in 5th on *pointe*, right foot behind [start of 302] as she beckons with her right hand to the nuns on her right, and again with her left hand to those on her left [302]. The same lowering into an undercurve step backward, now on the right foot, leads to a *développé* into *attitude* [303]. A slow full turn to the left follows, during which both arms rise into 5th and the left leg gradually draws into *passé* [304] before it unfolds forward. As she turns her arms come in crossed, fairly close to the chest, before moving to 3rd *arabesque*, the right arm higher than the left, as the left leg does a *développé* forward. At the end of this gesture the wrists fold backward, the palms facing forward [305]. A rapid forward *bourrée* follows [306] as the arms open sideward in preparation for a full *port de bras* ending with the greeting gesture, coming to rest in *bras bas* as she steps forward on the left foot, now facing front. A brief *fermata* in the music [start of 307] separates this ending from the allegro-like section which follows.

H: [307-313] Looking at Robert, who is still seated downstage left, she performs a quick *glissade* into a *piqué* on the right foot to low *arabesque* traveling toward downstage right, her arms making a low spreading gesture as they open to the diagonals, led by the palms. With a swift step across on the left foot she begins a circular path as she repeats the quick *glissade*, the *piqué* and the arm gesture [307, start of 308]. Three *coupé chassé* steps follow as she continues the circling, her left arm making a full *port de bras* as she inclines to the left. The last *coupé chassé* which completes the full circle is followed by a *temps levé battu* on the right foot, the beat ending with the left foot in front [308, start of 309]. Looking again at Robert, she repeats the *glissade*, *piqué* and the circling all to the other side, ending facing downstage right, right foot *cou de pied devant* [309, 310, start of 311]. The *glissade*, *piqué* is now taken to the right side, traveling toward upstage right. On the *piqué* her right arm rises quickly to 5th. On the repeat of this *glissade, piqué*, the *piqué* turns three-quarters to the right, the right arm coming to a low 1st, with inward rotation, the palm facing forward. Now facing downstage left she steps diagonally backward on her left foot, her right performing a *petit battement* (front, back), her left arm forward in a low 3rd position, as she turns her upper body to the right. The diagonal step and *petit battement* are repeated twice more, alternating sides [312]. She then turns quickly to face downstage right and steps back with her right foot into a lunge, both arms now side low [start of 313]. With her head inclined to the right and turned to the left, looking at Robert, she makes a quick gathering arm movement, the arms crossing diagonally low in preparation for a slower scattering gesture, the arms opening diagonally middle, led by the heel of the hand. This gesture ends at the start of [314].

H: [314-323] Turning quickly to face downstage left, she starts a series of four open diagonal *piqué* steps, each followed by *petit battement* behind and in front, thereby approaching Robert on a zig-zag path, her arms in *demi-bras* [314, start of 315]. On each step her upper body turns and leans slightly toward the *petits battements*, her arms reacting passively. Stepping on her right foot into a forward lunge, her torso inclined diagonally forward right, she brings her arms down and into a sagittal gathering movement, a supplication to Robert. This gesture is repeated enlarged as she sinks lower on her right leg, her left knee almost touching the floor [315, 316]. At the end of [316] she steps back on her left leg into a *développé* to *arabesque*, her arms gathering in across her chest. The *penché* that follows is addressed to Robert [317]. Coming up [318], she brushes her right leg through to forward middle, her right arm following the leg movement into a high *arabesque* line as she springs into an *assemblé*. This is followed at once by a *relevé* on *pointe* turning slowly to the left to end facing stage right, her arms coming to a low 1st [319]. Lowering her right heel, she raises her left leg to *attitude*, and inclines into a crescent shape, her chest twisted to the left while the whole torso inclines diagonally forward right, her left arm overhead, her right arm down in the opposite direction. With her head inclined to the right and turned to the left, she looks under her left arm at Robert [320]. Turning slowly to the left in this position, her torso gradually coming up, she ends facing upstage right [321]. Sinking on her right leg into a kneel, she arches backward toward Robert, unfolding her arms to extend diagonally backward. Her chest is twisted to the left and her head turned left toward Robert [322]. As she takes her weight forward to rise from the kneel, she turns to face downstage right and, leaning her torso forward rounded and looking down, she starts a full *port de bras* rising into 5th on *pointe*, left foot in front as her arms lift to 5th, led by the back of the wrists. She ends with head inclined to the right looking to the left at Robert [323].

H: [324-331] Bringing her right arm down to the side as she steps across toward stage right with her left foot, she performs a *glissade ouvert battu* with her arms in low 3rd, her left arm diagonally back. As the *glissade* is completed [324, count 2] her chest inclines slightly to the right diagonal, and her left arm moves through 1st up to 5th as she takes a diagonal step toward stage right, her chest now inclining slightly to the left. The beaten *glissade* is now repeated but without the body movement, instead the arms open to high 2nd coming down to *bras bas* as the *glissade* concludes [start of 325] and her head turns to the left to look at Robert. This is followed immediately by a small *assemblé* over which provides the start of three *entrechats quatres*. During these she is looking at Robert. As she lands on the third one [start of 326] she leans forward looking down as her arms open side low in preparation for an upward unfolding, led by the back of the hands. The arms pass close to the body as they lift and she rises to 5th on *pointe*. Her head ends inclined to the right as she looks to her left at Robert [326½]. With a quick *bourrée* to her right she travels on a seven-eighths clockwise circular path ending facing front. As she circles she leans to the left and opens her left arm toward Robert, palm up. Halfway through the circular path she leans to her right as her right arm lowers to the side, palm up. During this circling her gaze remains on Robert. After the *bourrée* [327½] her arms lift slightly and then lower, led first by the outer arm surface and then by the inside of the wrist, a small soft wave. The last four measures are then repeated to the other side, starting facing front and ending facing downstage right [328-331].

A4, A5, B2, B3: [330-331] The four upstage left girls *bourrée* forward, passing through the three girls in front of them to join Héléna, arriving in 5th position as she concludes her circling in 5th. During [332-335] they do the same movements as Héléna.

H: [332-335] Bringing her left arm in front to low 1st she unfolds it on a forward curve to side low as her left leg opens to side low on a similar curved path while she sinks slowly in *fondu* on her right leg. During this she looks diagonally downward toward her left leg. This sustained movement is followed by four rapid *bourrée* steps traveling slightly to the right, the left foot behind [332]. A *coupé* under on *fondu* leads to a repeat of the curved arm and leg gestures and the *bourrées*, the *fondu* and the opening gesture now being faster. Again there is a *coupé* under and the faster curved gestures with the left arm and leg. The next *coupé* under on the left foot leads into a *glissade* to the right. This is a preparation for a *piqué* to the right, the left foot placed *cou de pied derrière*, both arms being taken across to the right led by the outer surface of the arms, as her upper body leans to the left and she looks at Robert. On the *coupé* under which follows she lowers her arms slightly with a soft wrist movement, her eyes looking downward with a slight forward inclination of her head. She then lifts them again on the repeat of the *piqué*, again looking at Robert [335]. After the third such *piqué*, the *coupé* under leads into a three-quarter *soutenu* turn *en dehors* to the right, her arms rising to 5th and opening out to 2nd, palms ending up [335].

H: [336-342] Now facing downstage left, her right leg unfolds forward in preparation for a *grand rond de jambe* into *attitude*. Her arms gather in across her chest so that her hands are near her heart, her left hand touching, then, as her leg opens into 2nd, she leans slightly forward, opening her arms, palms up, in a scattering movement out to 2nd before the right arm rises to 5th as a very slow turn in *attitude* begins [336]. During [337, 338] and into [339] she performs two and a half turns, ending facing upstage right, her left arm rising to 5th via 1st before she sinks into a backward kneel on her right knee. She twists her body far to the left and leans diagonally backward to look at Robert as her right arm opens sideward and her left arm unfolds in a gesture to him. This gesture ends at the start of [340]. She then brings her left hand to her mouth and 'blows him a kiss', gesturing out toward him again [340]. Her torso then returns to normal and, facing upstage right, she brings her arms in front of her, fairly close to her chest before, with a pushing motion, gesturing toward the upstage right part of the stage, her index fingers indicating the branch. She then twists and leans toward Robert, again 'blowing a kiss'. Once more her torso returns to normal, facing upstage right, and she gestures toward the upstage right stage area, pointing with both index fingers, her right arm raised forward high. Rising on her left foot, she closes into a half *soutenu* turn *en dehors* to the right, her arms in 5th [342].

GROUP: [334-339] While Héléna and the four girls perform the repeated *glissade, piqué* to the right, the group rises and walks forward, then runs swiftly into a diagonal line from upstage right to downstage left, their paths being shown in the floor plan. All end with a step forward on the right foot, the arms in a high *arabesque* line. They hold during [340-342].

R: [334-342] He gets up and walks forward, as if called by Héléna. He responds to each of her 'kisses' with a similar gesture [341, 342].

H: [343-346] (Note that, starting with [343], the unit for each beat is changed in the dance score to accommodate the movements for the slower pace used here.) A little unfolding gesture with her right leg begins a swift *bourrée* forward, her arms opening side high. The soft unfolding gesture and the *bourrée* are repeated three times, the third one leading into a longer *bourrée* as the arms slowly lower through *demi-seconde* [343, 344]. At the end of [344] she takes two forward steps, right, then left, before kneeling backward [345] on her right knee, her arms rising sagittally from down to forward, and then coming toward her in an upward curve, a gathering movement, as though beckoning to Robert to come toward her. As she does this gesture she leans diagonally forward right, turning slightly left [345]. Her last gesture is to lean backward as she gathers her arms forward, upward and then opens them to the side with outward rotation as though in abandon. Her final movement is to turn her arms inward, palms now facing down as her head inclines and turns away to the right [346].

GROUP: [343-346] On the last count of [342] they start a swift canon, this is begun by B1, the upstage right girl. She turns left to face downstage left, her arms across her chest and then steps forward on her left foot into a kneel. This ending is suitable for smaller stages as an ending tableau. For larger stages and in an operatic context the nuns step into *pointe tendue* so as to be able to move on more quickly. The canon is completed by the end of [344].

R: [343-346] As Héléna *bourrées* toward him, he 'runs' slowly past her to St. Rosalie's tomb and picks the branch from it [343, 344]. He turns and triumphantly waves the branch above his head [345, 346] as the curtain falls.

LABANOTATION GLOSSARY

Measure number reference is to the first time the usage occurs.

Key: ✛ unless ✧ is specified.

Orientation

R Robert	R ⫮ Turn right or left (the shortest way) to face Robert	• Face focal point (center of circle or semi-circle) (m.6)
R̲ Face Robert		

Parts of the Body

⩗⃝ Temples (m.11)	⃝ Mouth (m.83)	⊠ Lungs (m.12)	V̯⊠ Breath in

⊡ Front of chest (either side of breastbone) for both hands touching (m.25)	▷̇⊠ = ▷̇⊠) Chest inclines half way from normal (m.51)	

Inside of wrist (m.11)	⊟ Heel of hand (m.24)	⊔, ⊓ Inside edge of base of hand (m.176)

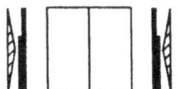   Either hand touching either shoulder (m.274)

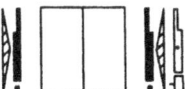 =   Pointing finger (m.21)

Shorthand for: (m.8)		Low 1st position (m.43)
Shorthand for: (m.28)		Arm at waist level (H, m.334)

Timing

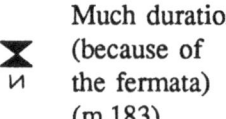 Much duration (because of the fermata) (m.183)

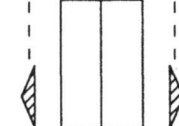 For the arms, a slight after-flow into final destination, drifting into ending position (m.32)

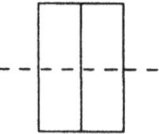 Demarcation line helpful in showing area of repetition (m.43)

Arm Gestures - Details

 SPECIAL USAGE: Rotation occurs at start of gesture and remains (but is cancelled with the next gesture) (m.313)

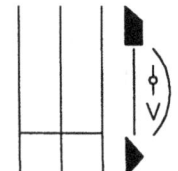 Both succession and an overcurve occur on way to new direction (m.15)

 Guidance is still in effect at end of gesture (m.3)

 Guidance ends before end of arm gesture (m.330)

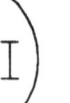 Straight path gesture (m.24)

 Palms press slightly to the left (H,m.279)

 A slight downward succession is followed by a slight upward lift (m.38)

Paths

 Follow A1 (m.1)

 See floor plan for modification of path (m.1)

 Wheel around center of the group (m.19)

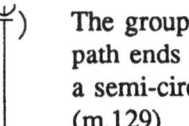 The group path ends in a semi-circle (m.129)

 End in a circle facing anti-clockwise (m.126)

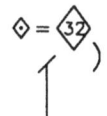 Resultant path (person is being led) (m.158)

Arrive at spot where you were on m. 32 (m.41)

 Dancers perform individual circles (m.38)

Right hand makes a sagittal circle around left hand (m.31)

GLOSSARY

Terminology

DL - Downstage left
DR - Downstage right
UL - Upstage left
UR - Upstage right

'Outside leg' - Toward wing
'Inside leg' - Toward center stage

Posé = An ordinary step on whole foot; may be in plié   *Piqué* = A quick step on pointe

'Run'

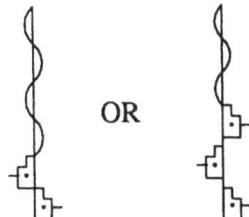 A 'run' in the word notes is usually a light, fast walk with a very slight lift between steps (rather than a real springing run) (m.1)

Travelling Brisé

  In a traveling *brisé*, to facilitate the beat, the body direction is a little less diagonal; instead of landing closed in 5th the second leg gesture passes through.

Here, for 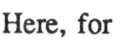 read

The adjustment in the body facing should be imperceptible

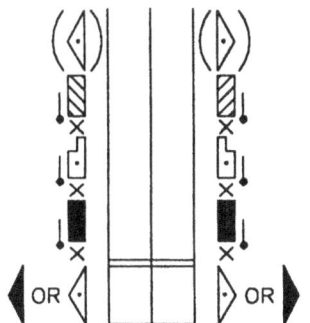 Full *port de bras* (m.6)

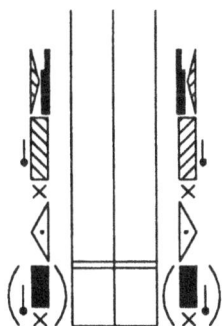 Reverse *port de bras* (m.91)

 Fast, light *glissades*, too fast to stress full foot articulation

(m.333,4) (m.37)

 Rest position (m.7)

Rond de Jambe

Abbreviation (m.233) 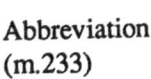 =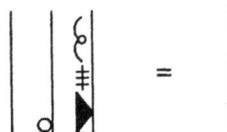

Miscellaneous

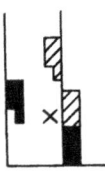 × shows distance off the floor for left leg gesture, i.e. only a little (m.145)

St.L:
St.R: ≃ St.R group does the lateral symmetry of St.L (m.1)

 Gathering movement (H,m.277)

ᔔ ᔕ Unemphasized (C1,2,m.21)

P Partner (m.13)

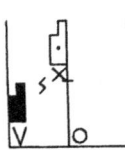 'Zed' caret meaning 'the same', connects gesture to new support, i.e. it is only a preparation for the step (H,m.212)

🍷 Goblet (m.199)

▨ The upstage right off stage area (m.21)

 (H,m.125)

↑
◯
↓
Design drawing; a horizontal circular path is 'drawn' in the air (m.183)

⊤ Floor (terra) (m.123)

 Aerial view of holding hands (m.16)

∧ No longer in effect (cancelled) (m.151)

⊣⊓, ⊓⊢ VALIDITY: Palm and thumb edge facings are automatically cancelled with the next movement

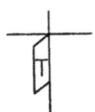 Turn to face upstage (m.90)

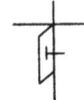 Turn to face stage right (m.90)

THE CHOREOGRAPHIC SCORE

OF

THE BALLET OF THE NUNS

FROM

ROBERT LE DIABLE

The photographs of the London City Ballet in the following section
were all taken by Peter Teigen in 1996.

An introduction of six measures from the previous *Procession of the Nuns* during which the curtain rises.

BACCHANALE

Bacchanale

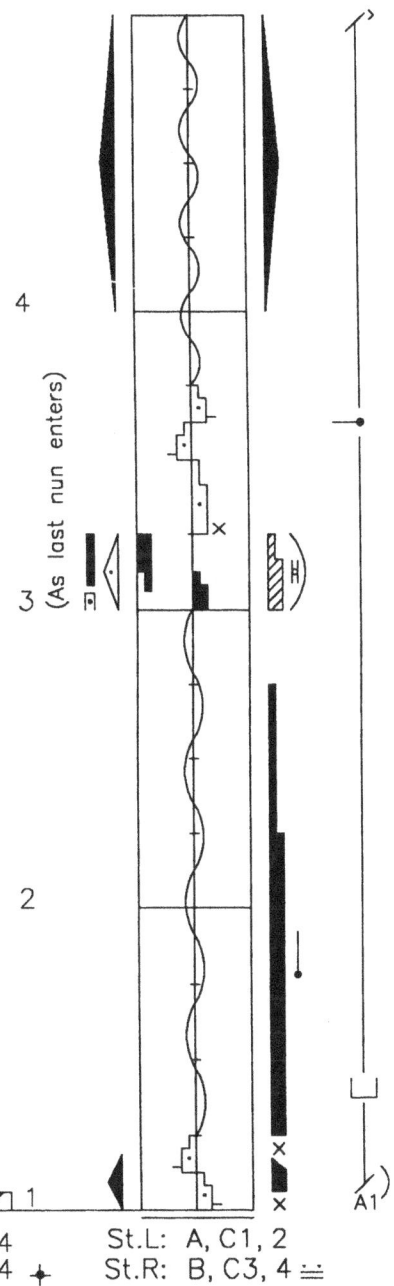

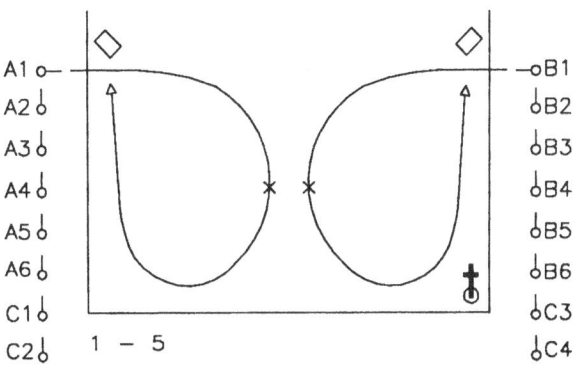

4   St.L: A, C1, 2
4   St.R: B, C3, 4

ROBERT LE DIABLE - THE BALLET OF THE NUNS

153

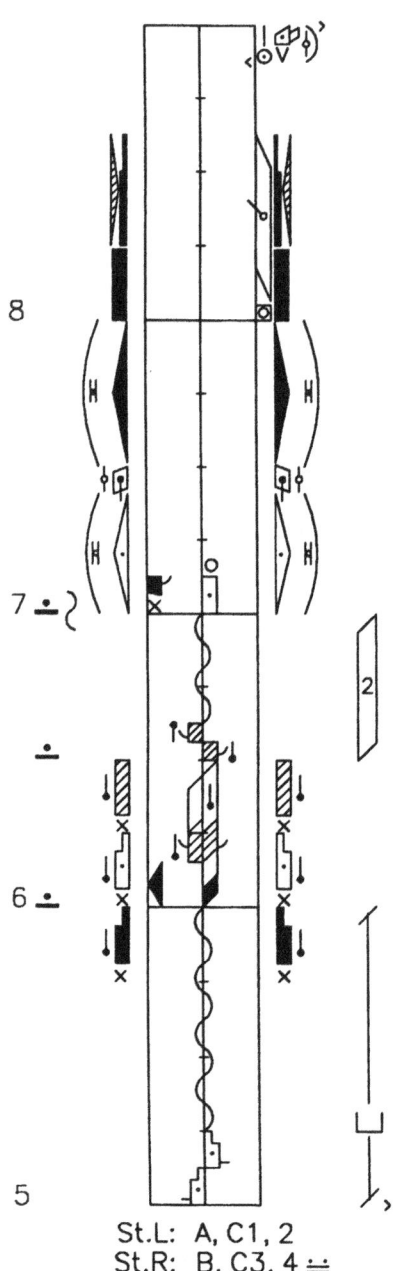

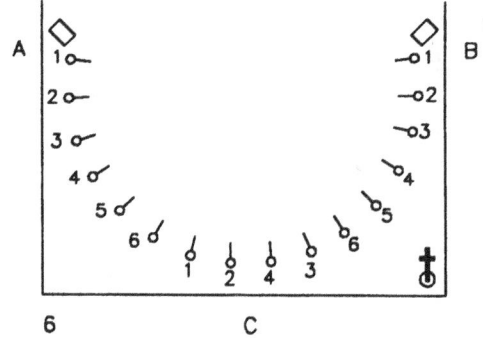

St.L: A, C1, 2
St.R: B, C3, 4

BACCHANALE

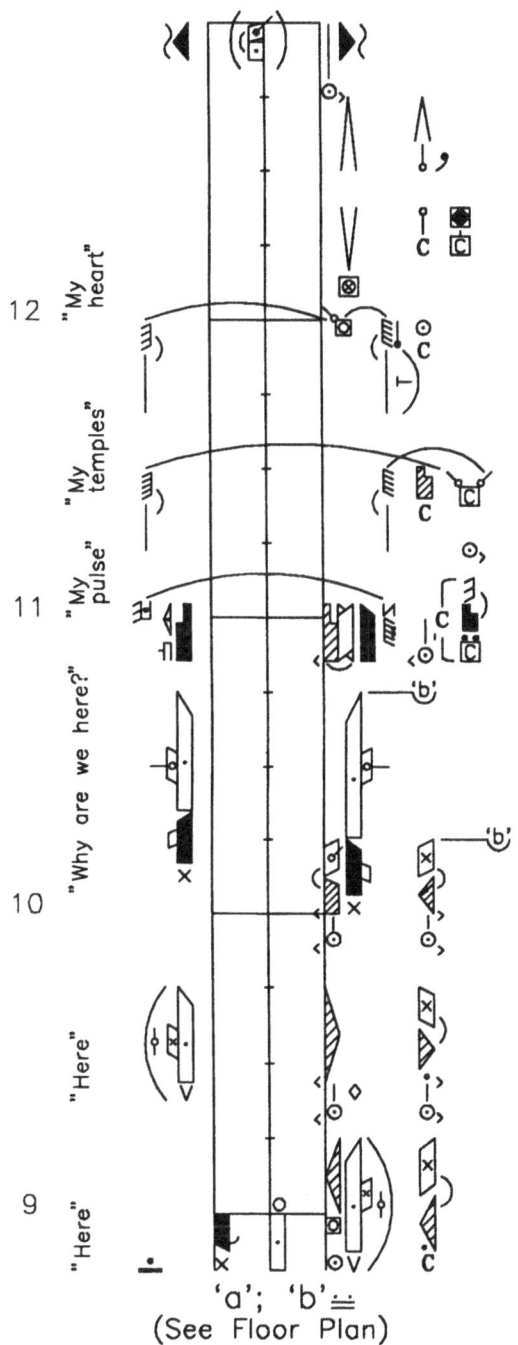

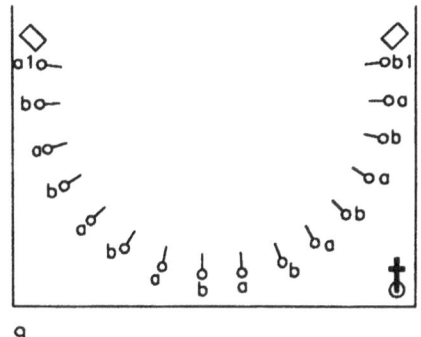

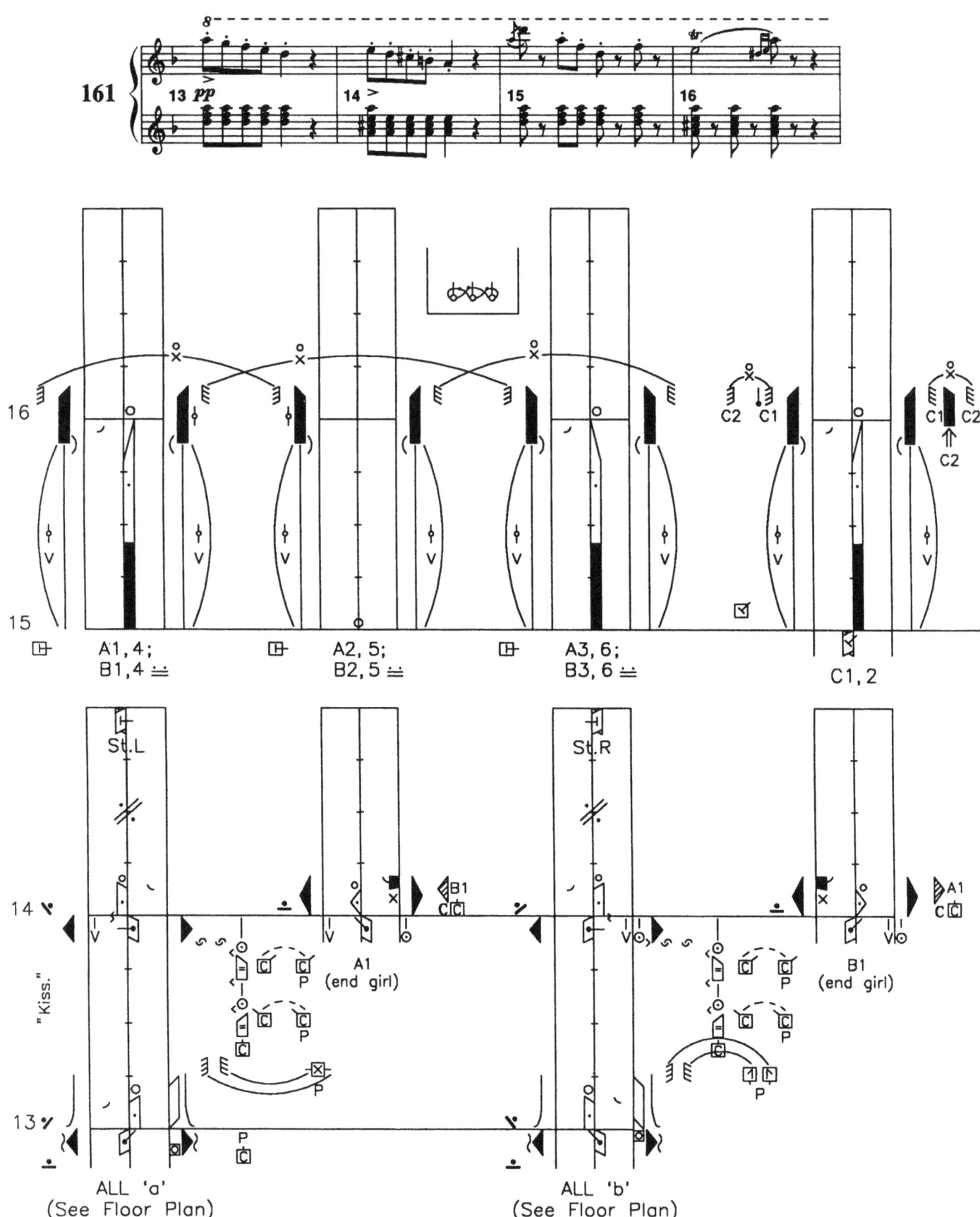

BACCHANALE

65

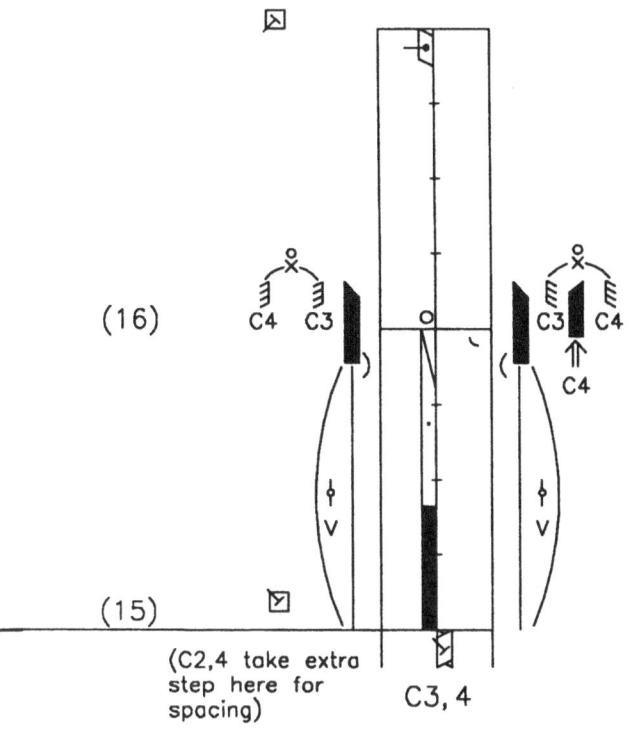

(C2,4 take extra step here for spacing)

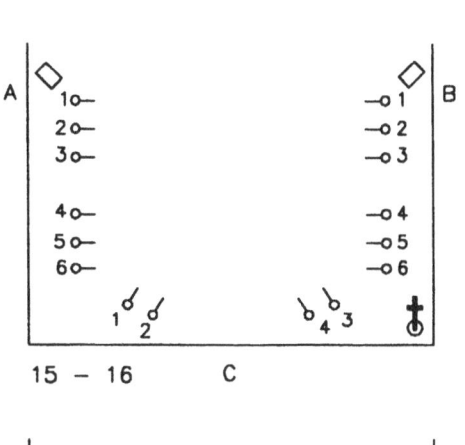

15 – 16

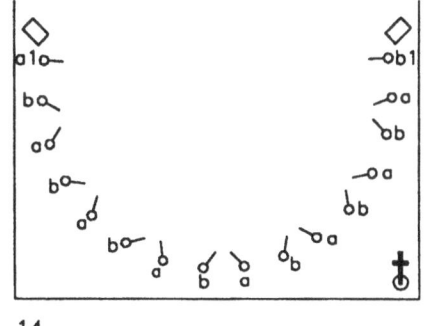

14

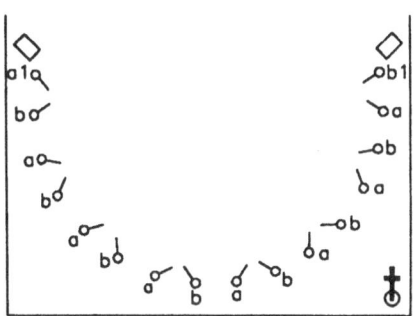

13

17 − 19 for C

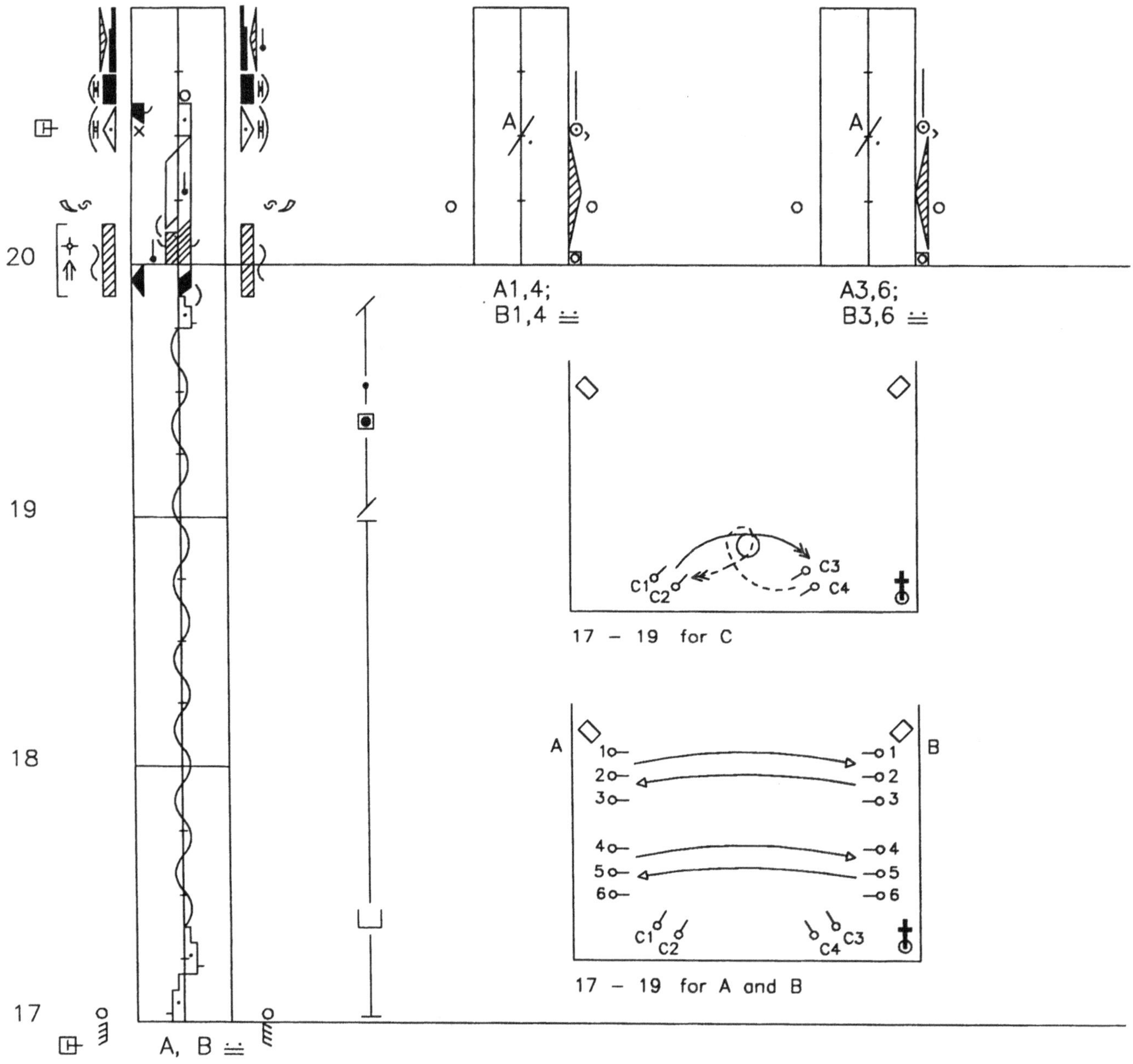

17 − 19 for A and B

BACCHANALE

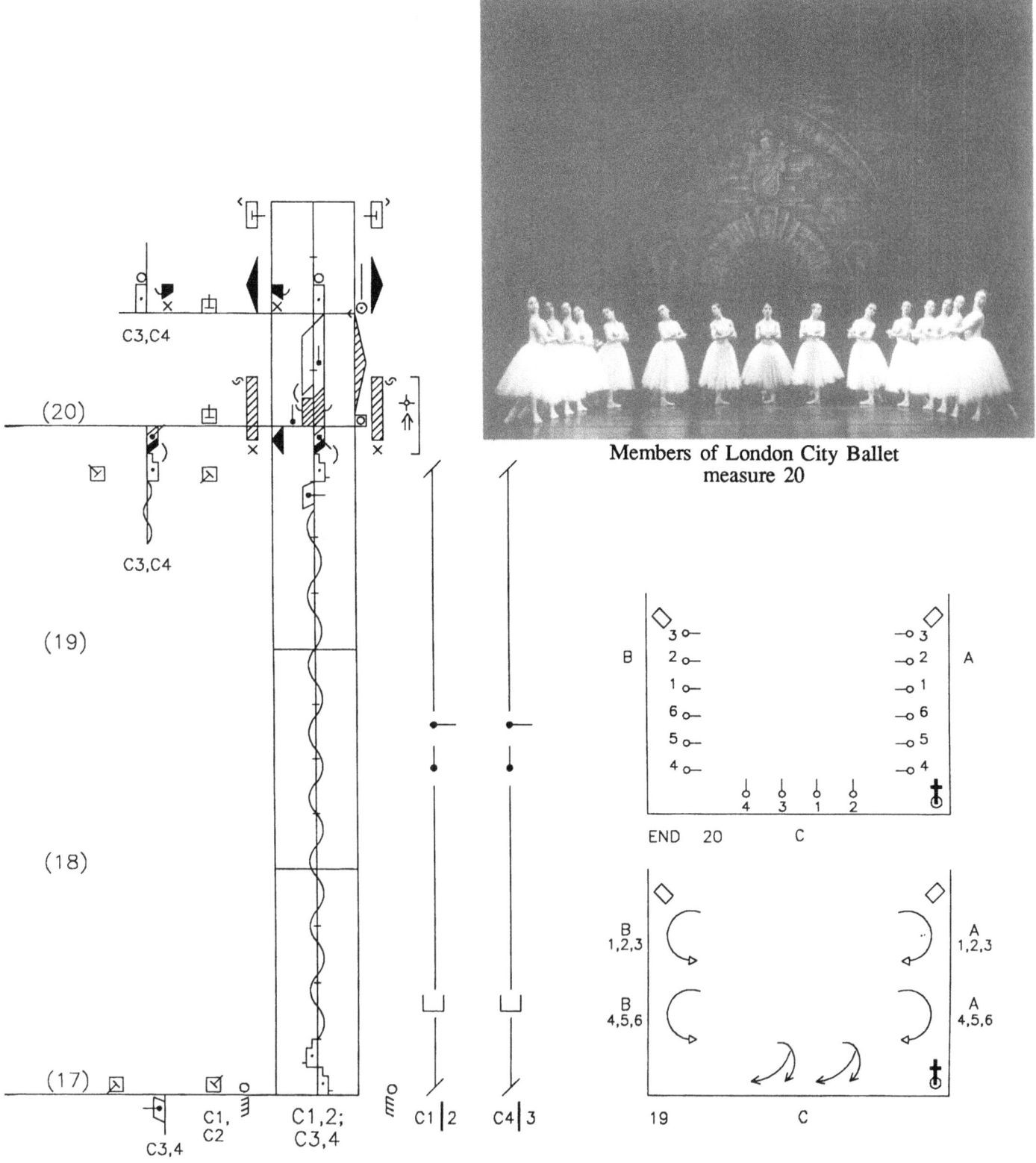

Members of London City Ballet
measure 20

ROBERT LE DIABLE - THE BALLET OF THE NUNS

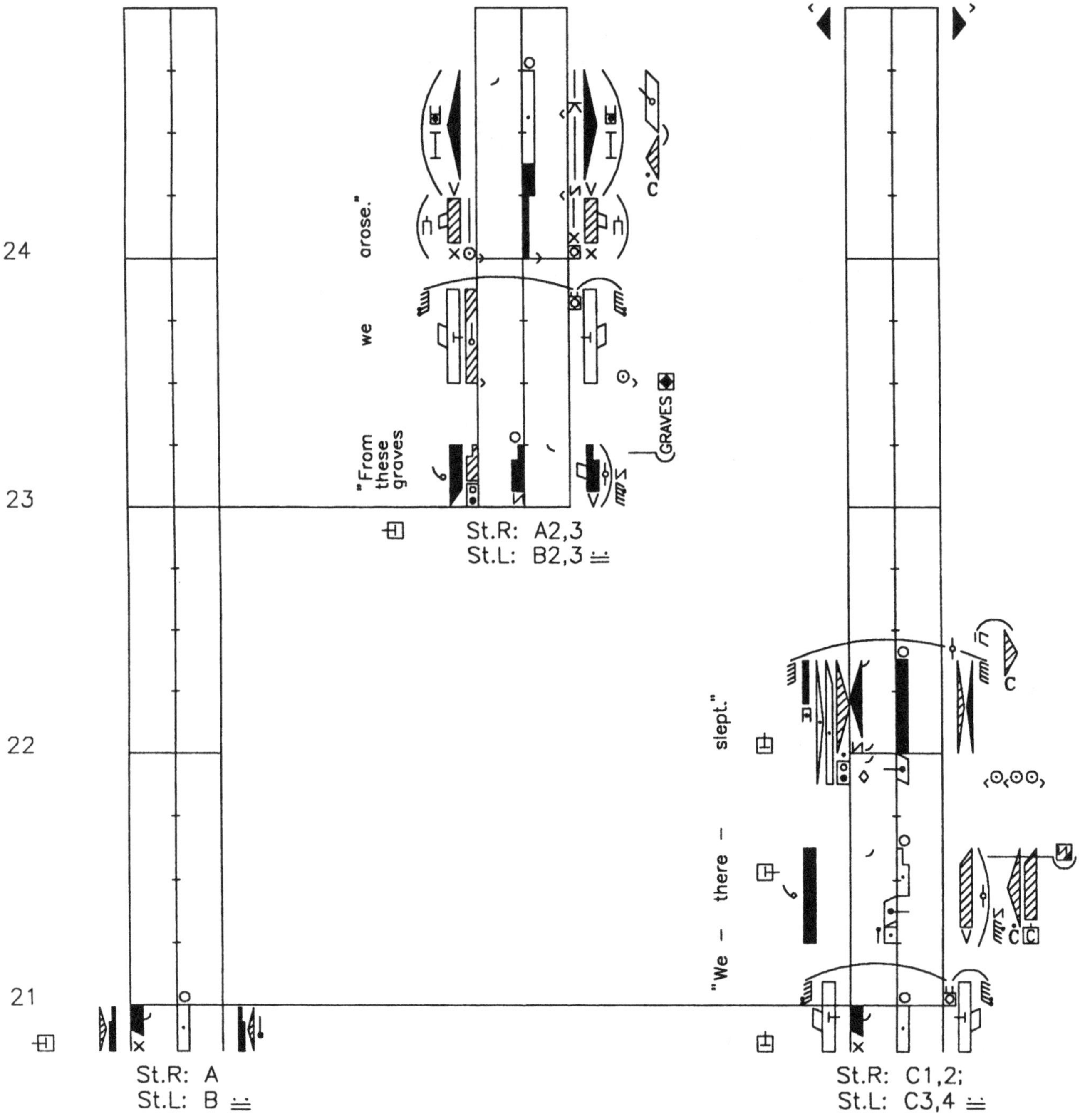

BACCHANALE

measure 23, count 1

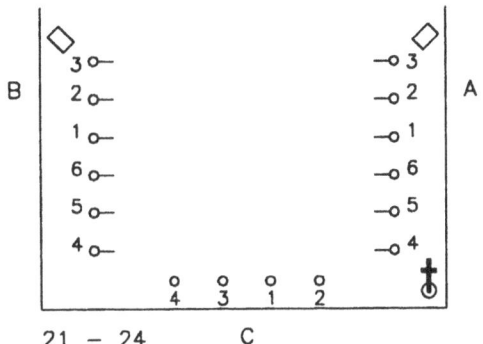

ROBERT LE DIABLE - THE BALLET OF THE NUNS

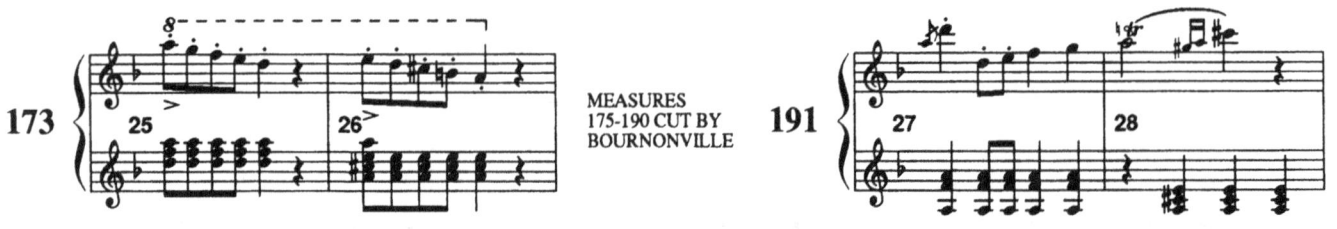

MEASURES 175-190 CUT BY BOURNONVILLE

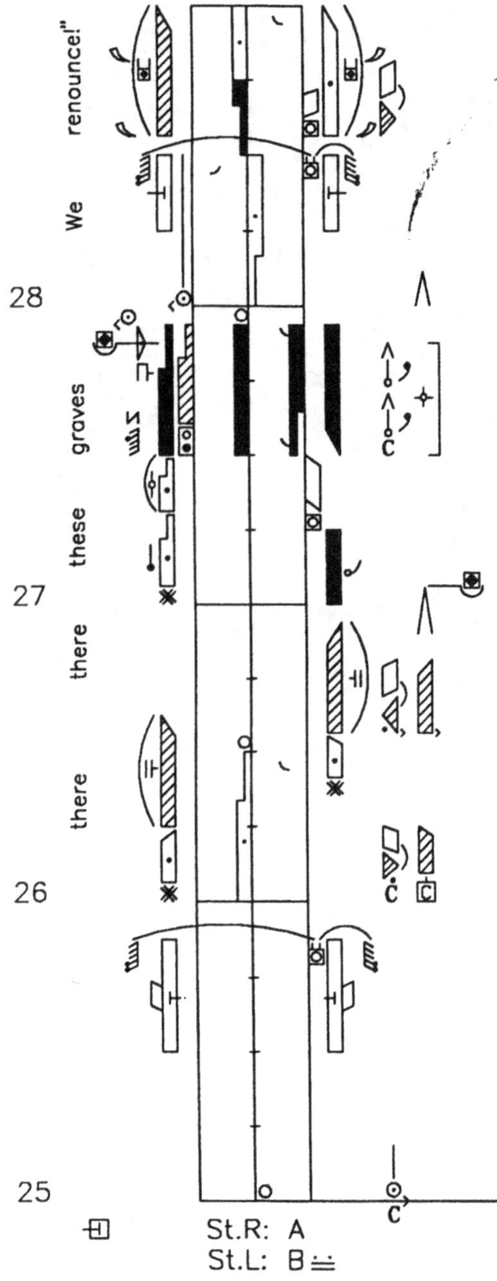

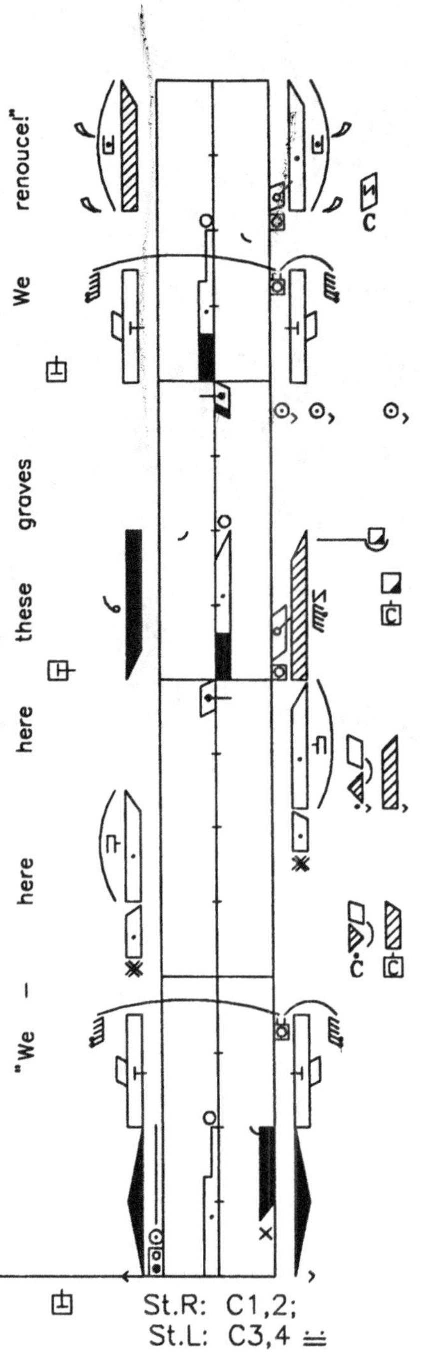

BACCHANALE

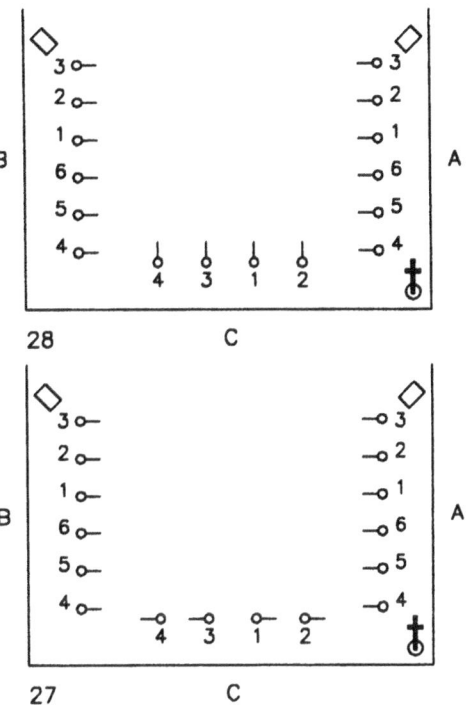

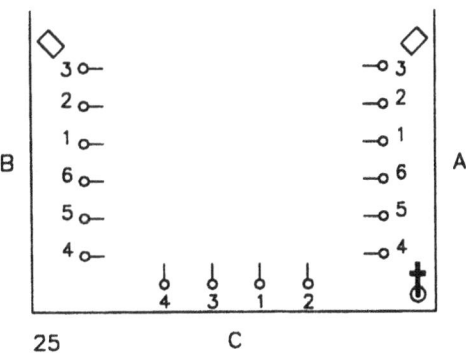

ROBERT LE DIABLE - THE BALLET OF THE NUNS

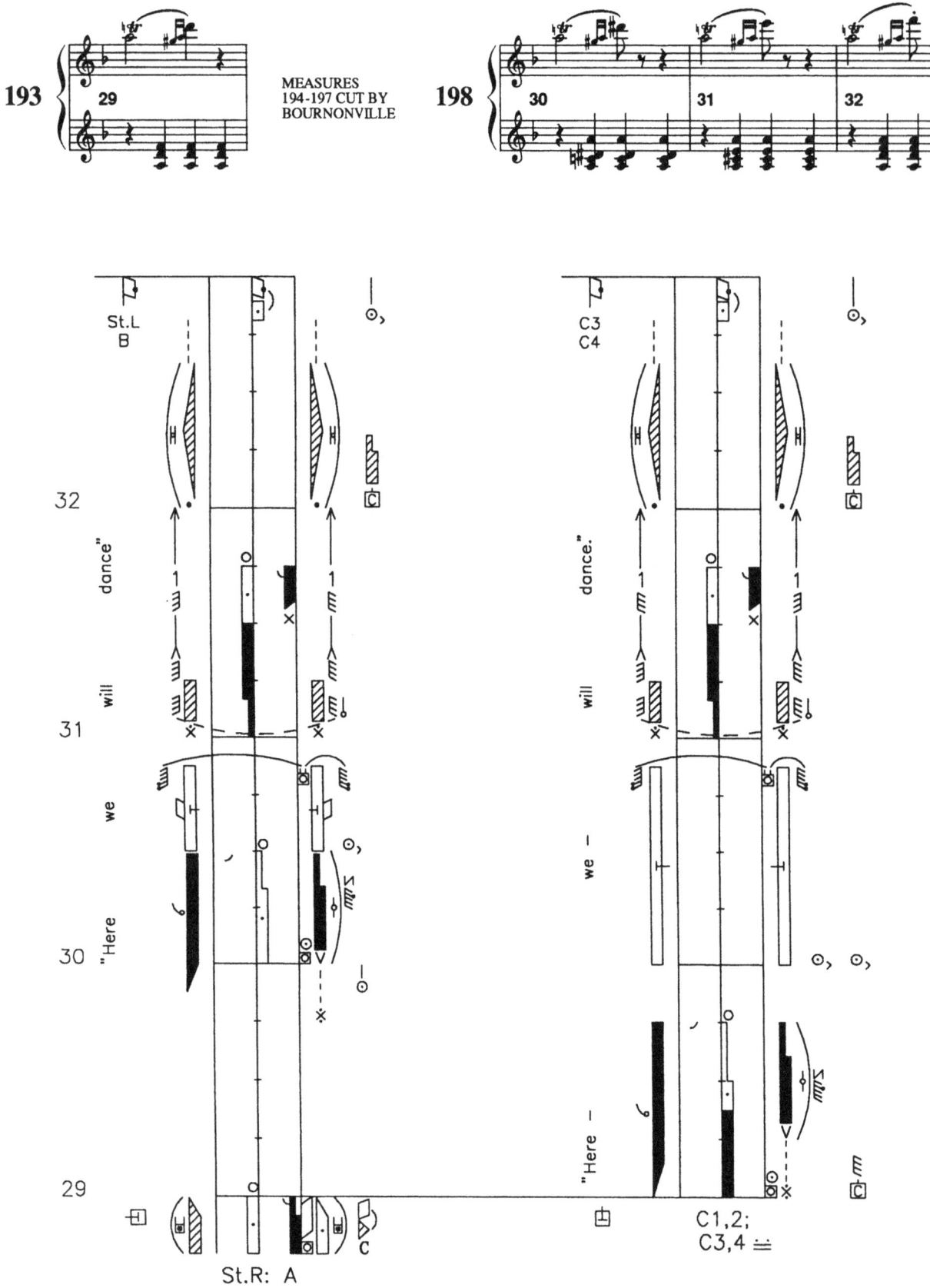

BACCHANALE

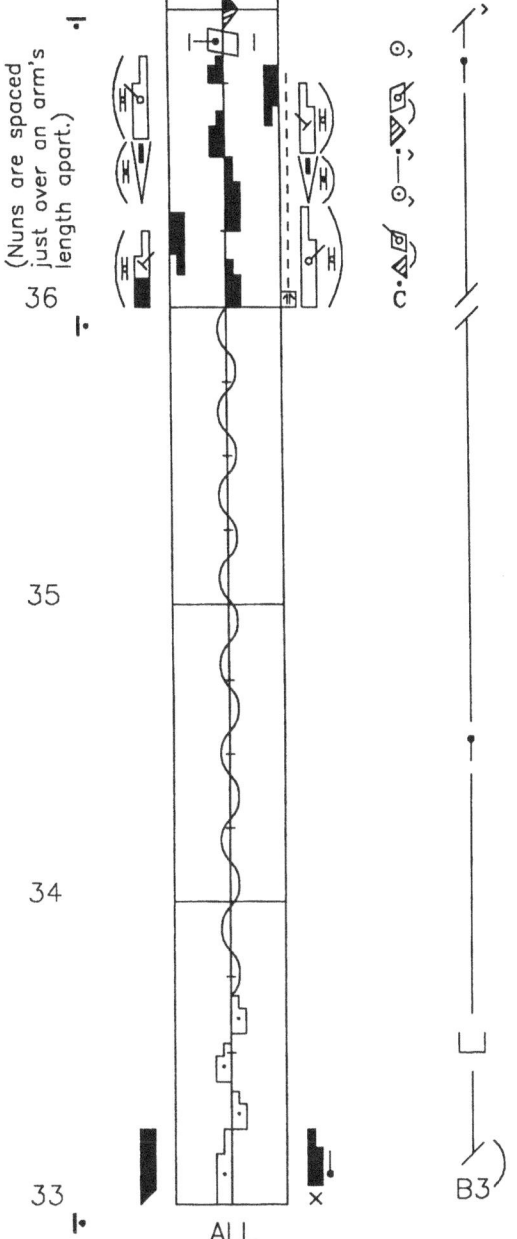

(Nuns are spaced just over an arm's length apart.)

measure 36, count 1

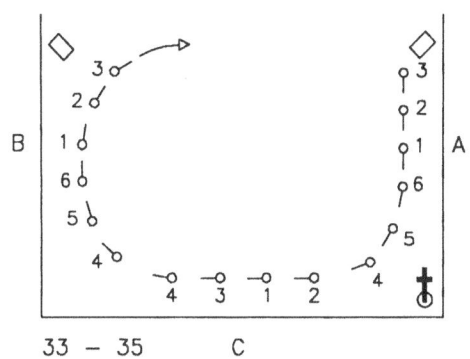

33 – 35

ROBERT LE DIABLE - THE BALLET OF THE NUNS

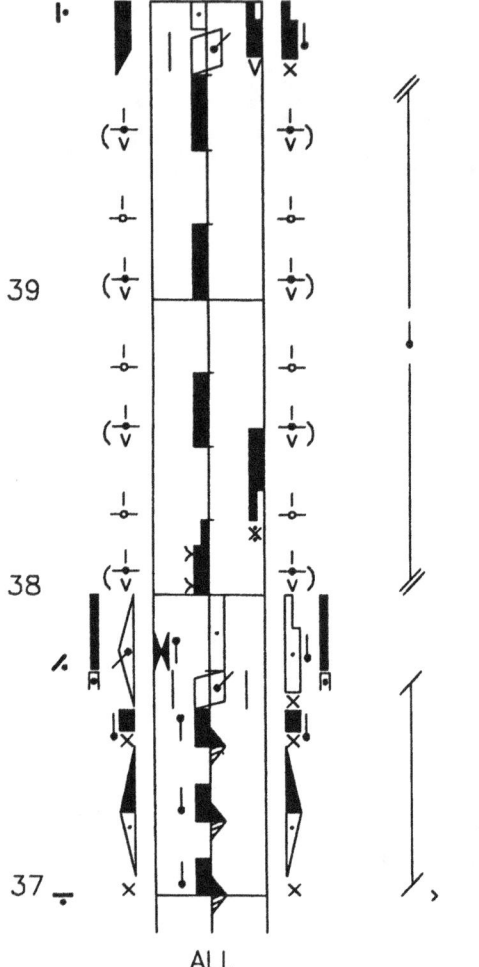

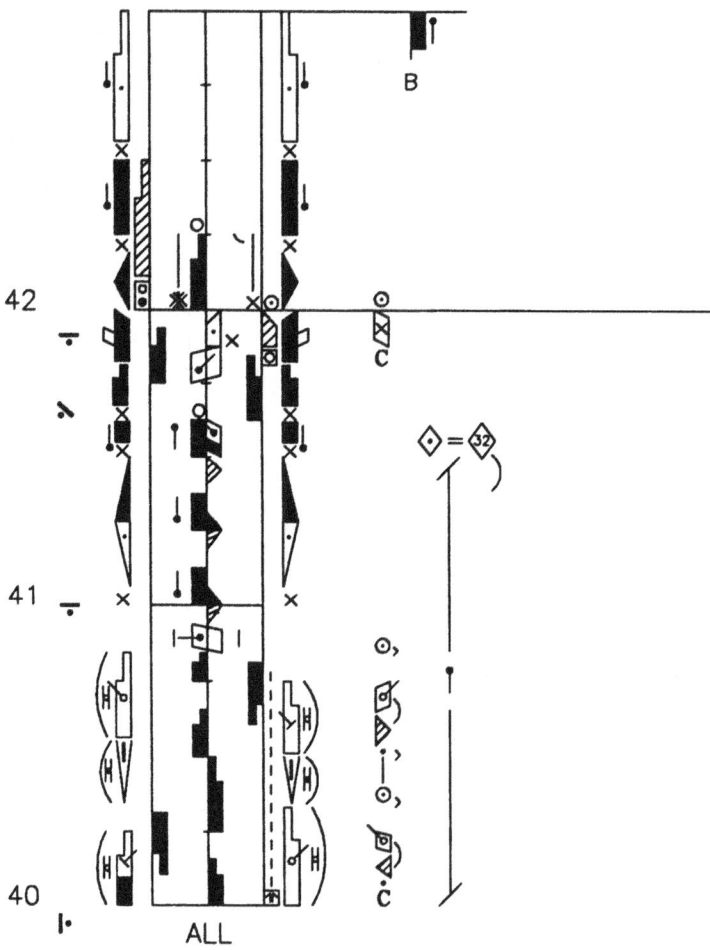

BACCHANALE

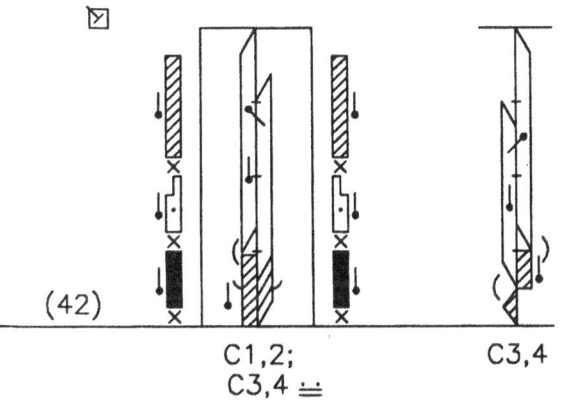

(42)   C1,2;
       C3,4 ≕   C3,4

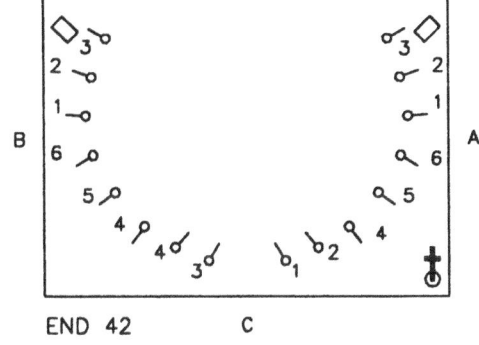

END 42   C

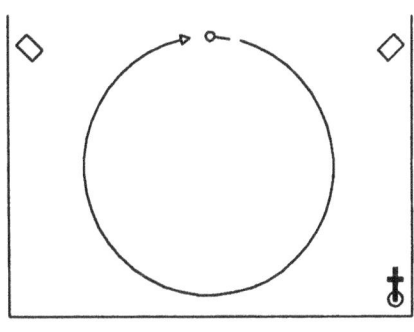

36 — 40

211
43
44
45
46

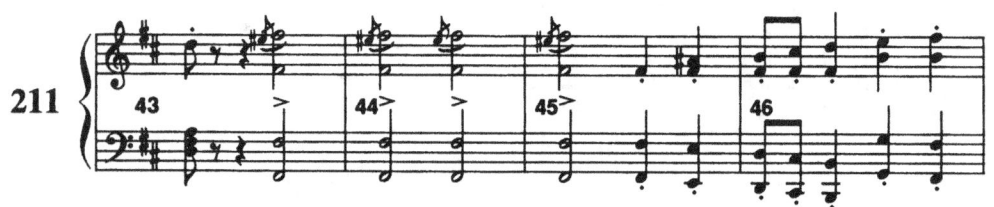

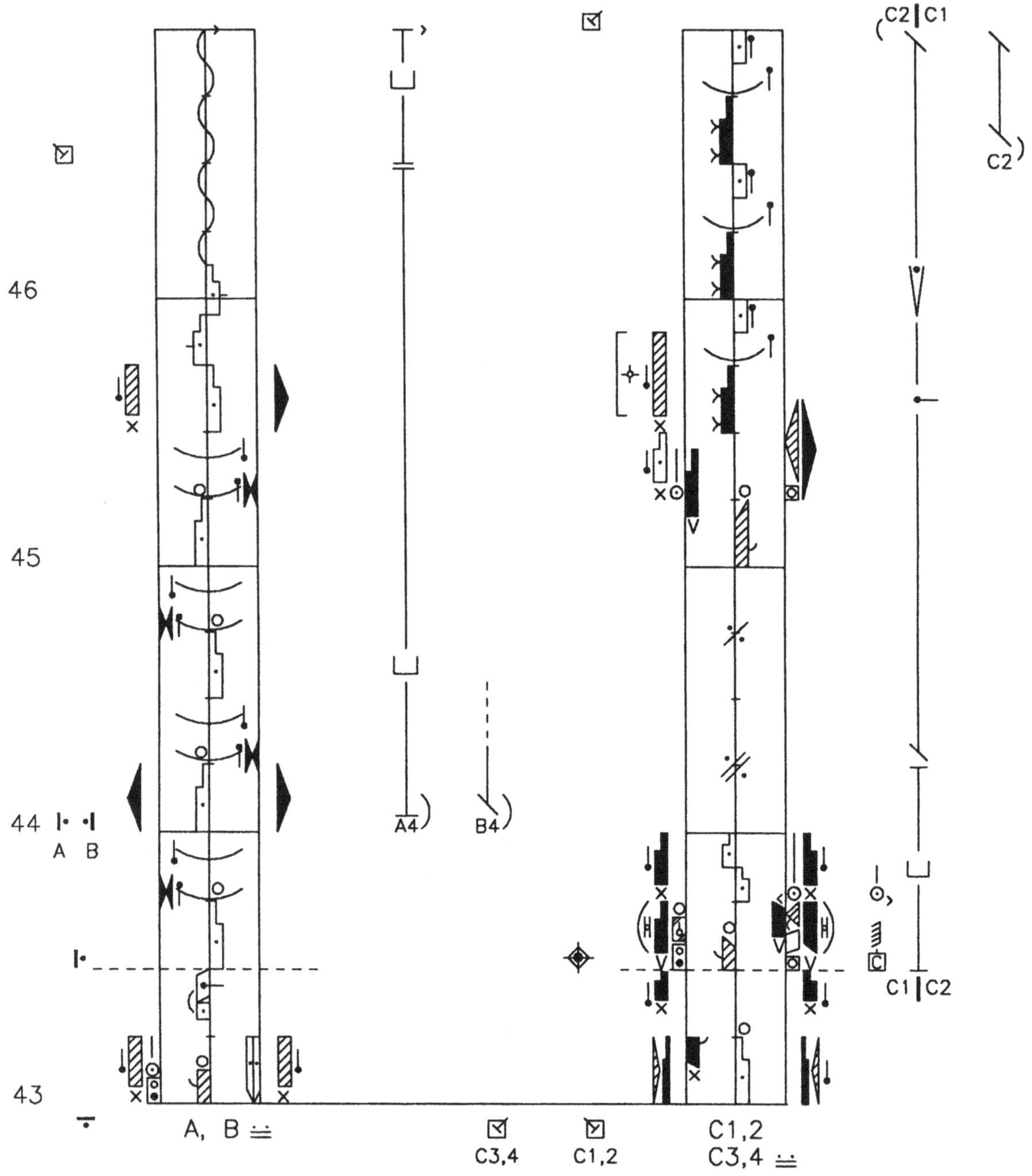
46
45
44
A B
43
A, B
A4
B4
C3,4
C1,2
C1,2
C3,4
C2 C1
C2
C1 C2

BACCHANALE

77

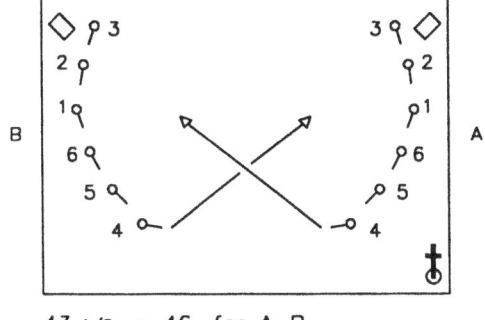

43 1/2 — 46 for A, B

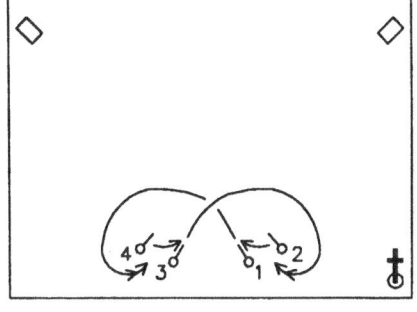

43 1/2 — 46 for C

ROBERT LE DIABLE - THE BALLET OF THE NUNS

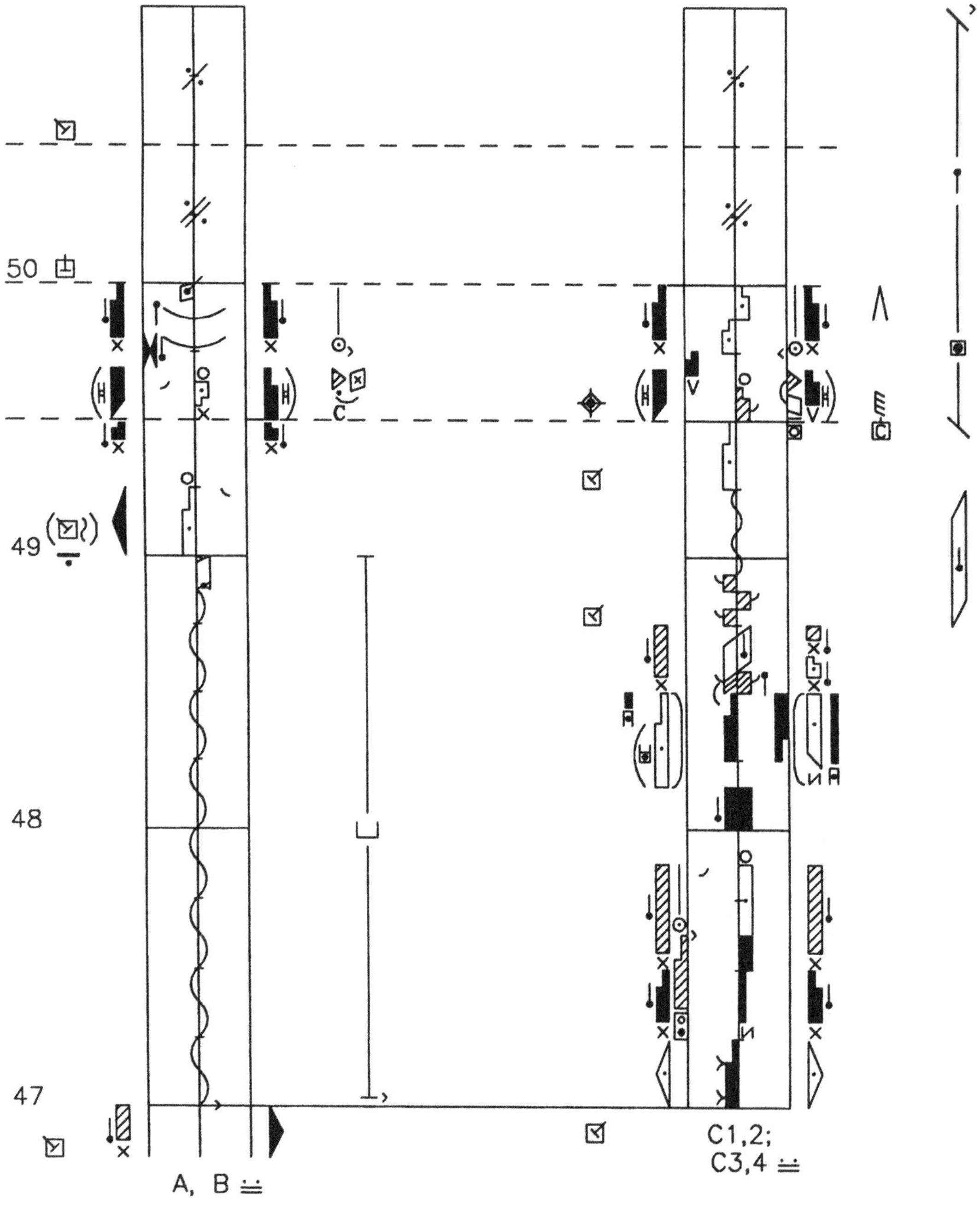

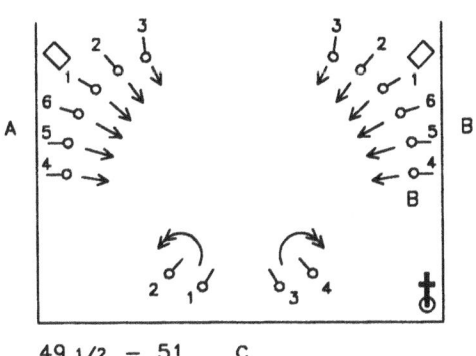

49 1/2 – 51

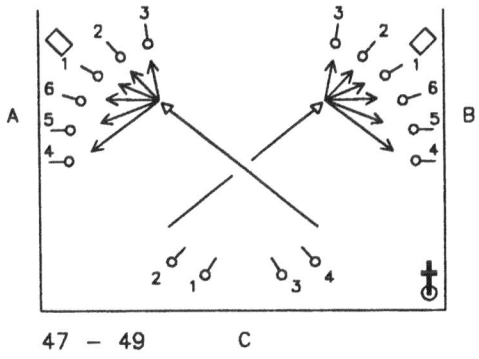

47 – 49

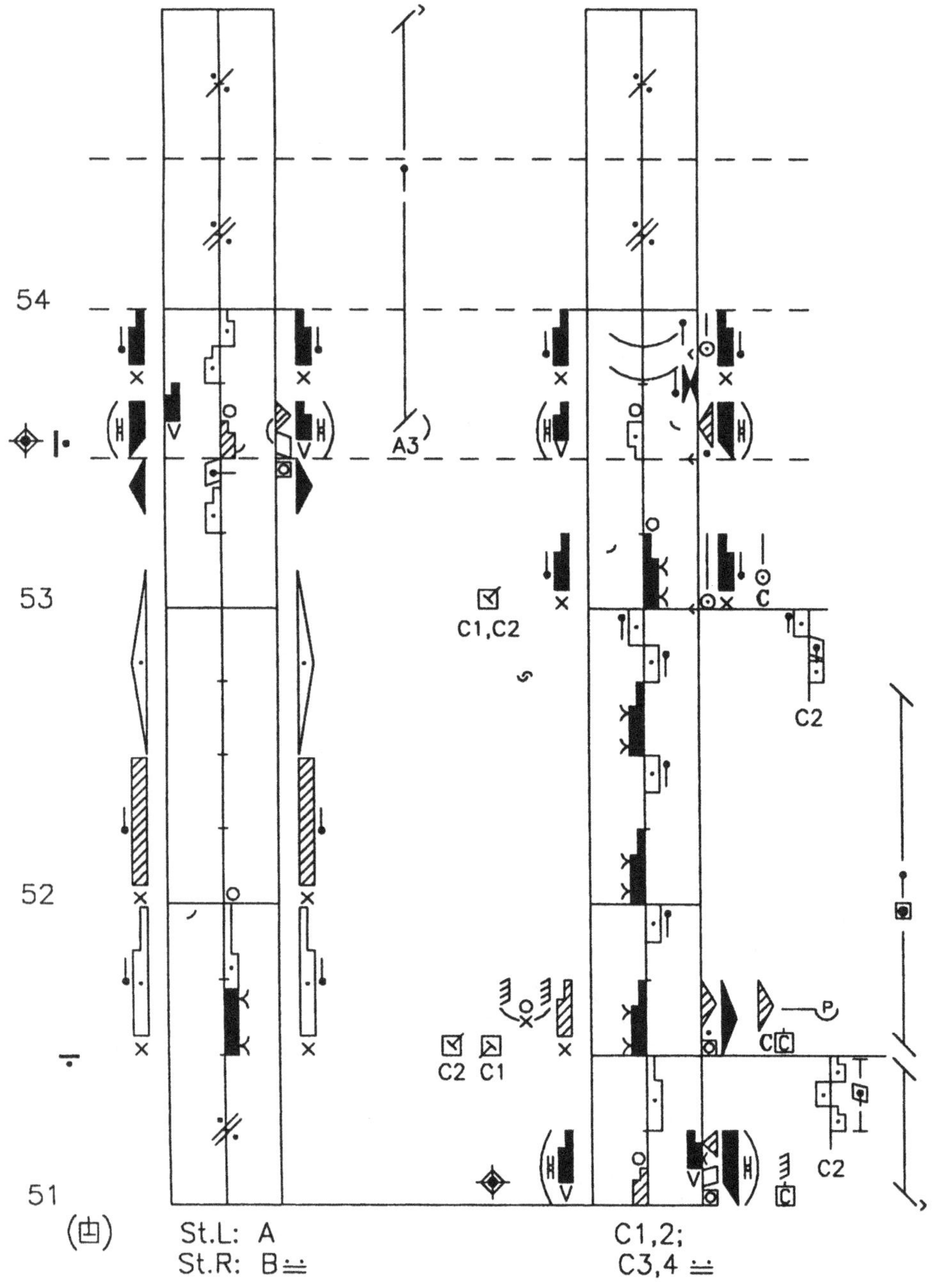

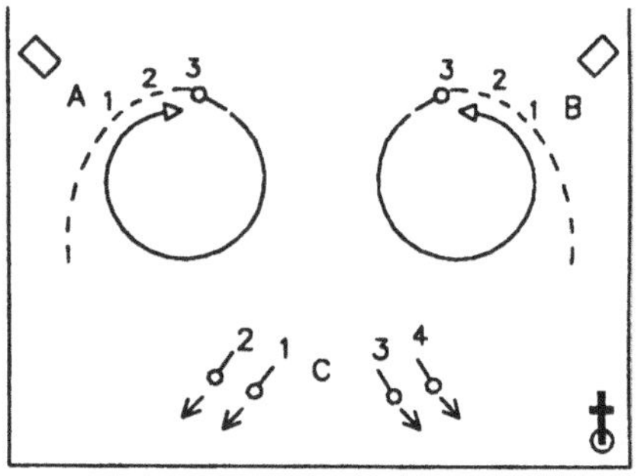

ROBERT LE DIABLE - THE BALLET OF THE NUNS

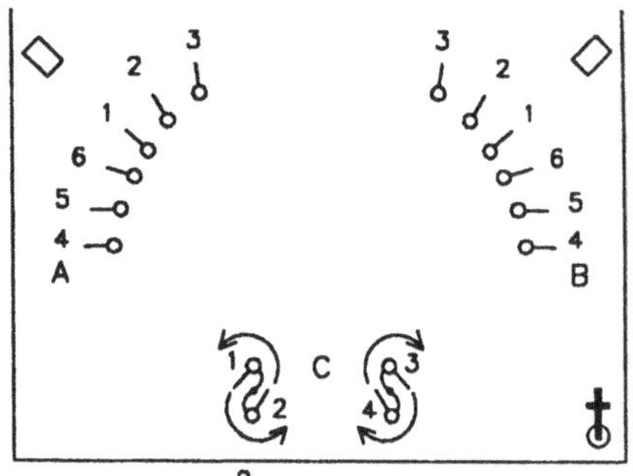

223

55
56
57

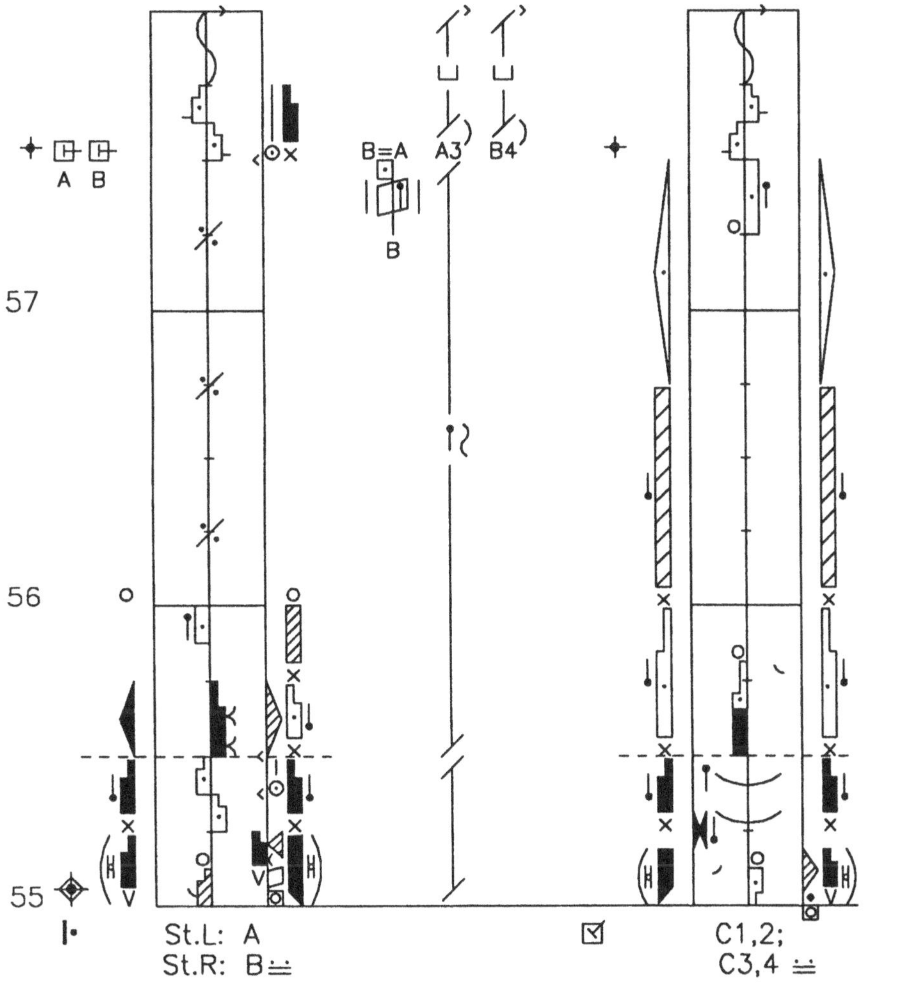
A B
B=A
B
A3
B4
C2
C3,4=C1,2
57
56
55
St.L: A
St.R: B
C1,2;
C3,4

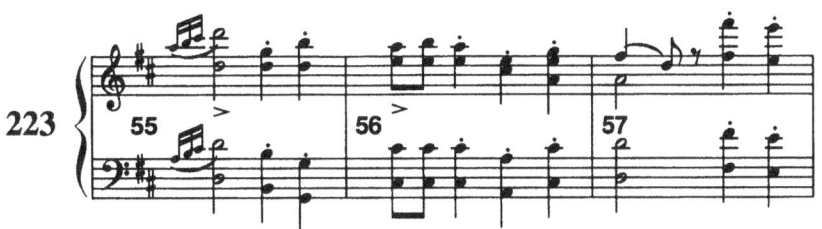

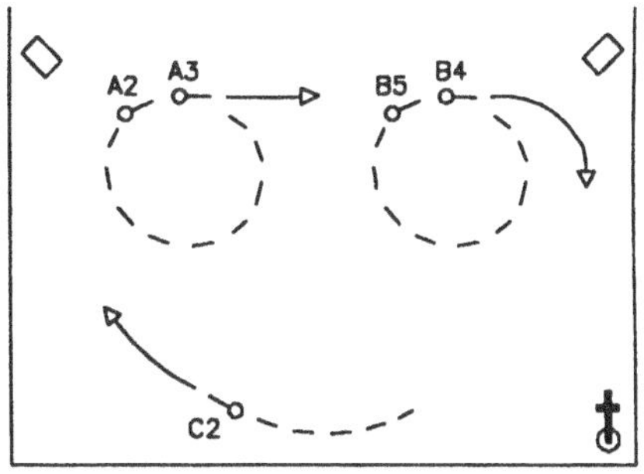
A2
A3
B5
B4
C2

57 1/2

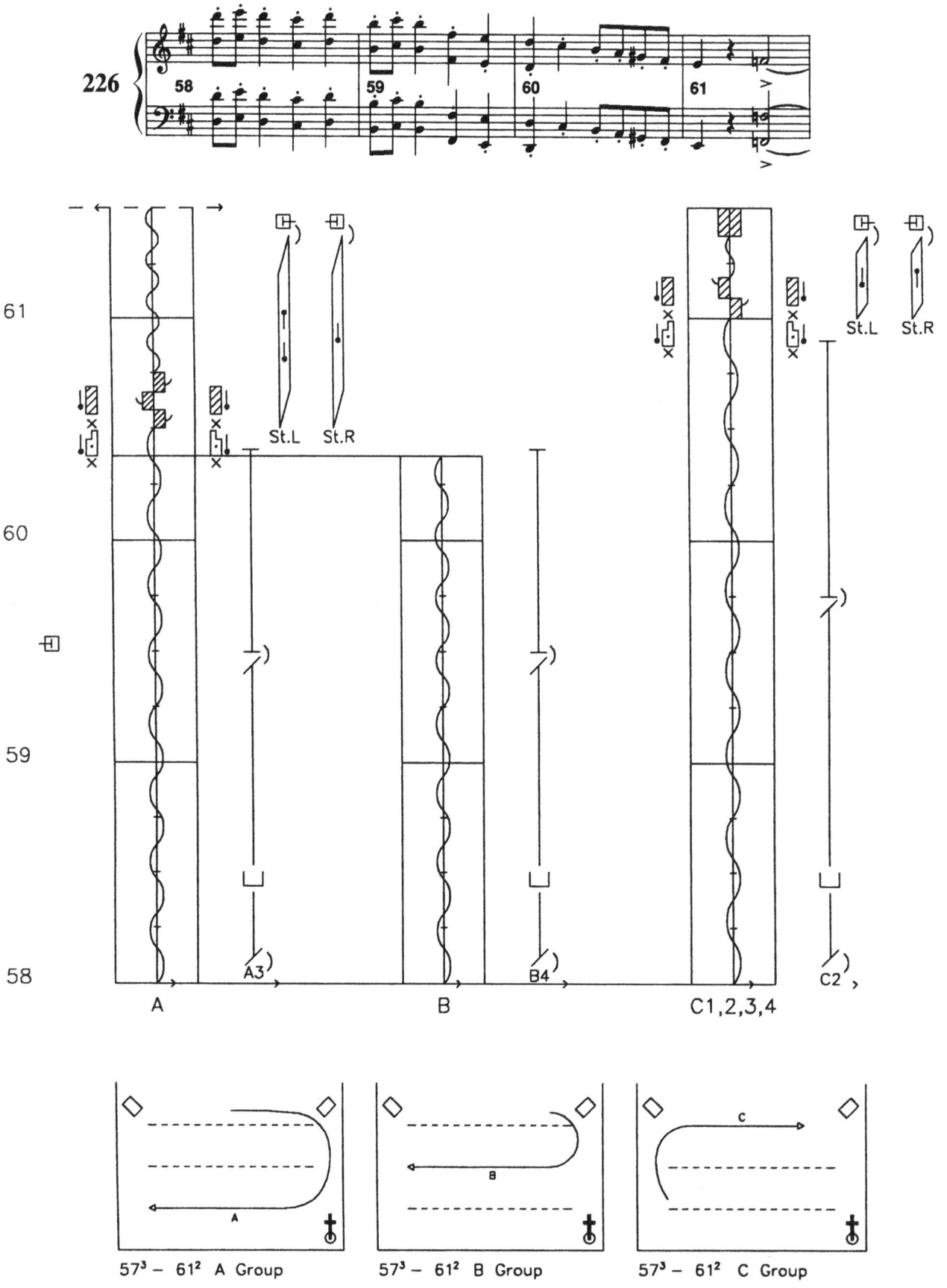

BACCHANALE

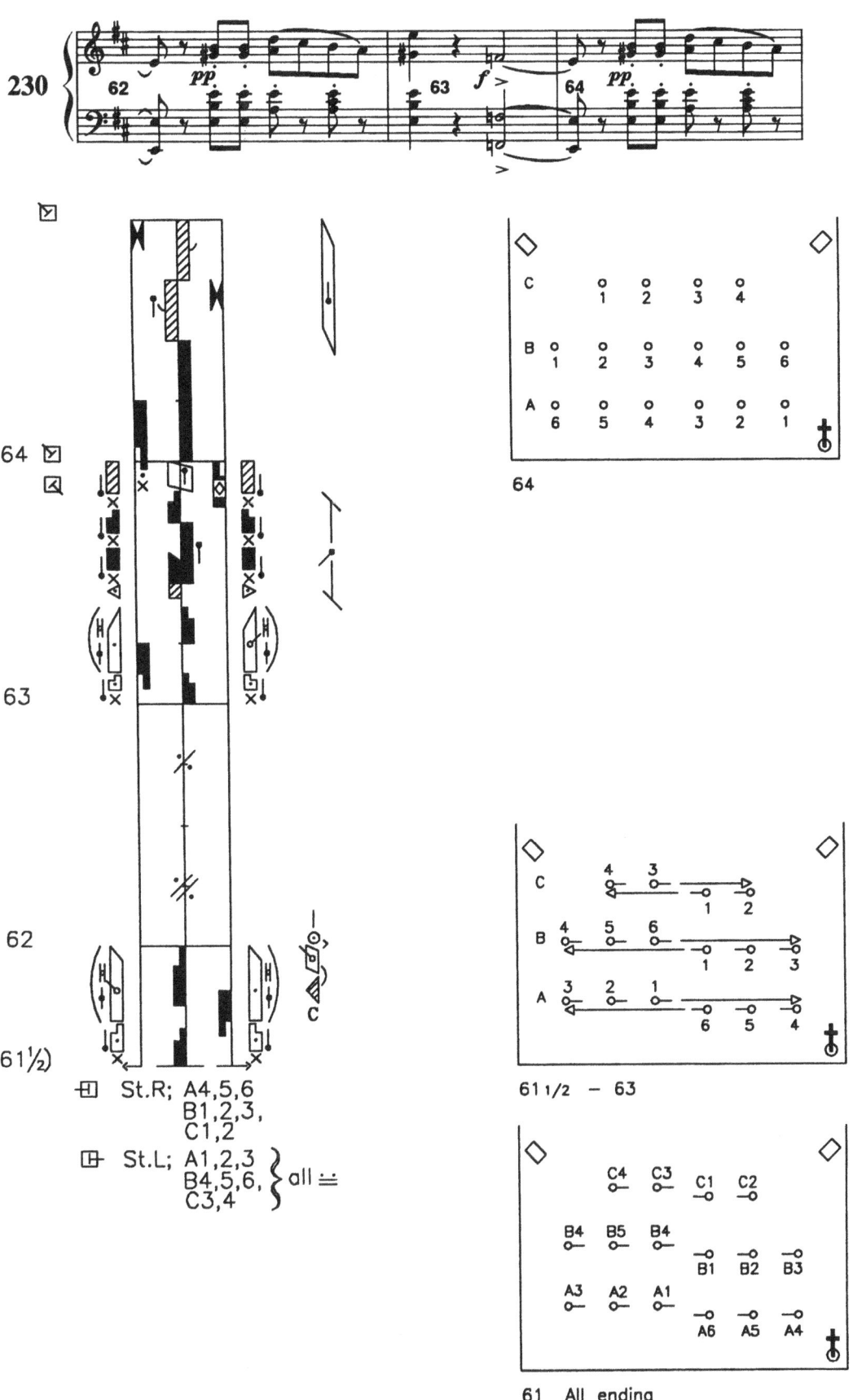

ROBERT LE DIABLE - THE BALLET OF THE NUNS

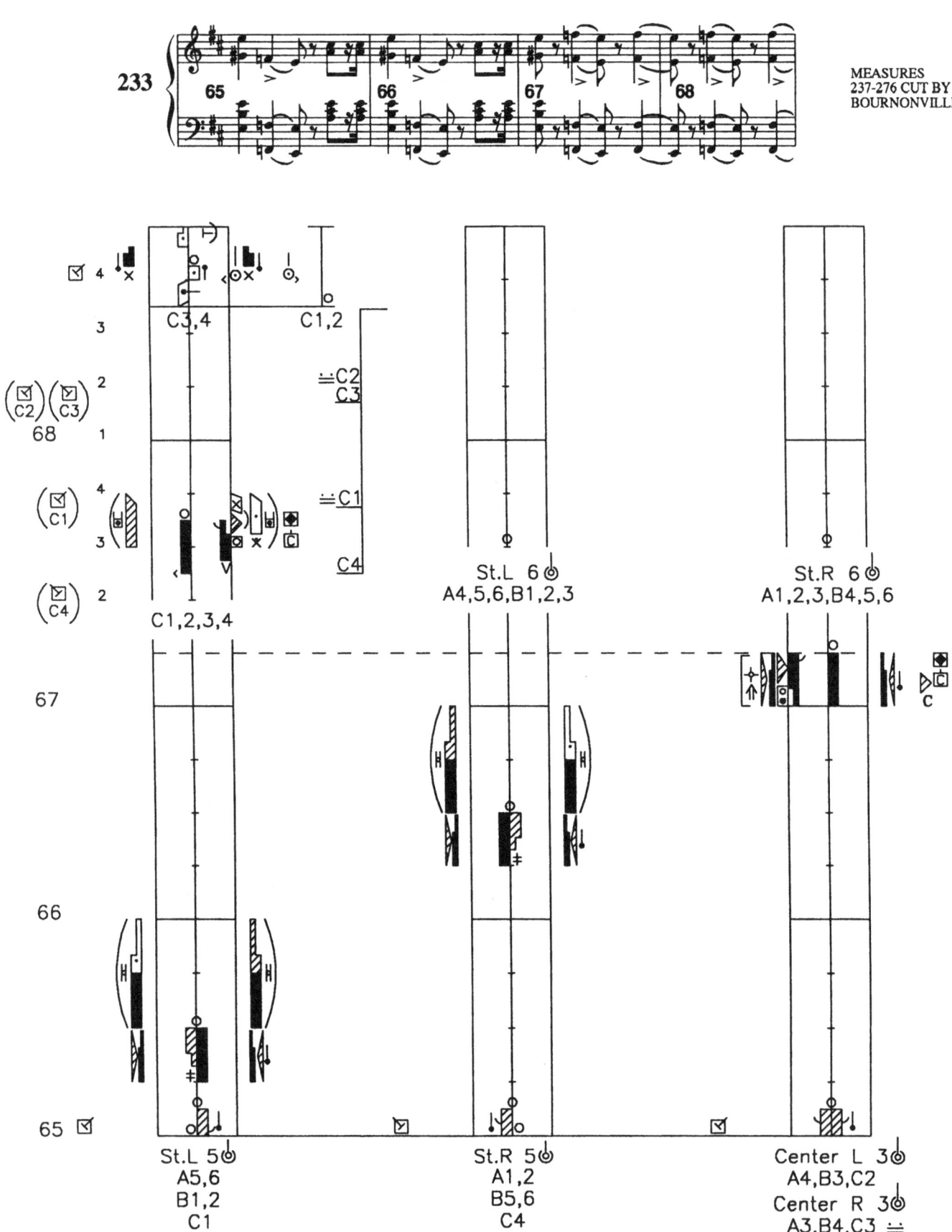

MEASURES 237-276 CUT BY BOURNONVILLE

BACCHANALE

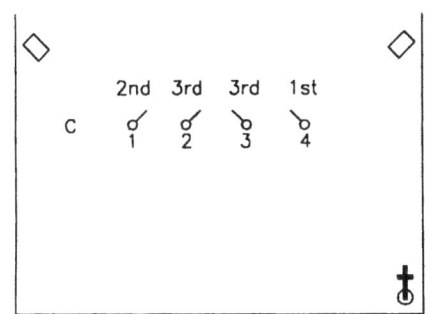

67 1/2, 68   C girls

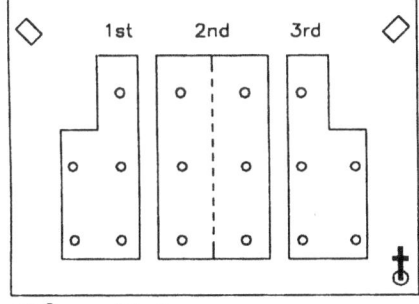

65^2 – 67 Canon

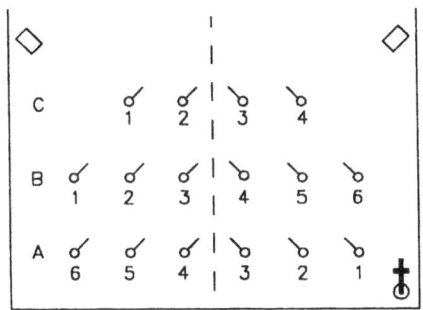

65

measure 67, count 1

86 ROBERT LE DIABLE - THE BALLET OF THE NUNS

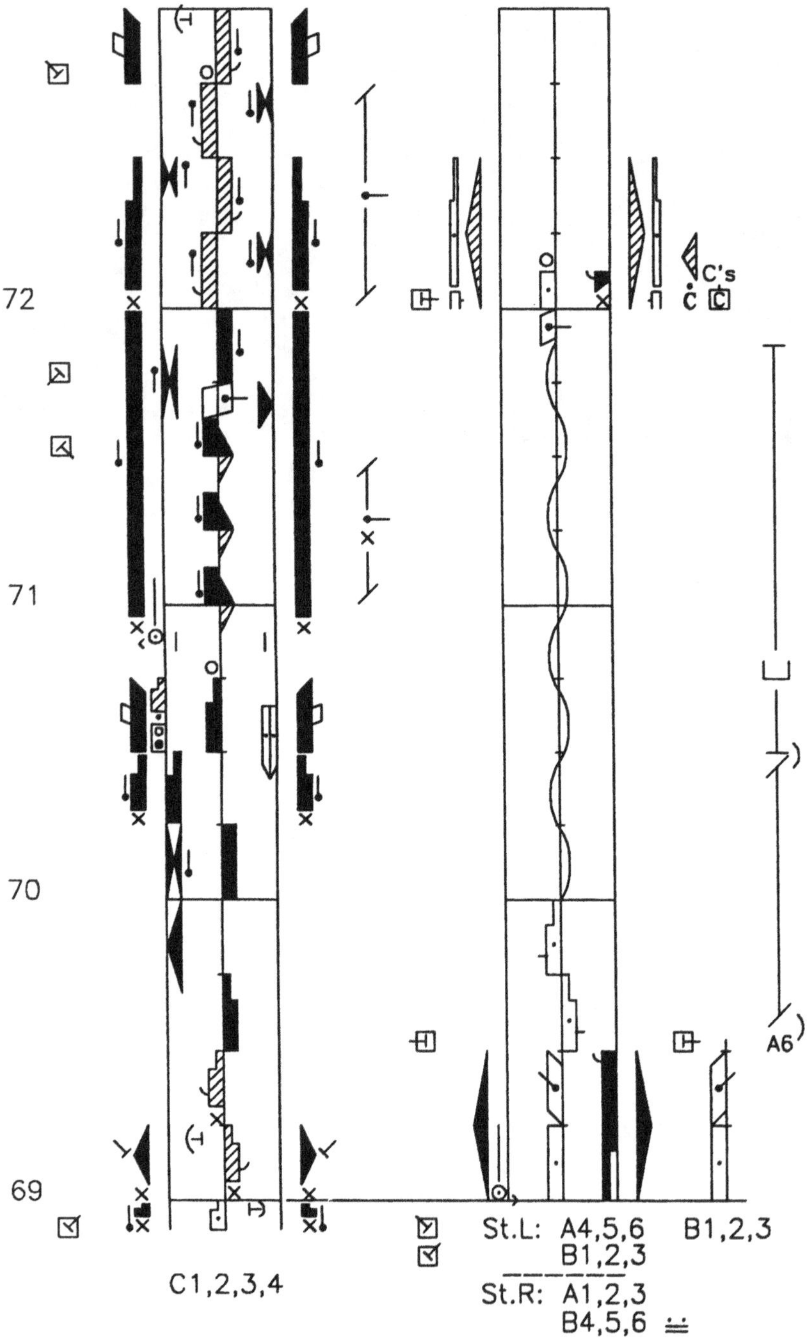

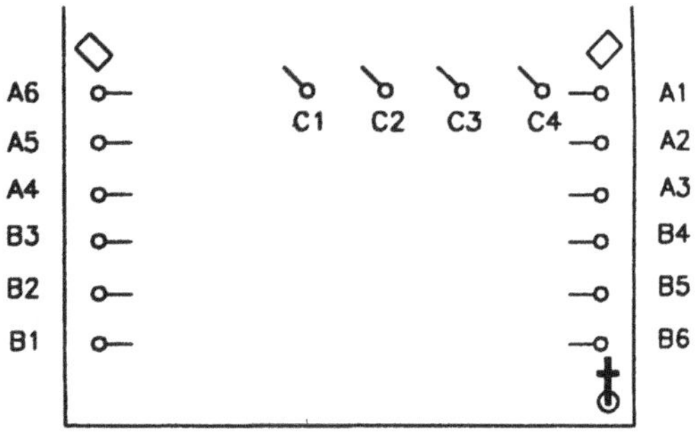

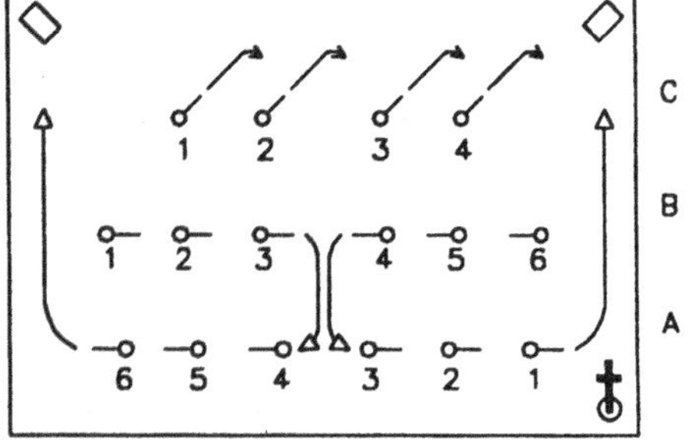

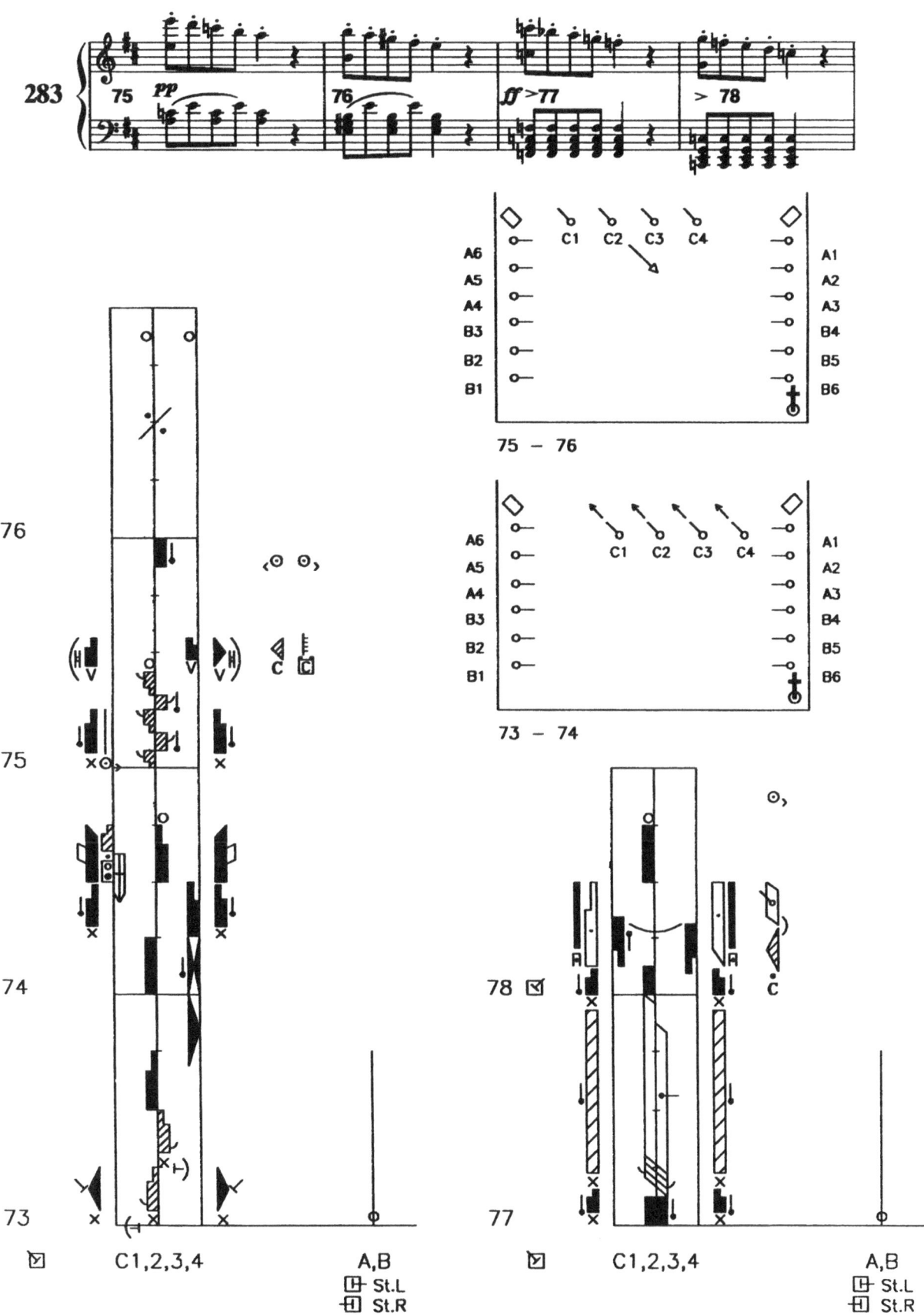

ROBERT LE DIABLE - THE BALLET OF THE NUNS

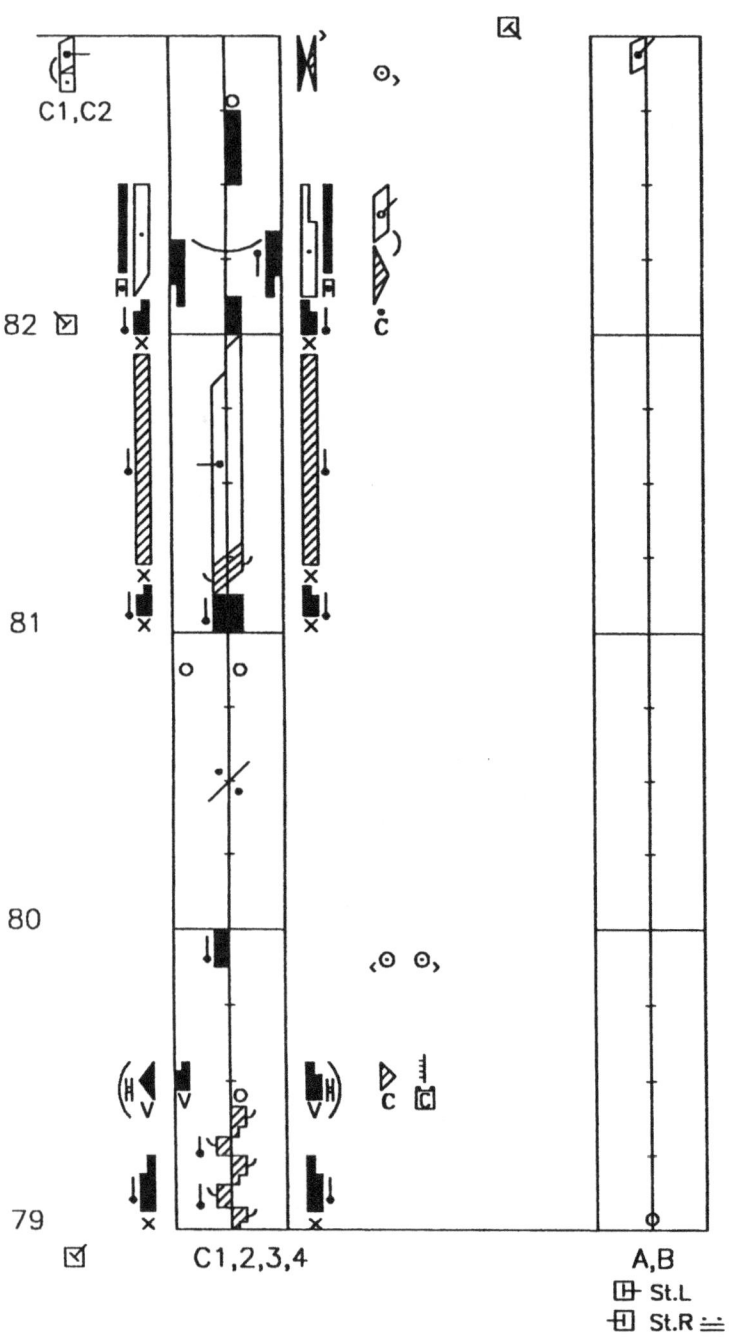

MEASURES
295-325 CUT BY
BOURNONVILLE

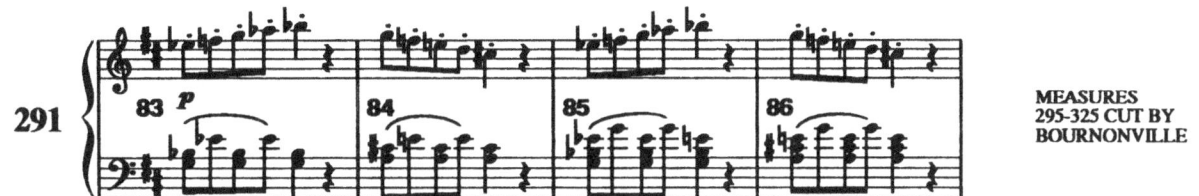

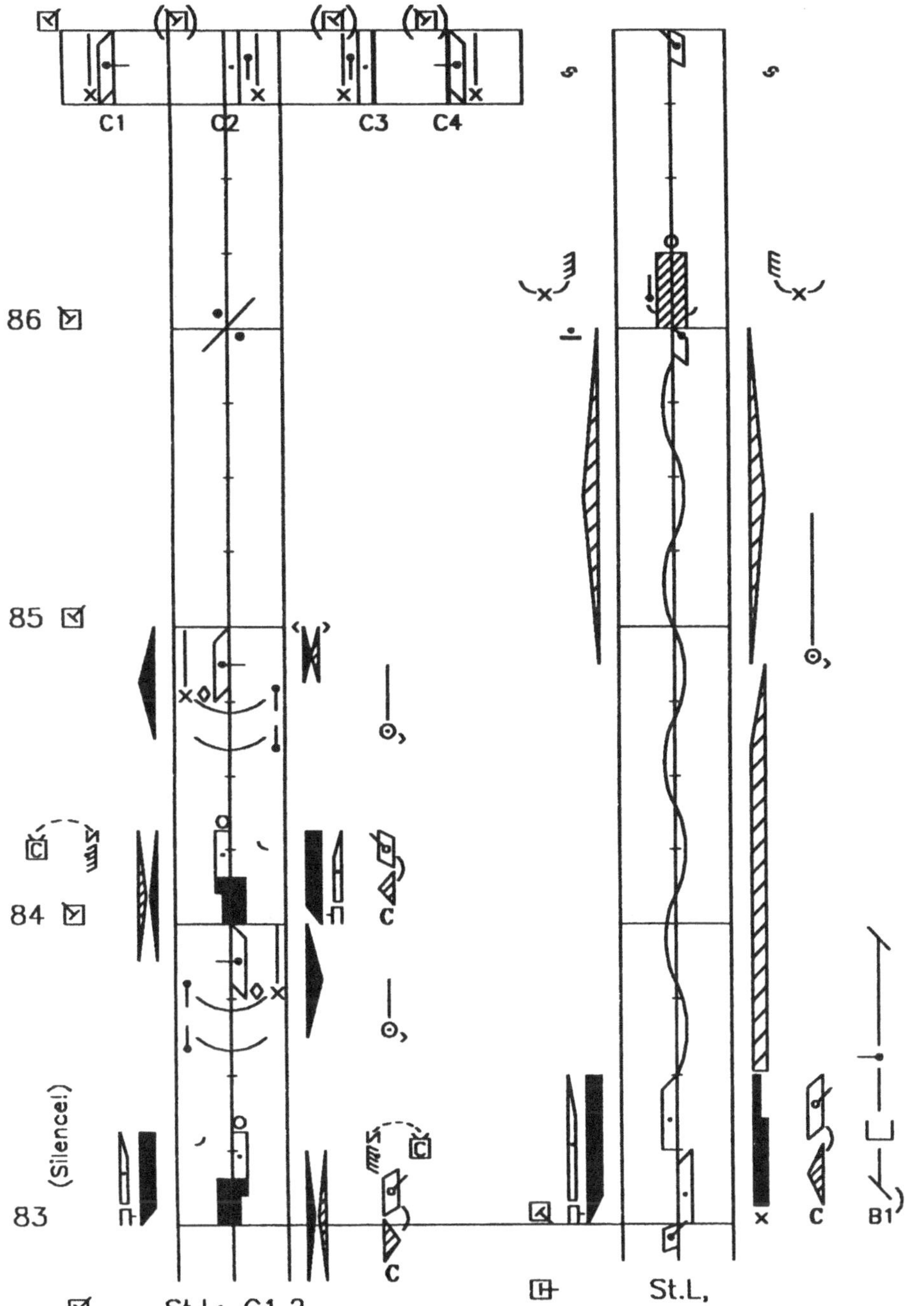

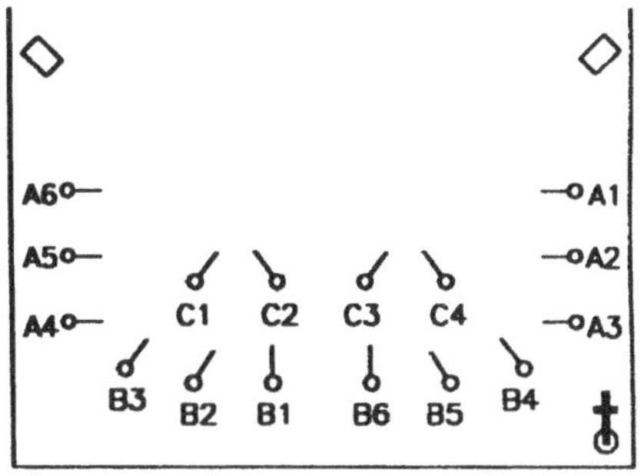

86

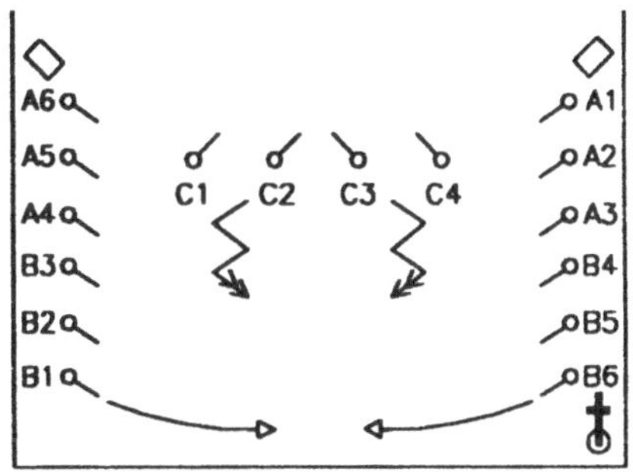

83 – 85

St.L: C1,2
St.R: C3,4

St.L,
St.R;

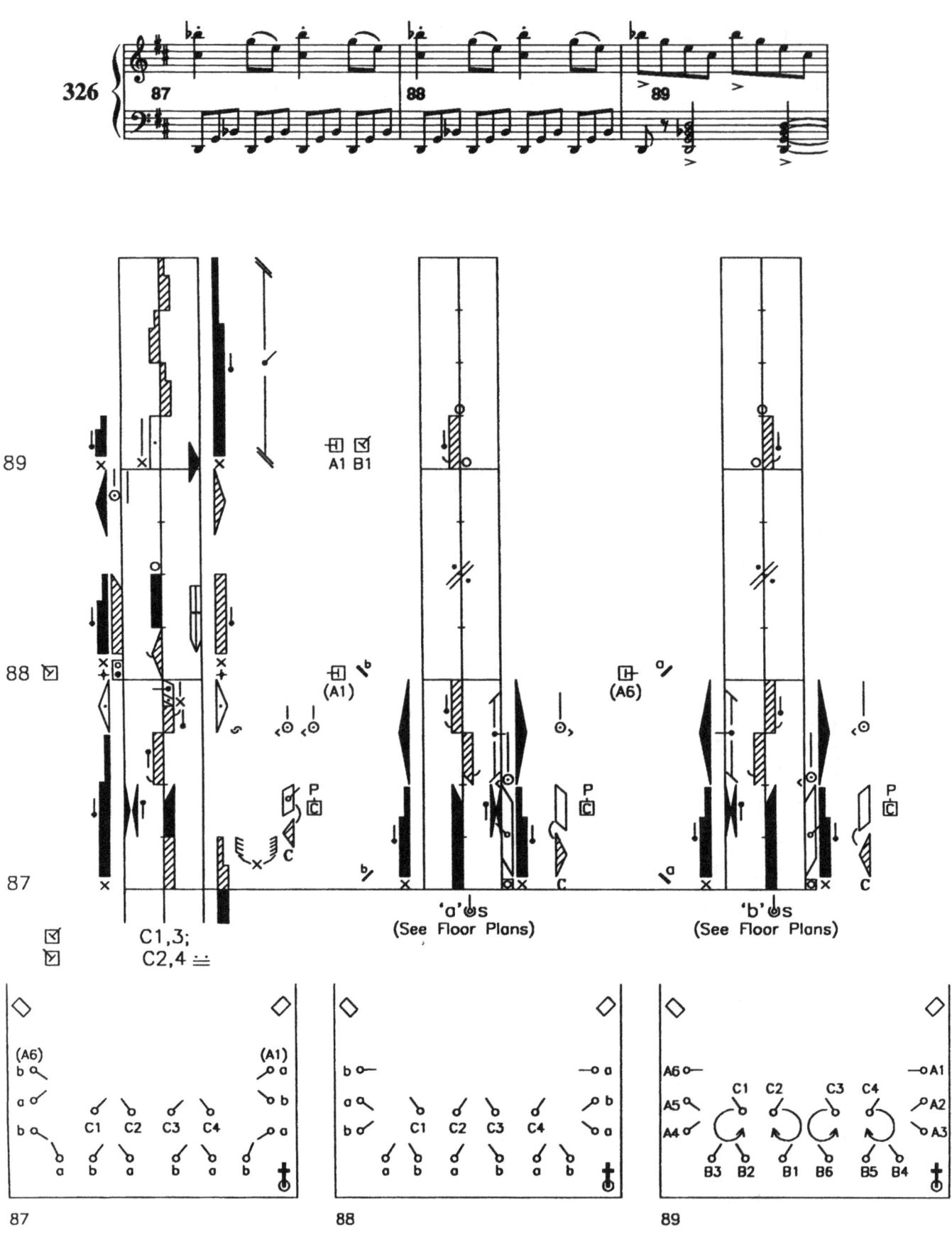

BACCHANALE

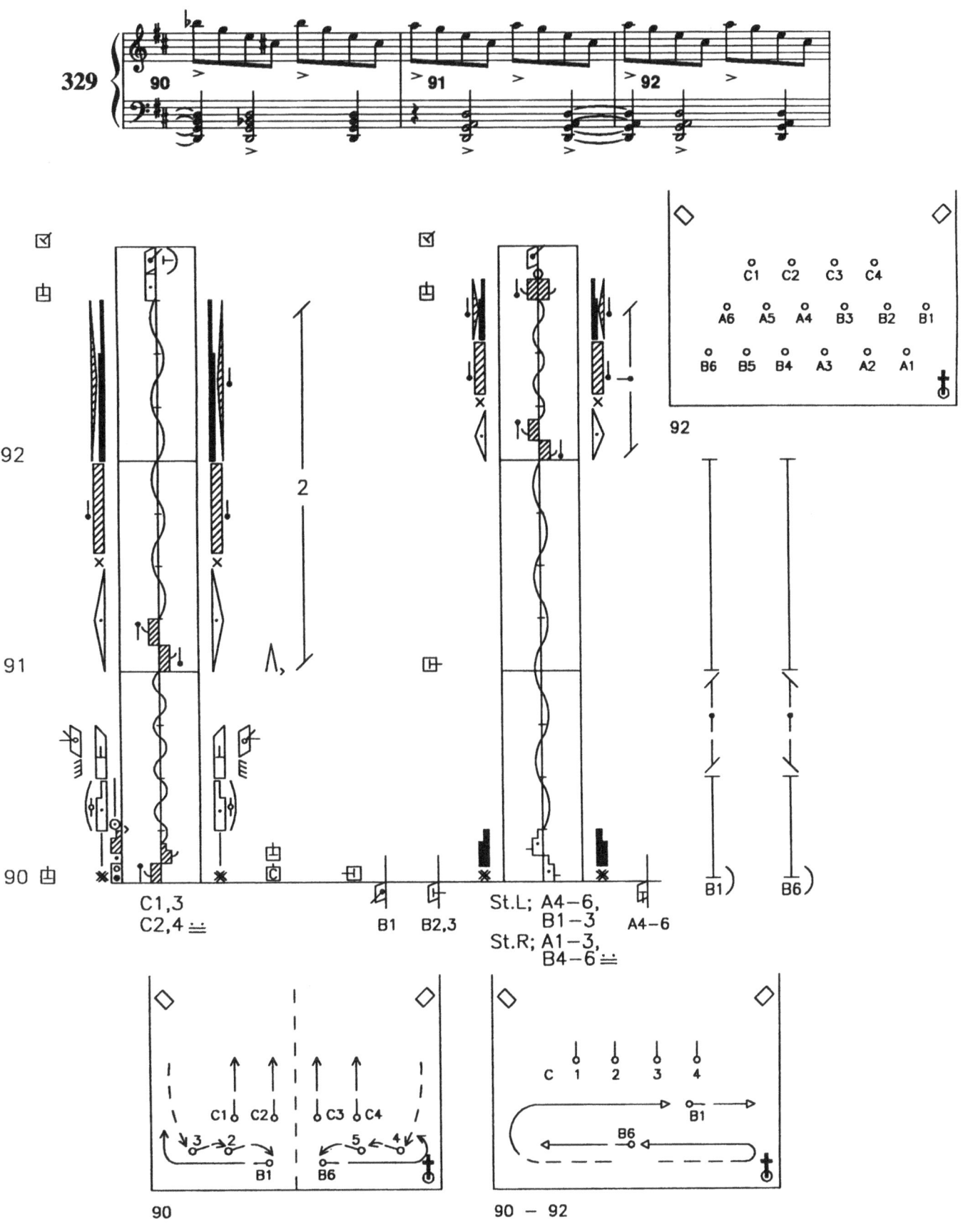

ROBERT LE DIABLE - THE BALLET OF THE NUNS

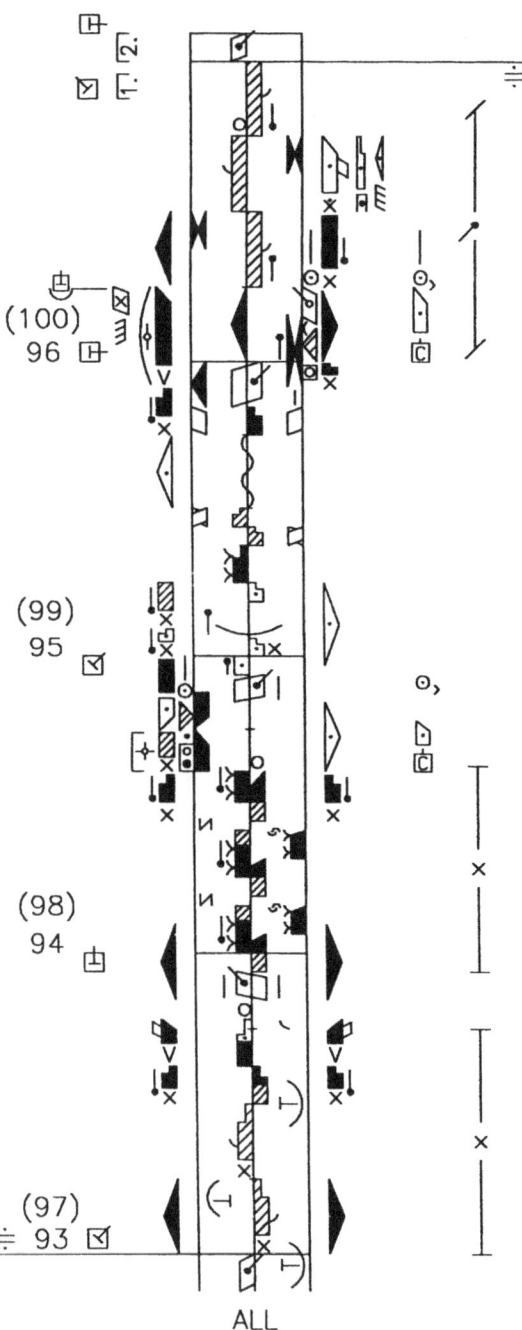

measure 94, count 4

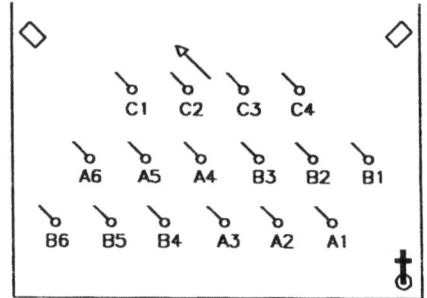

97 – 100

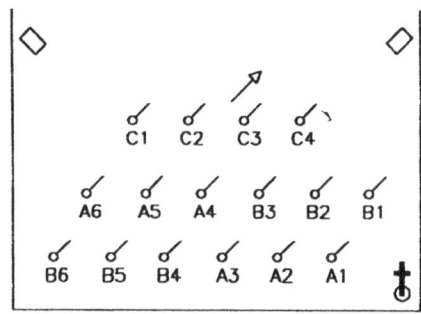

93 – 96

BACCHANALE

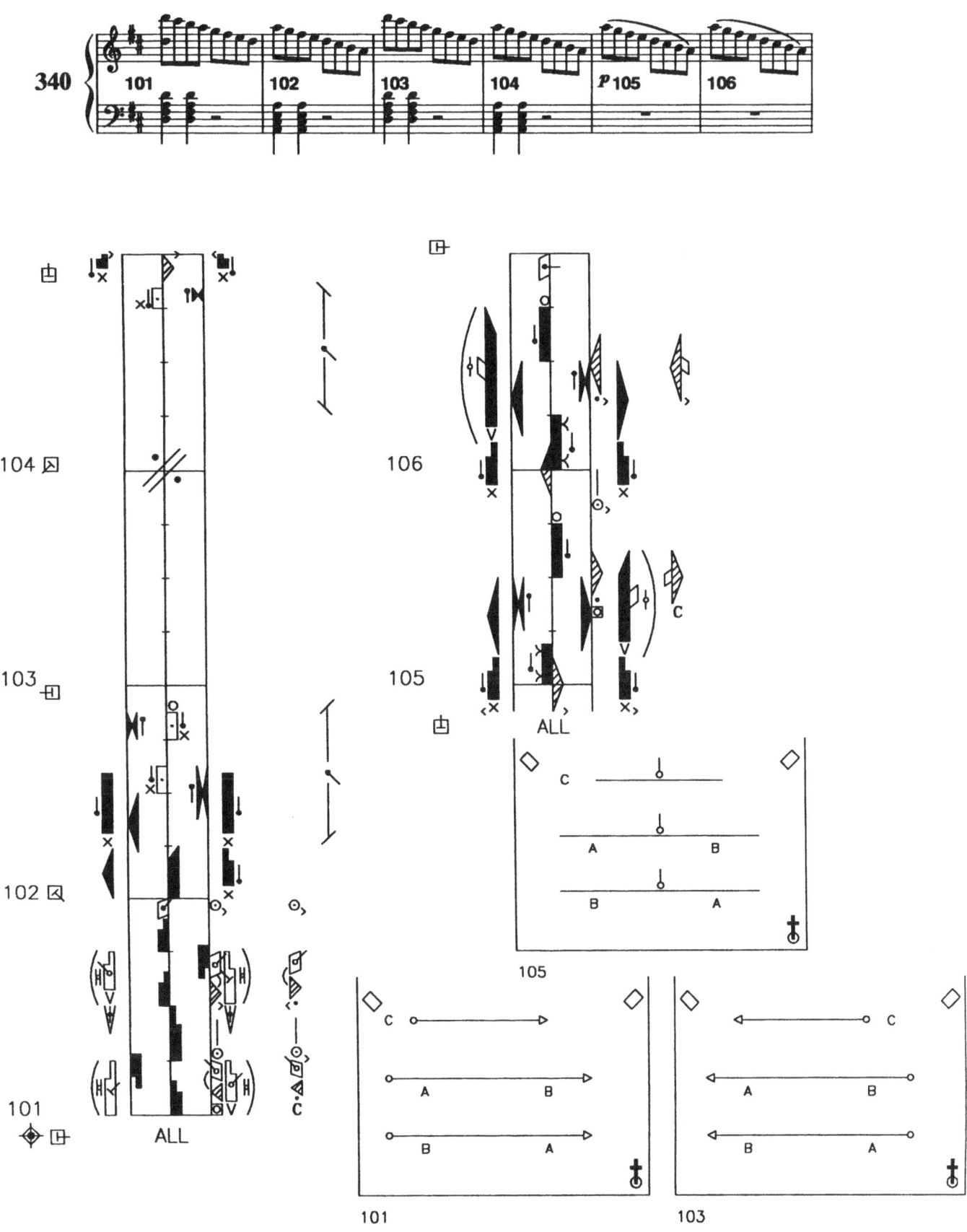

94 ROBERT LE DIABLE - THE BALLET OF THE NUNS

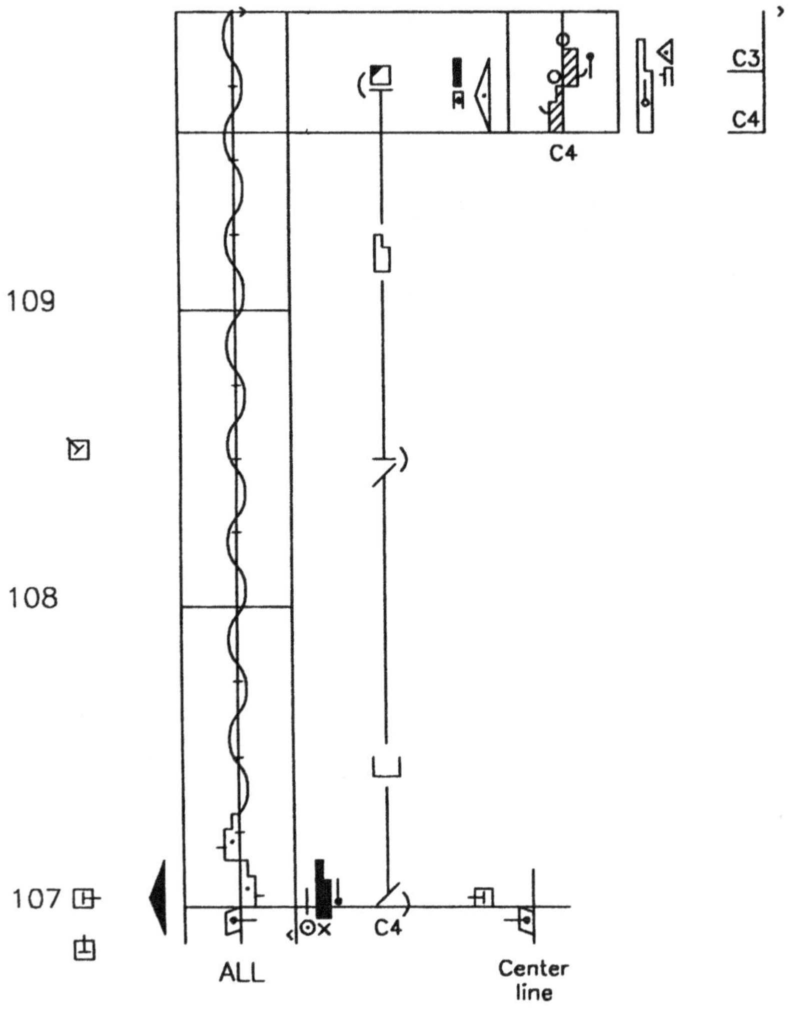

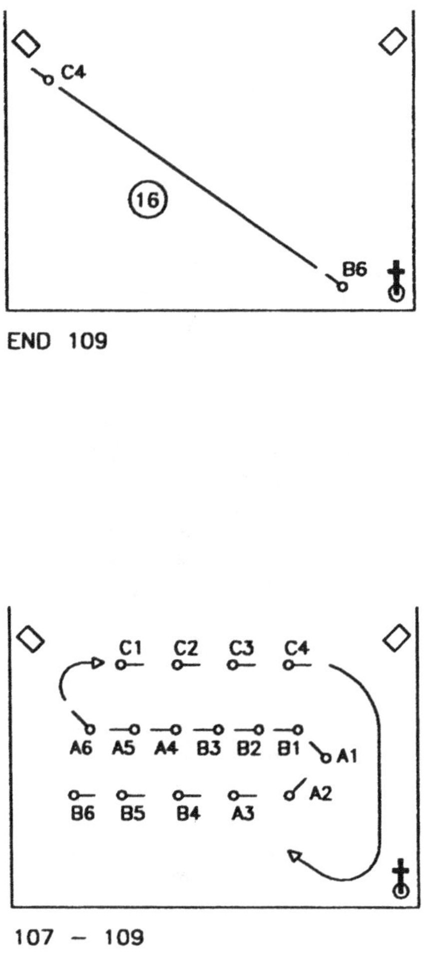

BACCHANALE

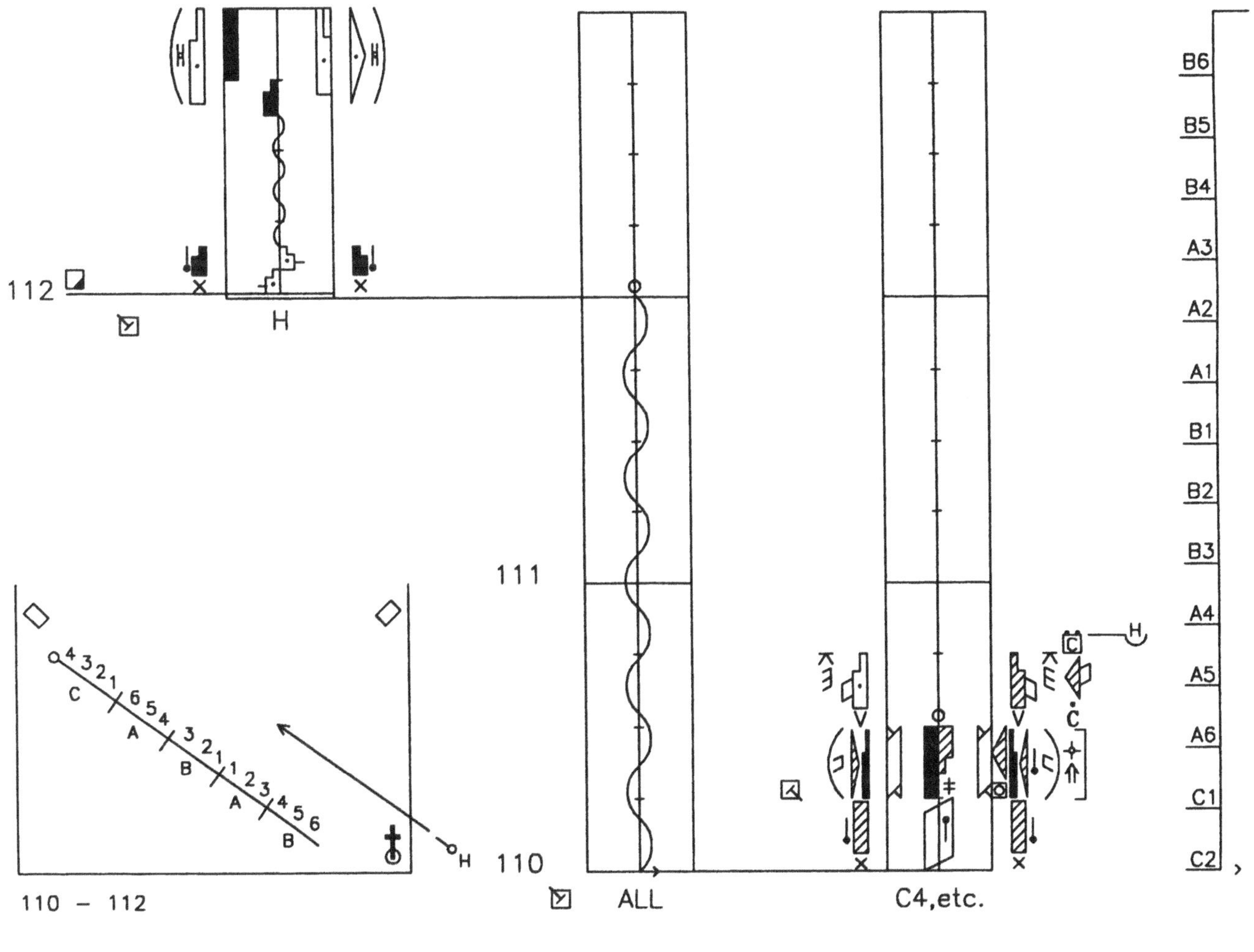

95

112

110 – 112

111

110

ALL

C4, etc.

ROBERT LE DIABLE - THE BALLET OF THE NUNS

Allegro Vivace

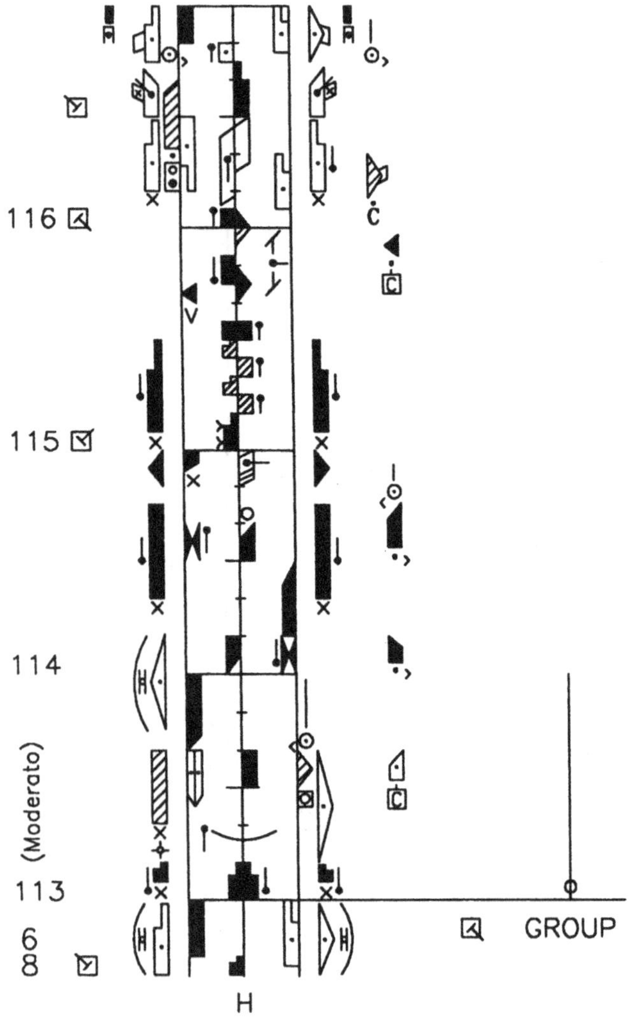

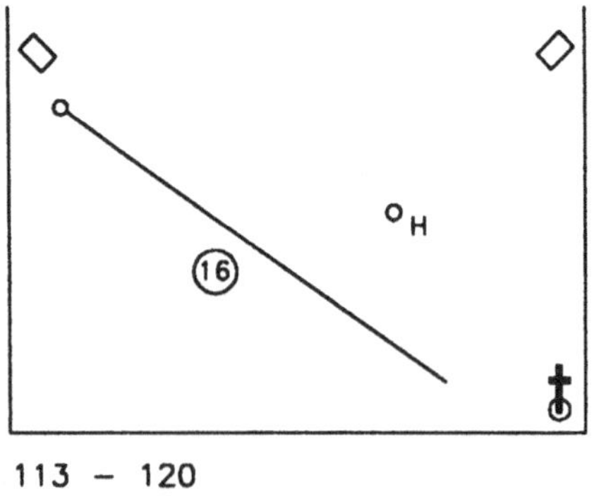

ALLEGRO VIVACE

Virginnia Viney as the abbess Héléna
measure 113 and 117

98 ROBERT LE DIABLE - THE BALLET OF THE NUNS

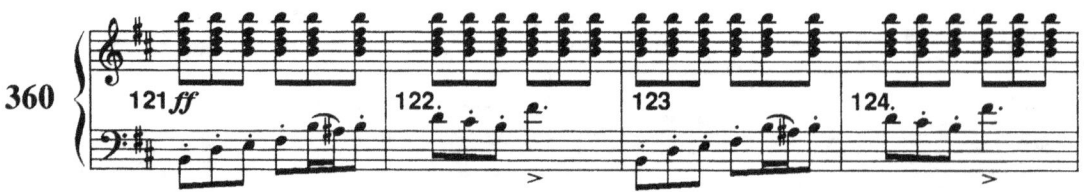

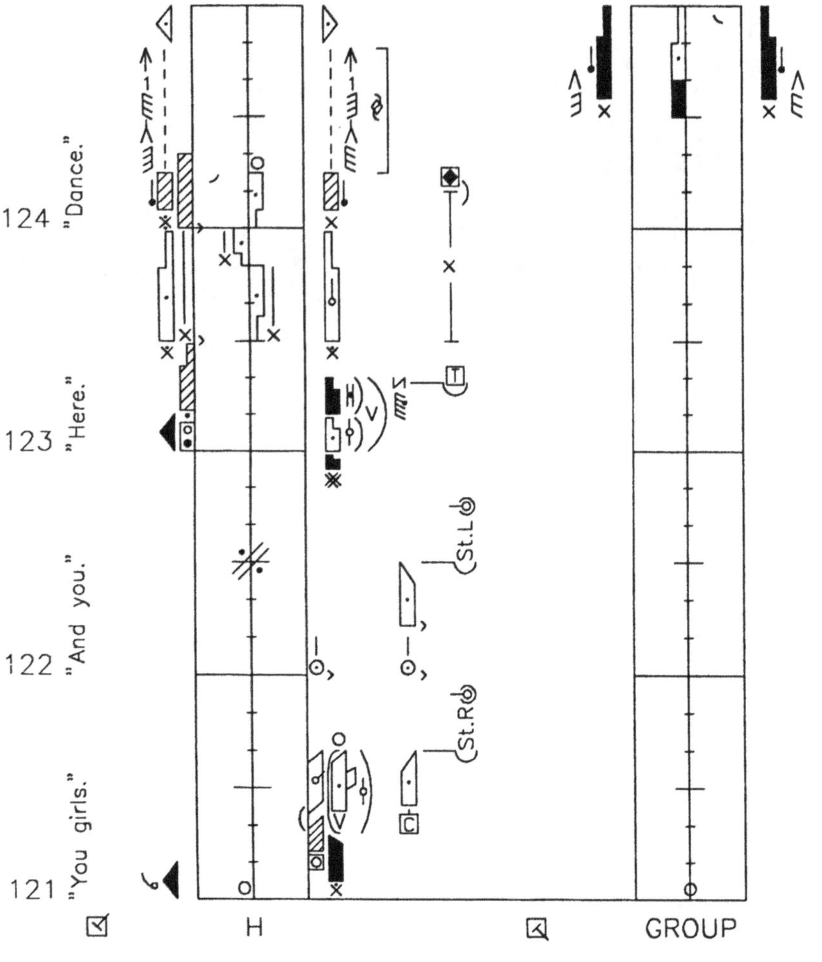

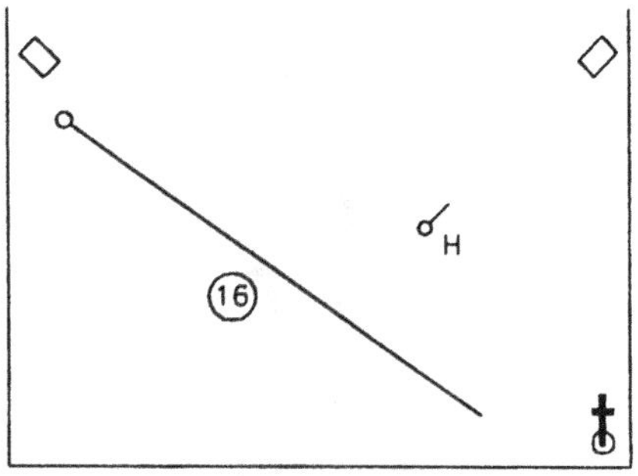

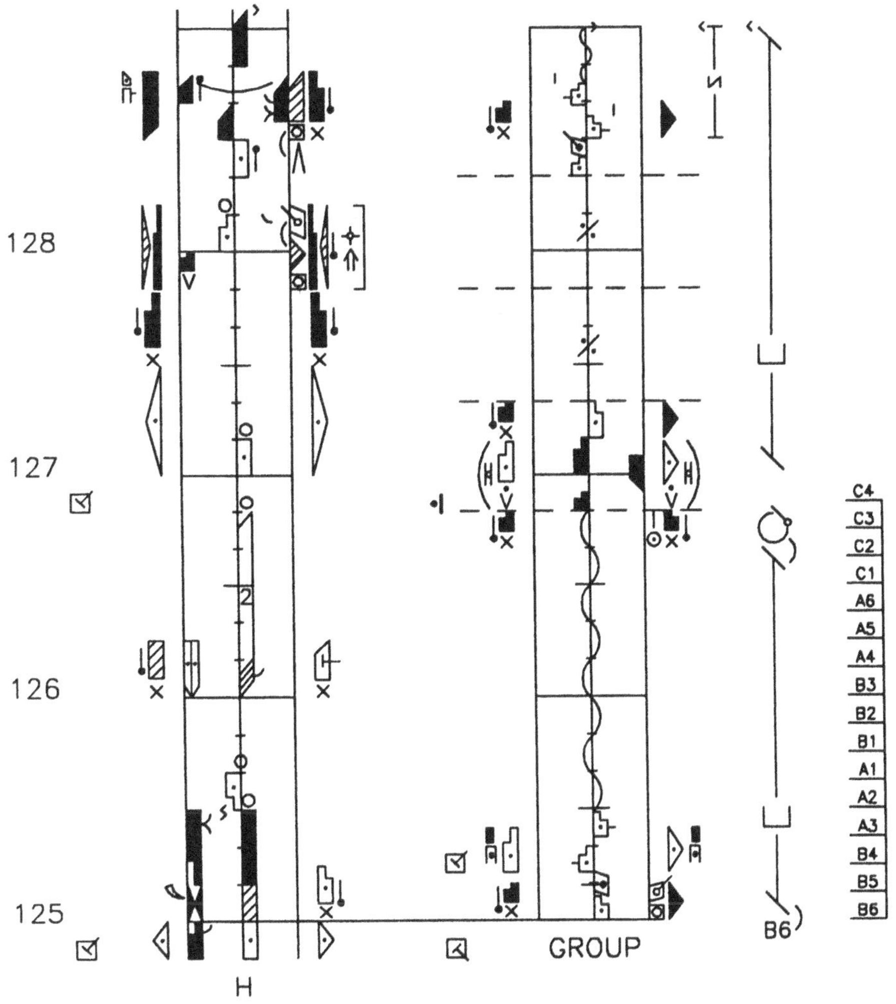

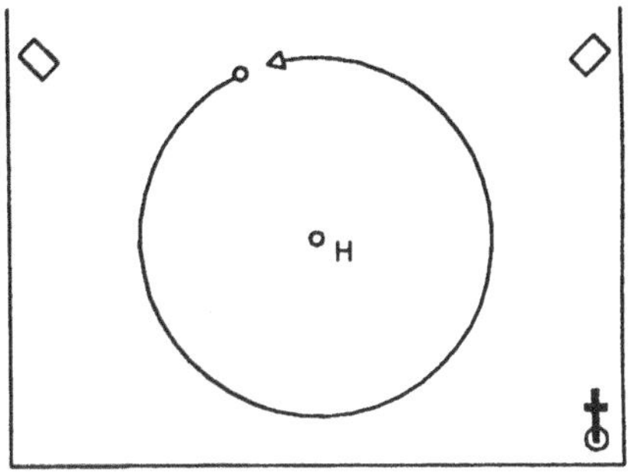

ALLEGRO VIVACE

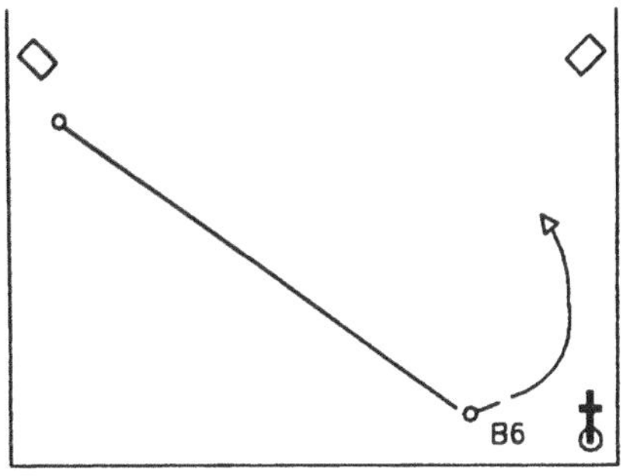

125 start

125 1/2 − 126

127 − 128

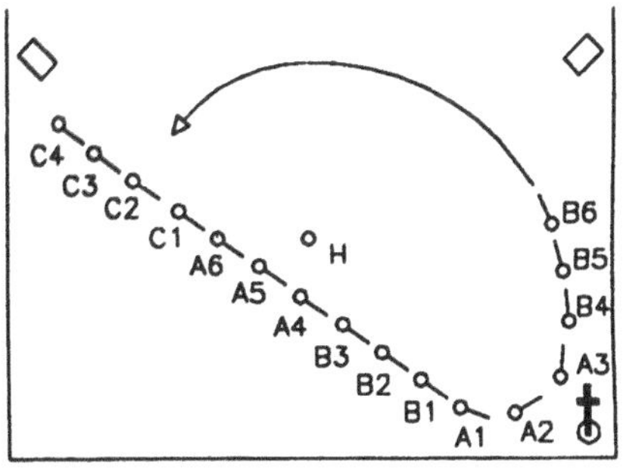

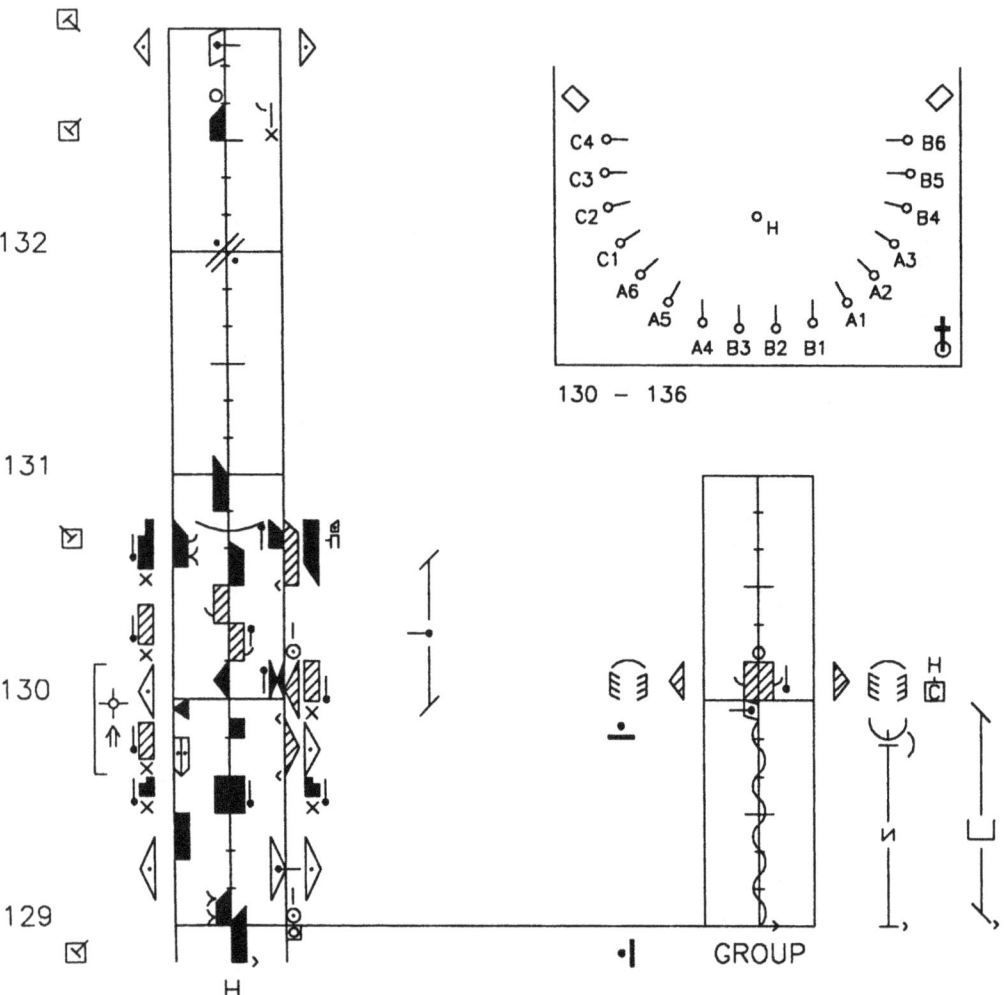

372
133
134
sfp
135
sfp
136

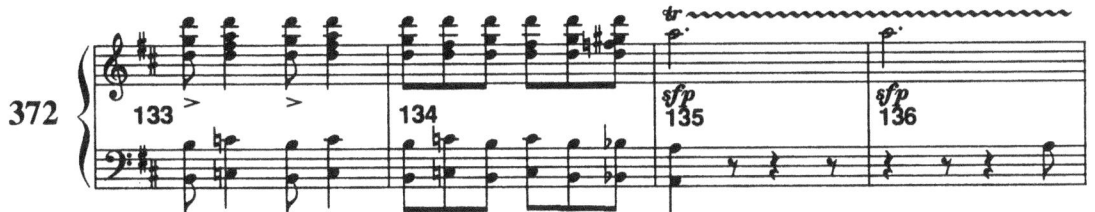

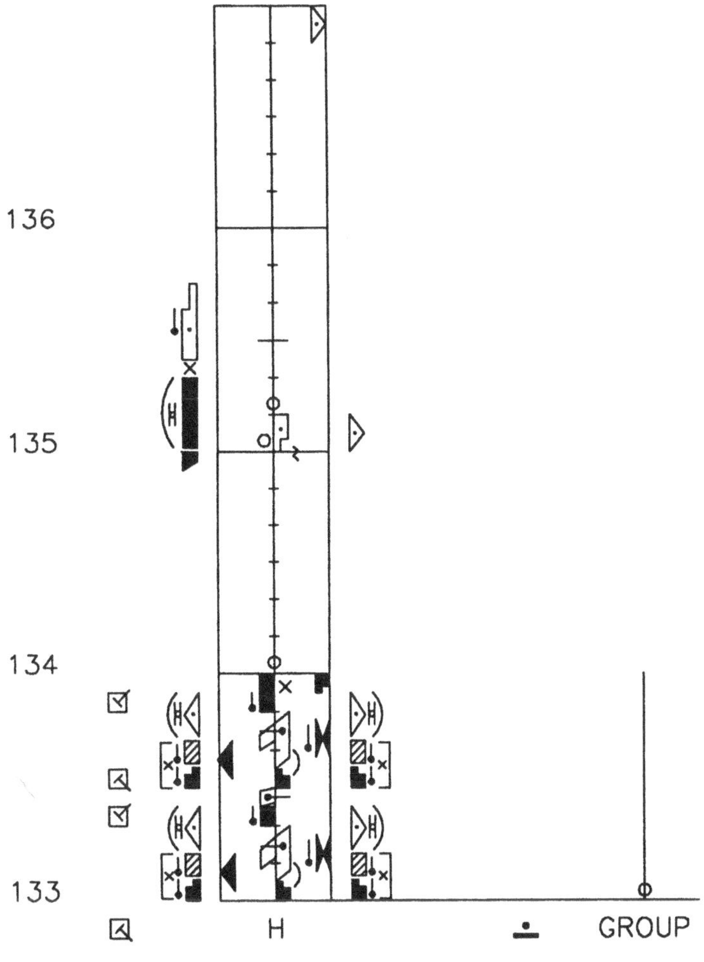
136
135
134
133
H
GROUP

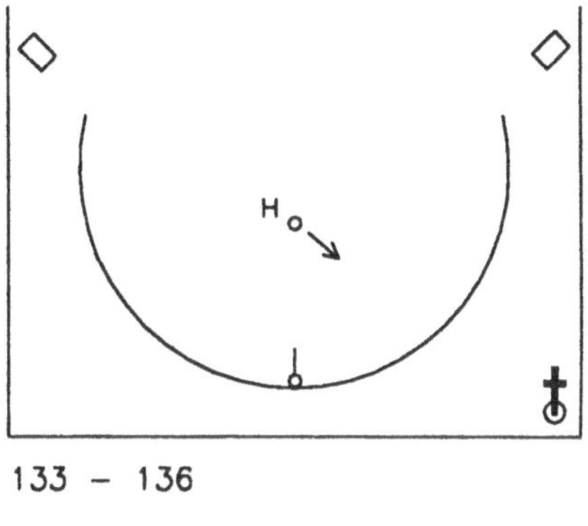
H
133 – 136

ROBERT LE DIABLE - THE BALLET OF THE NUNS

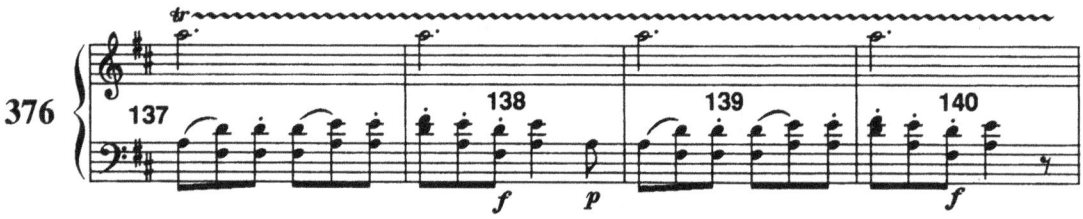

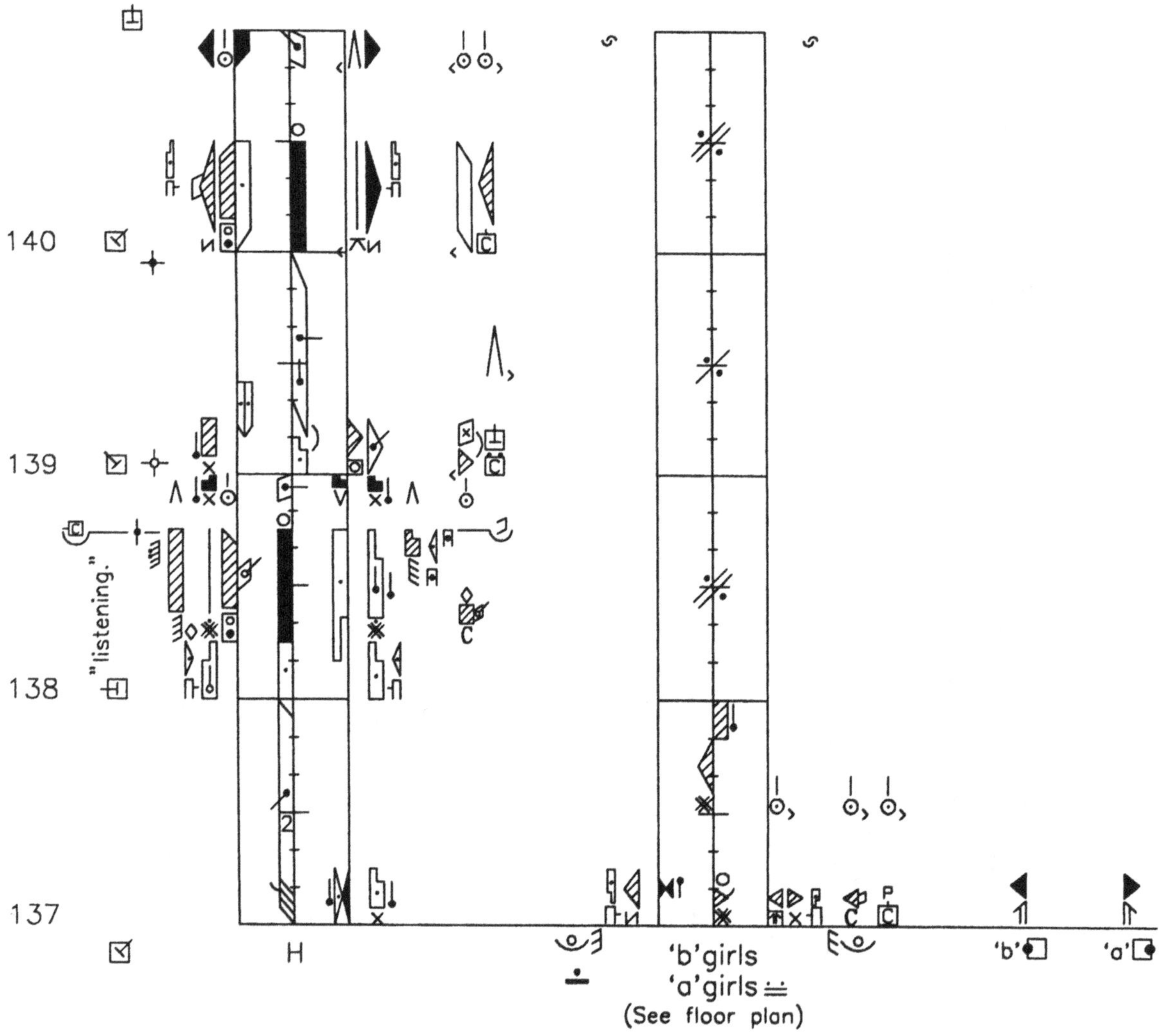

'b'girls
'a'girls
(See floor plan)

ALLEGRO VIVACE

103

measure 138

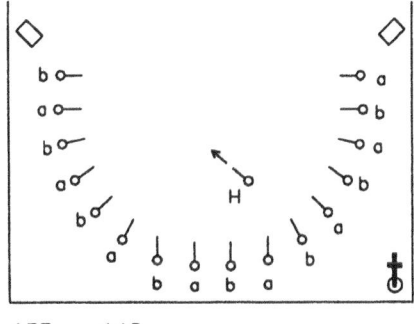

137 — 140

380

383

MEASURES
384-399 CUT BY
BOURNONVILLE

141 – 144

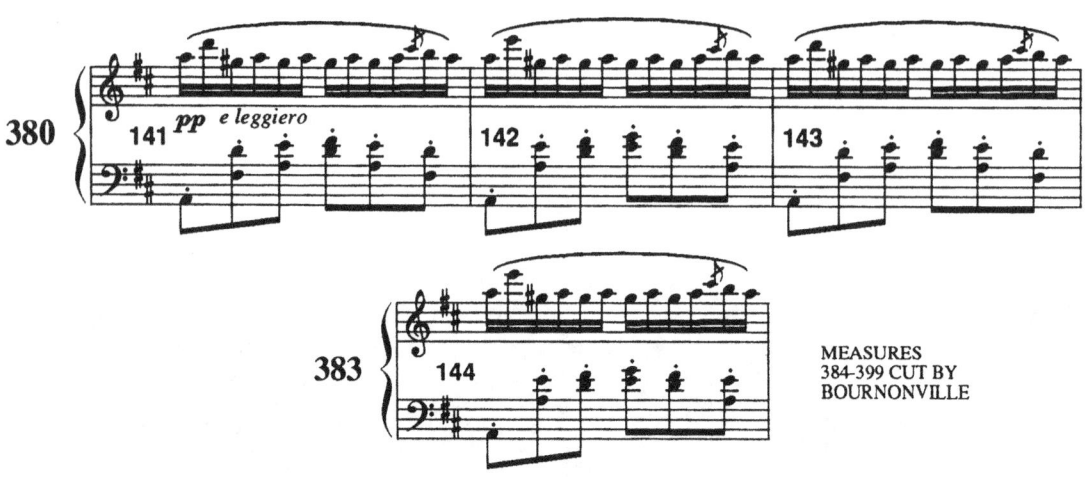

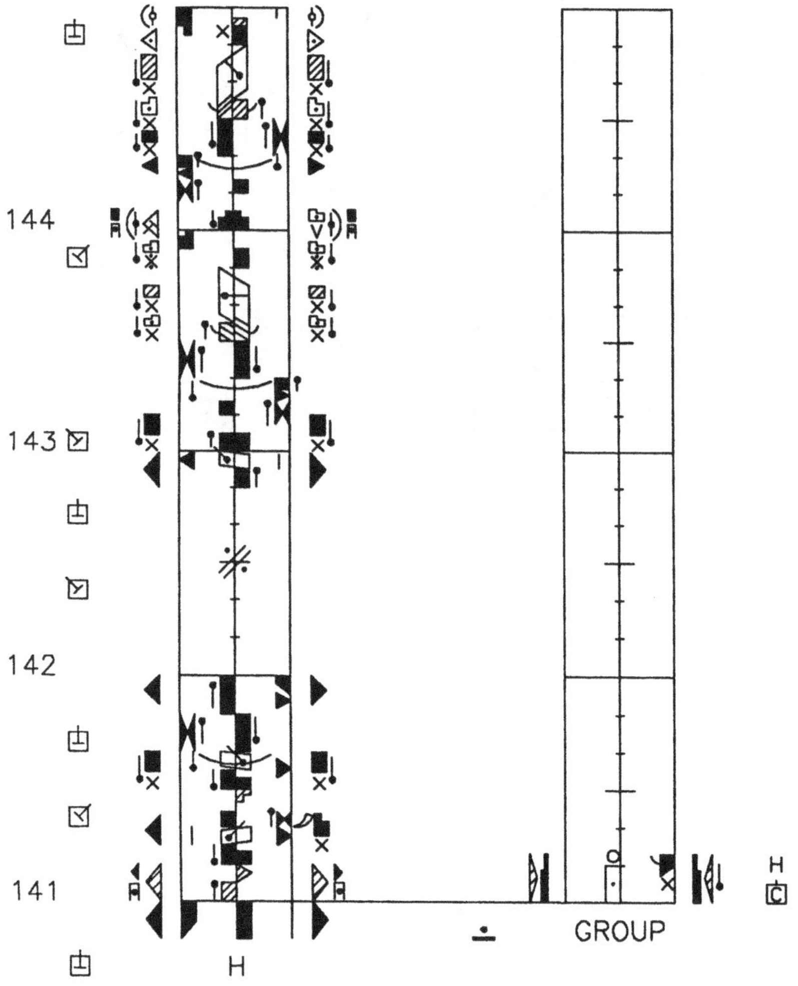

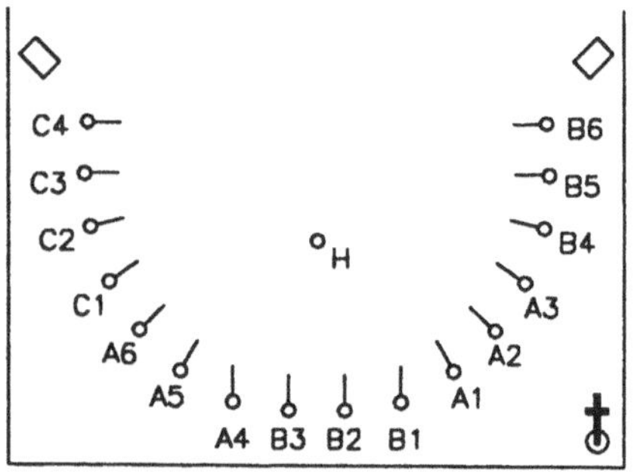

ALLEGRO VIVACE

105

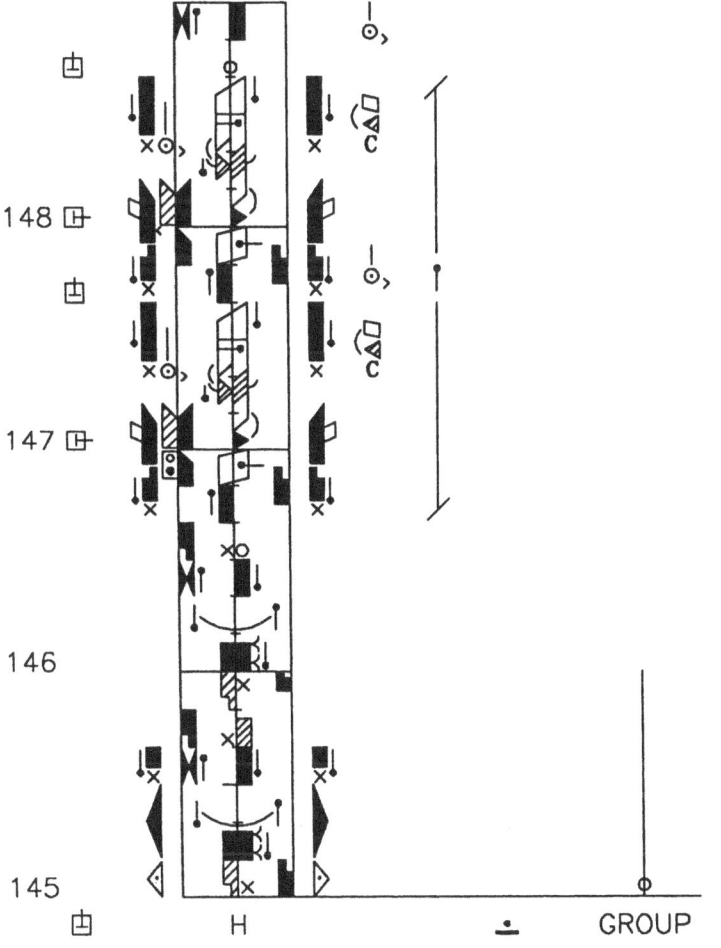

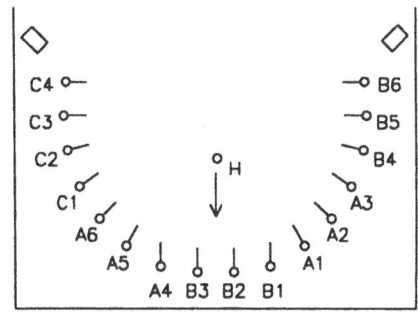

145 – 148

106　　　　　*ROBERT LE DIABLE - THE BALLET OF THE NUNS*

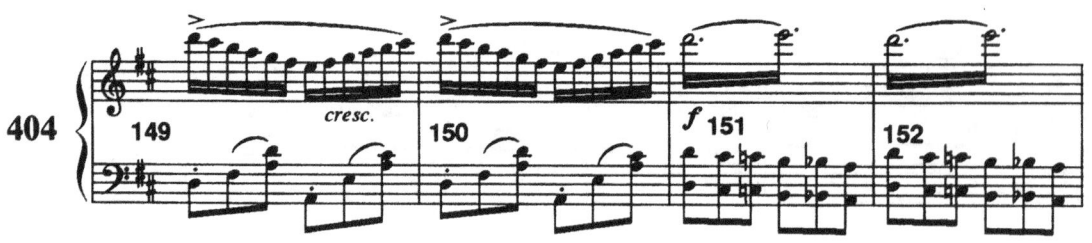

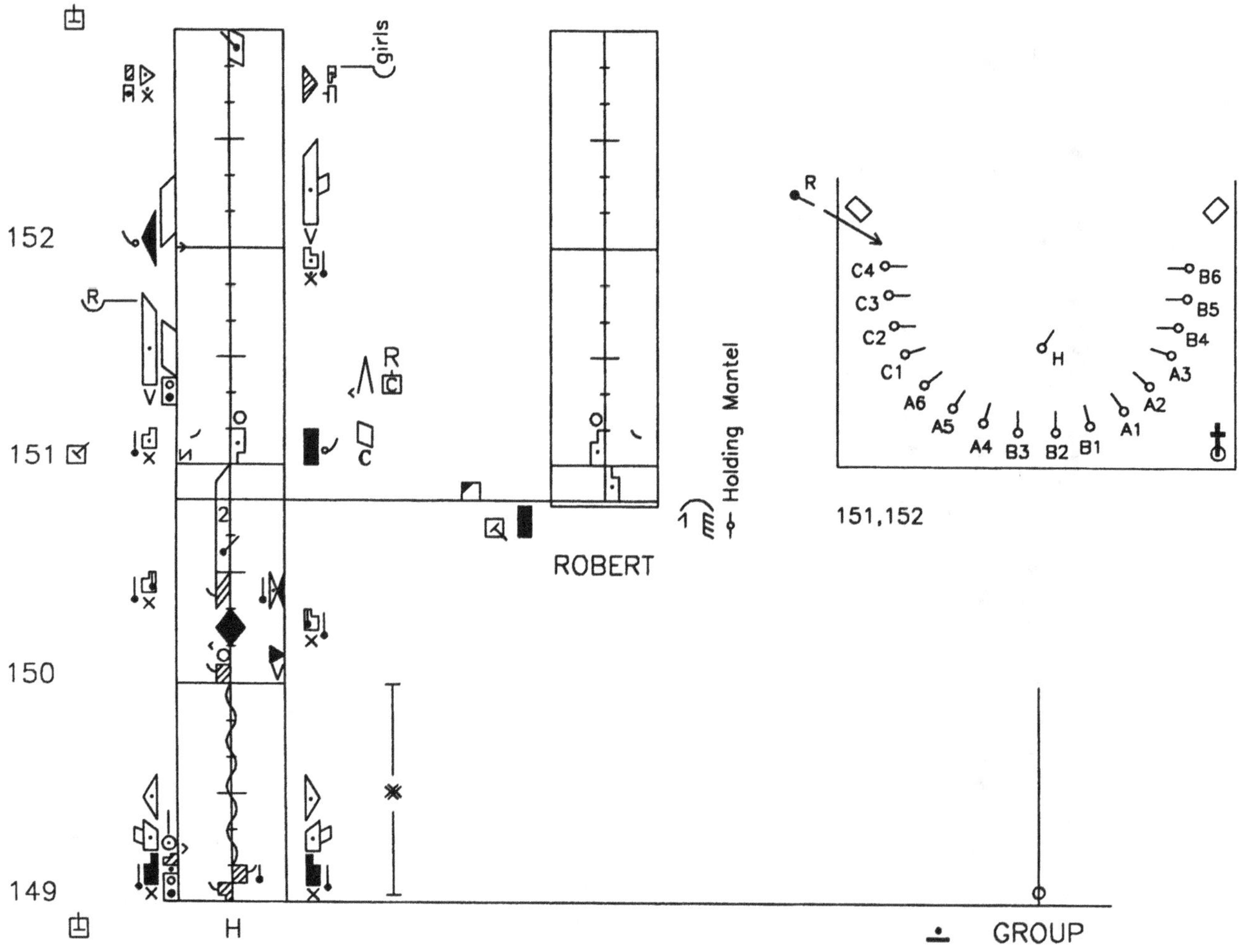

ALLEGRO VIVACE

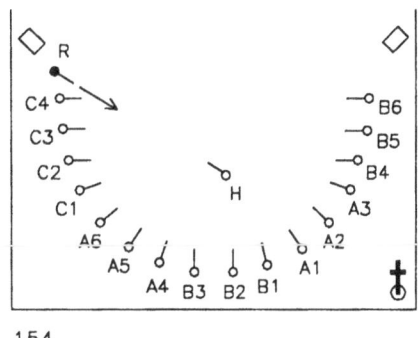

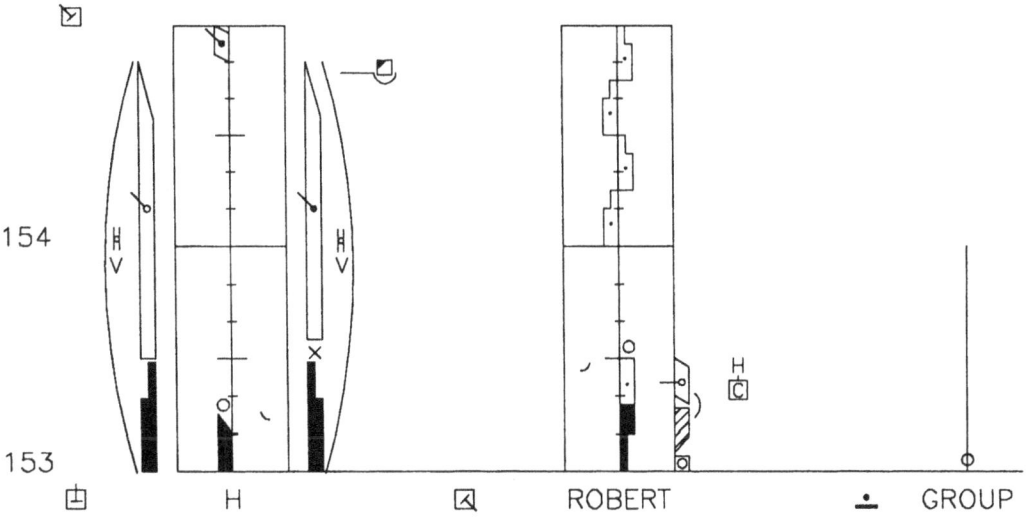

ROBERT LE DIABLE - THE BALLET OF THE NUNS

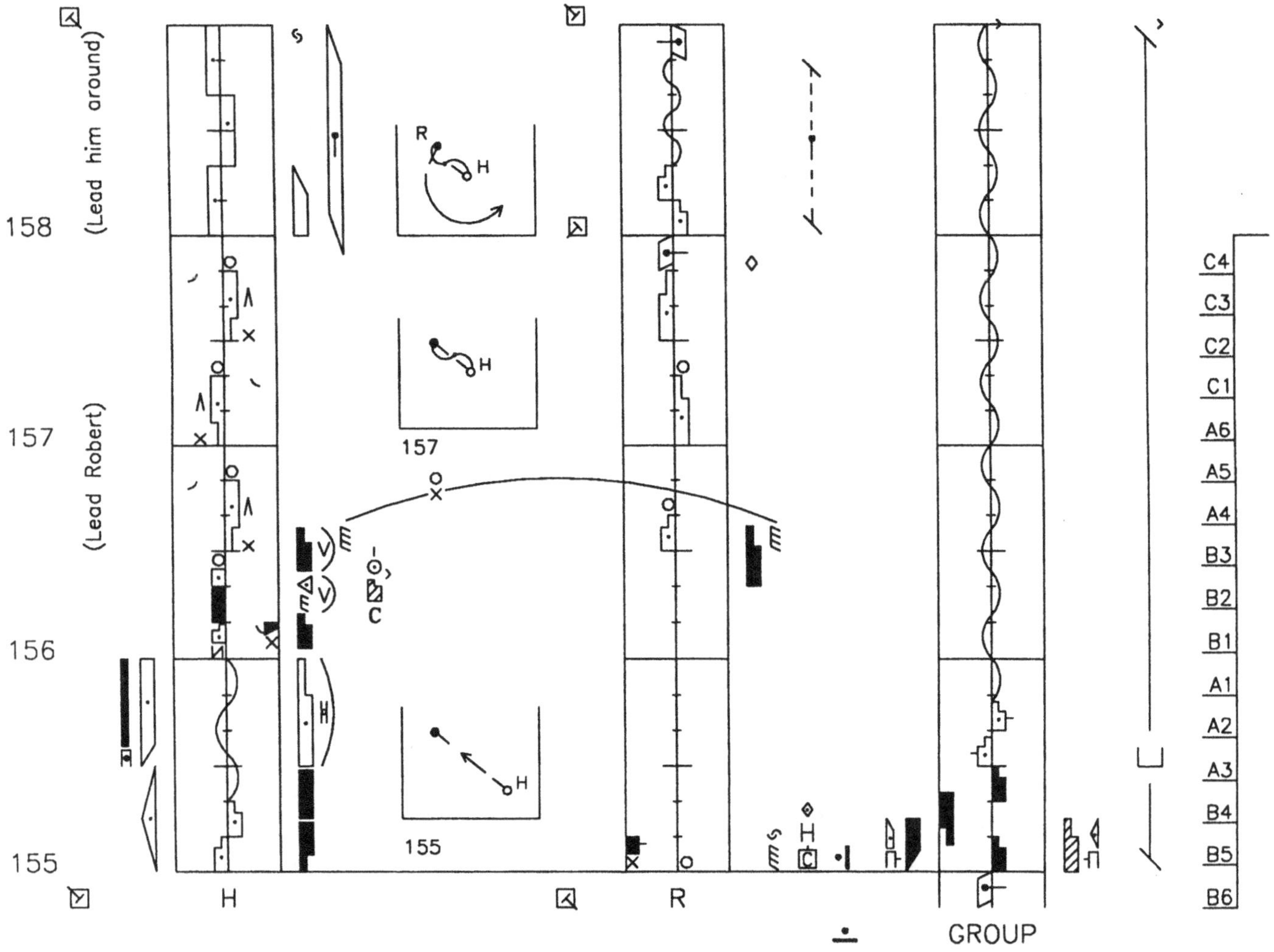

ALLEGRO VIVACE

109

Marius Els as Robert being drawn in
by Virginnia Viney as Héléna
measure 156

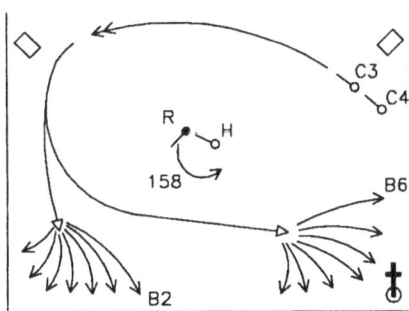

158, 159 (See plan for 160 for
ending positions)

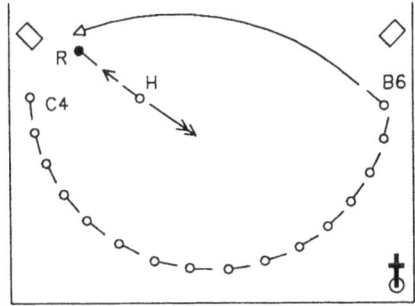

155 — 157

110 ROBERT LE DIABLE - THE BALLET OF THE NUNS

MEASURES 418-465 NOT RECONSTRUCTED

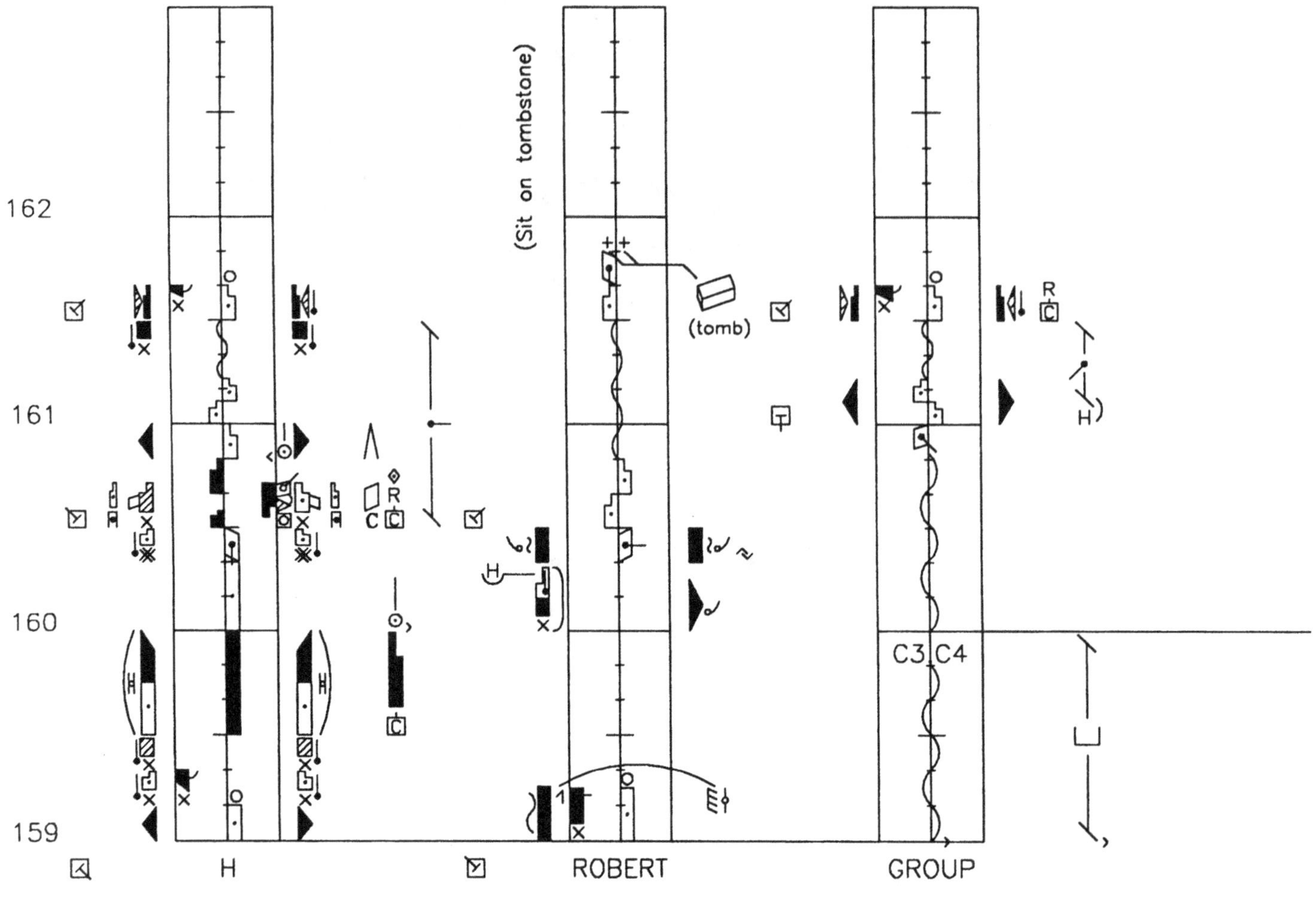

ALLEGRO VIVACE

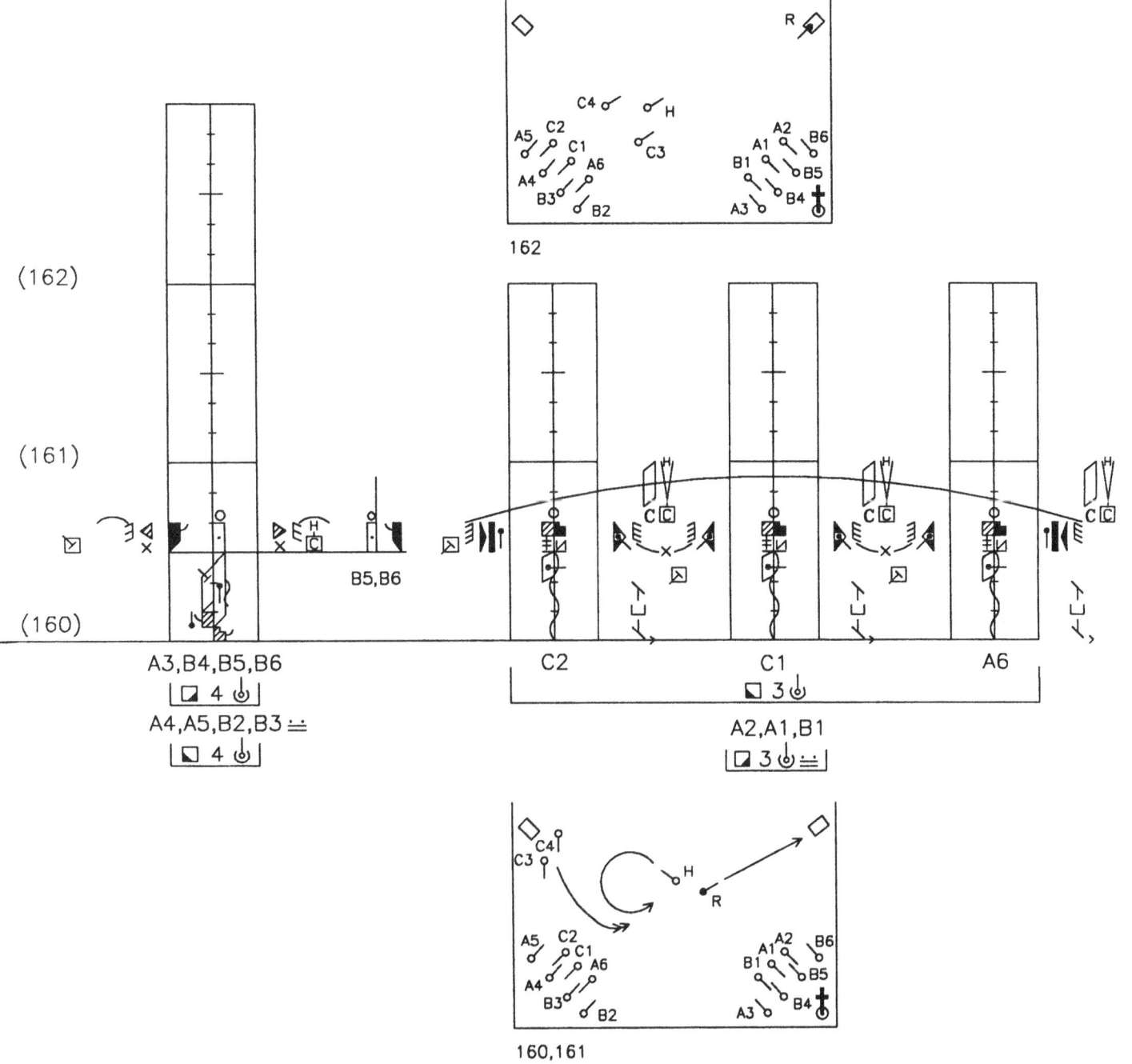

112 ROBERT LE DIABLE - THE BALLET OF THE NUNS

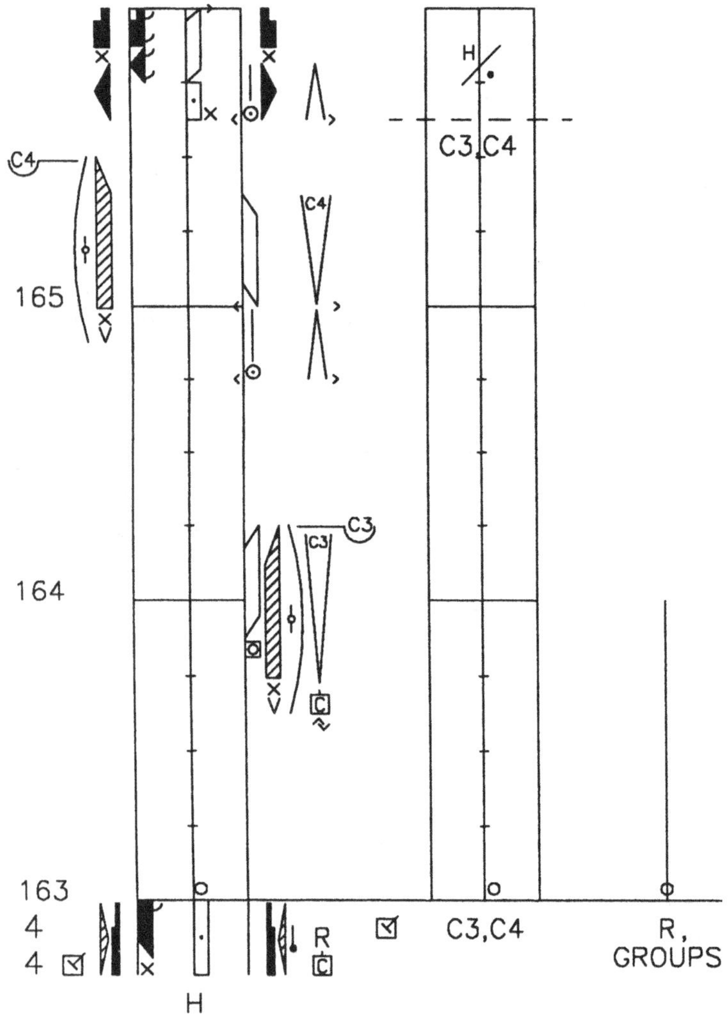

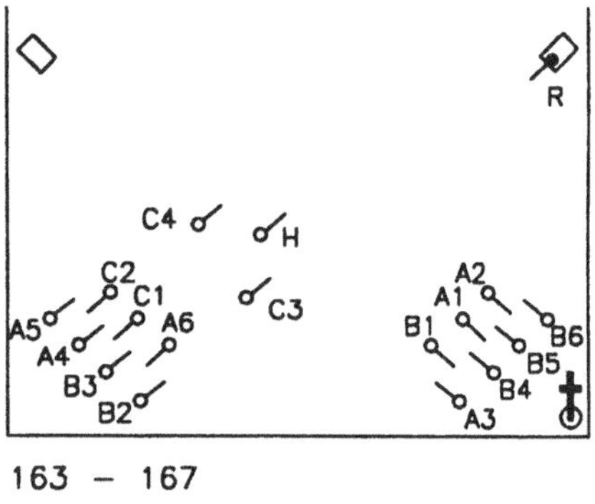

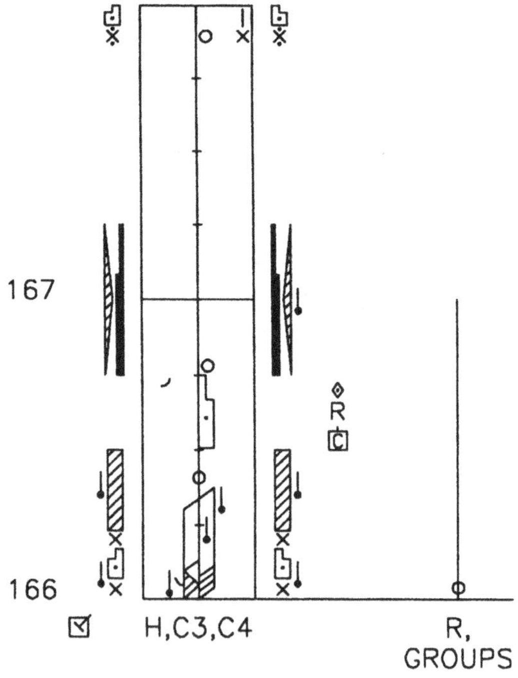

1ᴱᴿ AIR DE BALLET

1ᵉʳ Air de Ballet
Séduction par l'ivresse

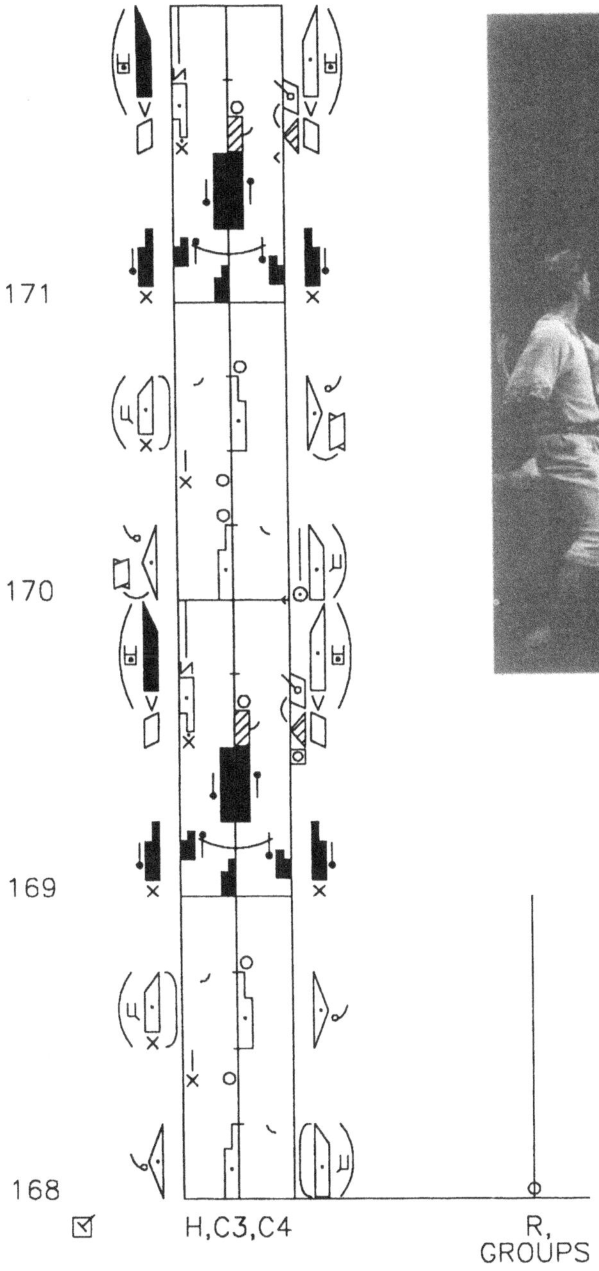

measure 169, counts 3, 4

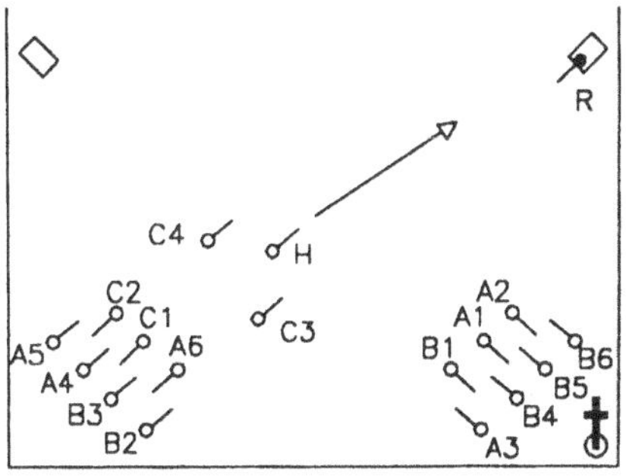

168 – 173

ROBERT LE DIABLE - THE BALLET OF THE NUNS

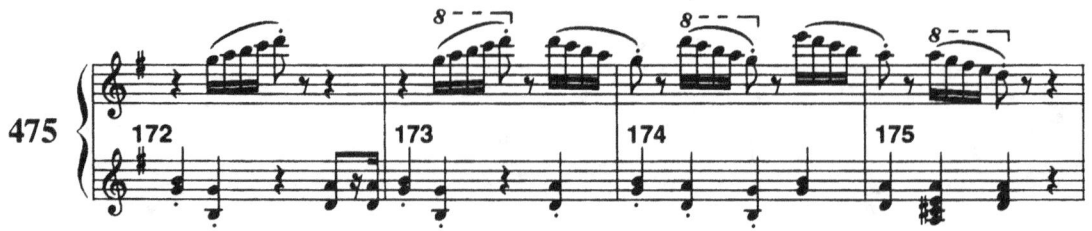

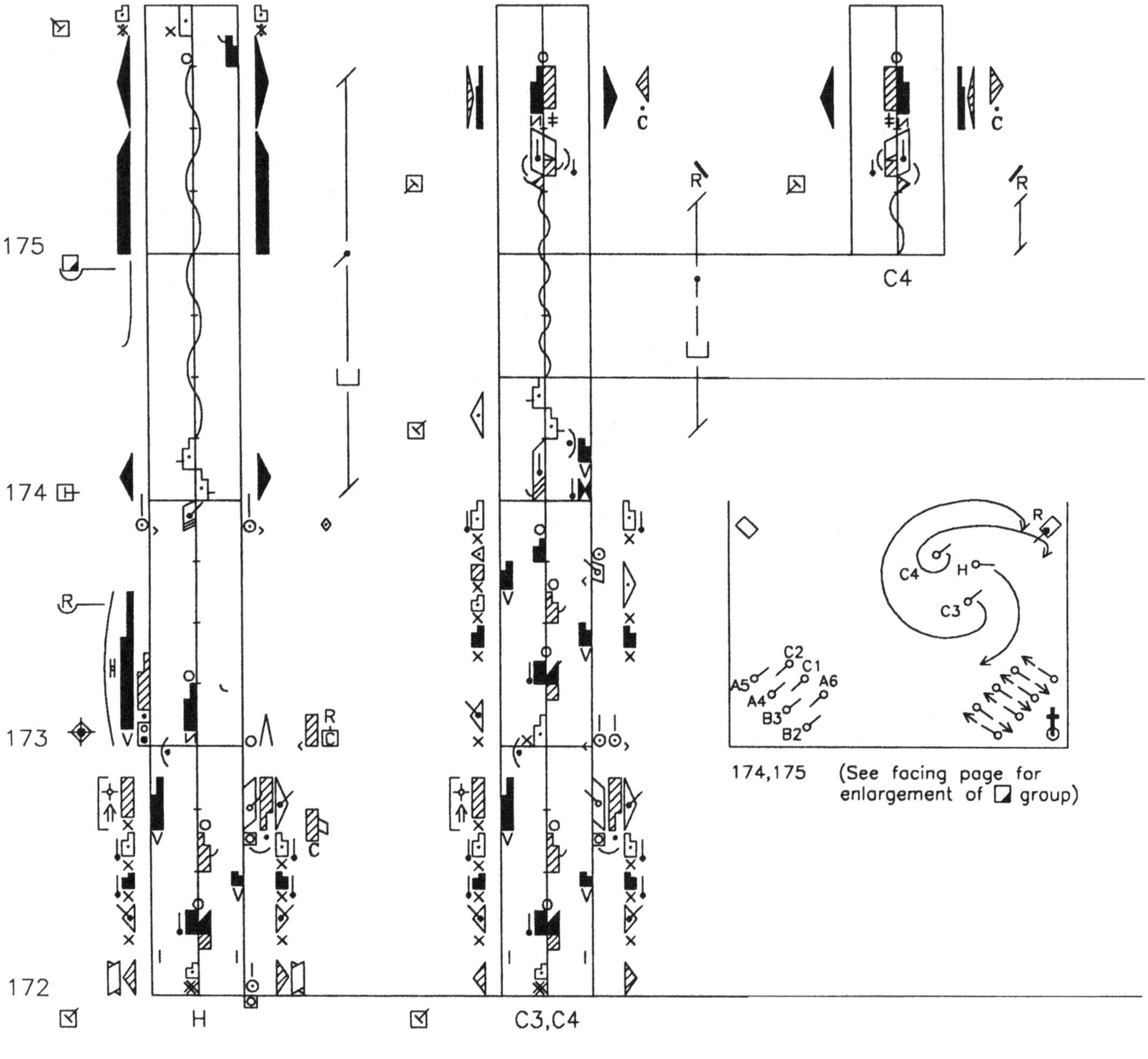

175

174

173

172

C4

174,175 (See facing page for enlargement of ▢ group)

H   C3,C4

1ᴱᴿ AIR DE BALLET

115

MEASURES
479-497 CUT BY
BOURNONVILLE

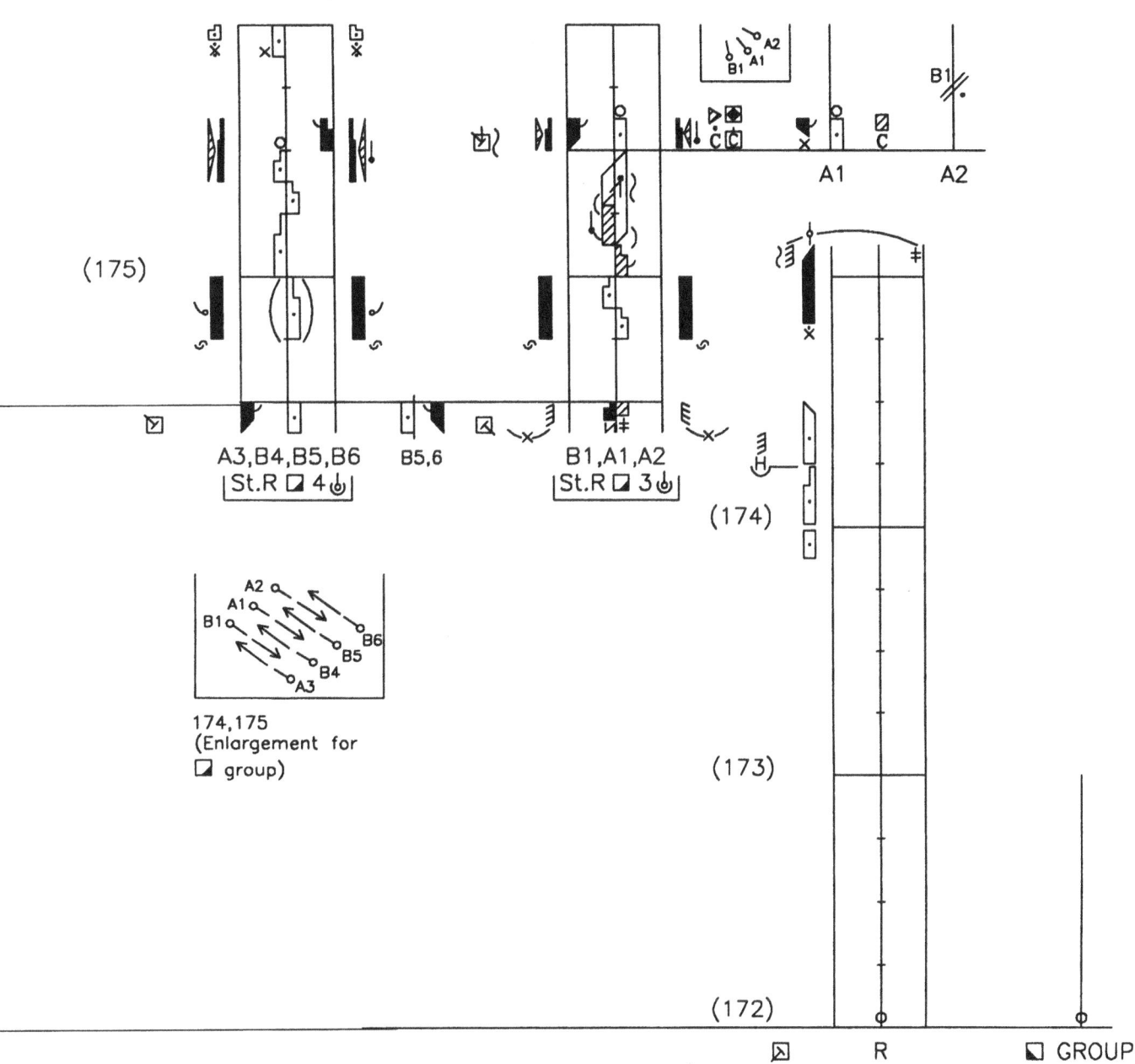

116 · ROBERT LE DIABLE - THE BALLET OF THE NUNS

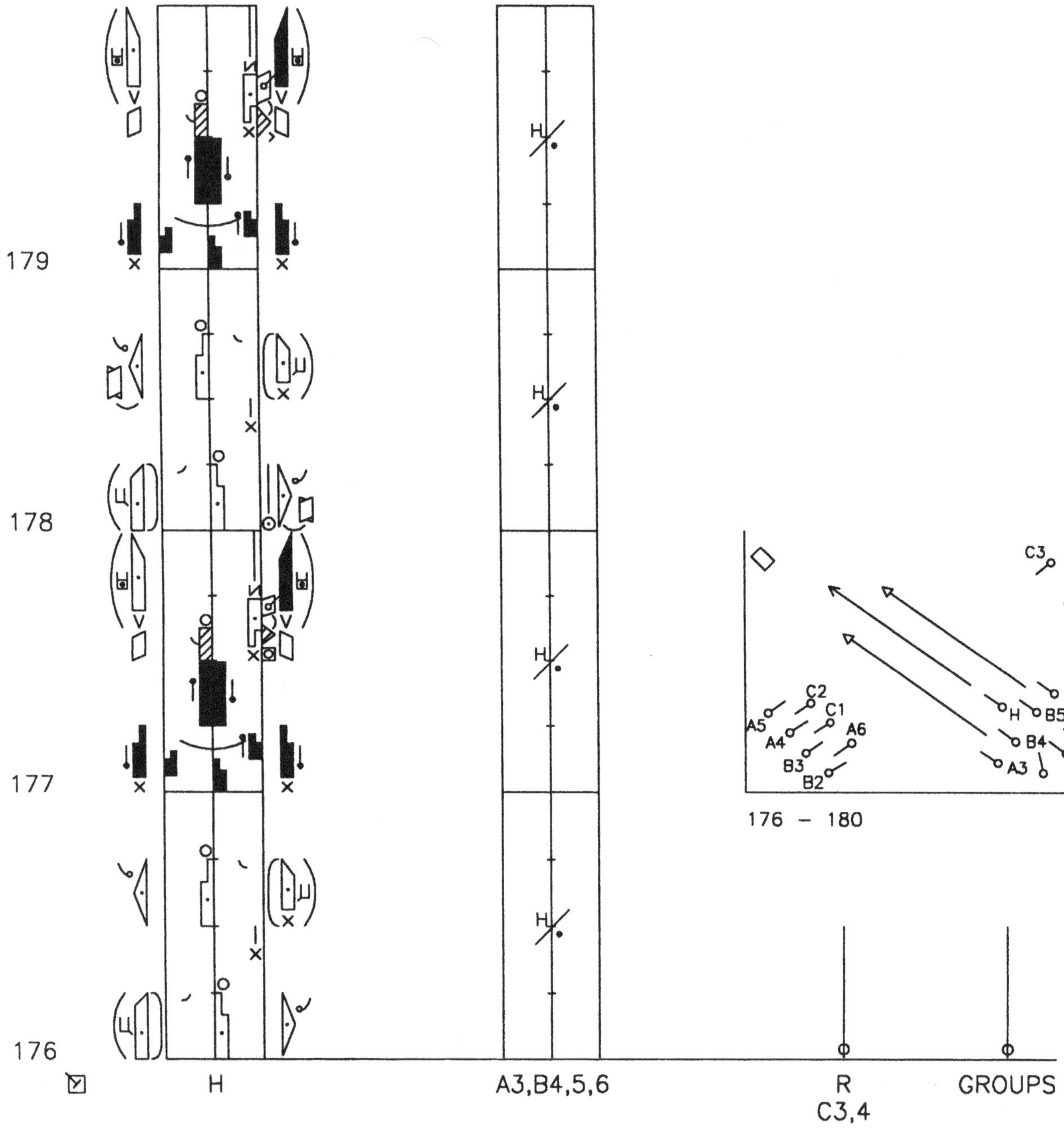

502

8
180
181
182

182
181
180
UL nuns
B6
B6
H
A3,B4,5,6
4
R
C3,4
GROUPS
B6
B5
B4
A3
182³ – 183
H
B6
B5
B4
A3
C3
R
C4
C2
A5
C1
A4
A6
B3
B2
A1
A2
B1
182,183

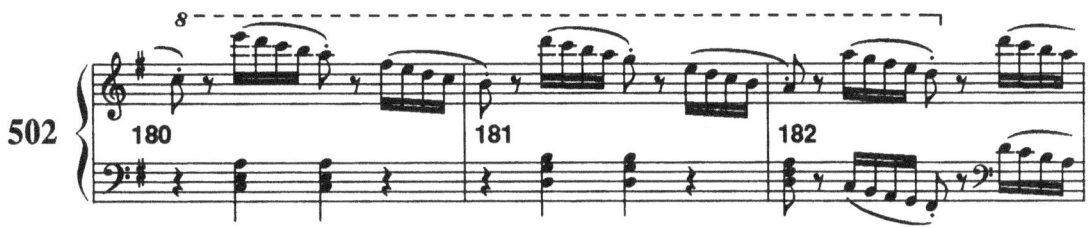

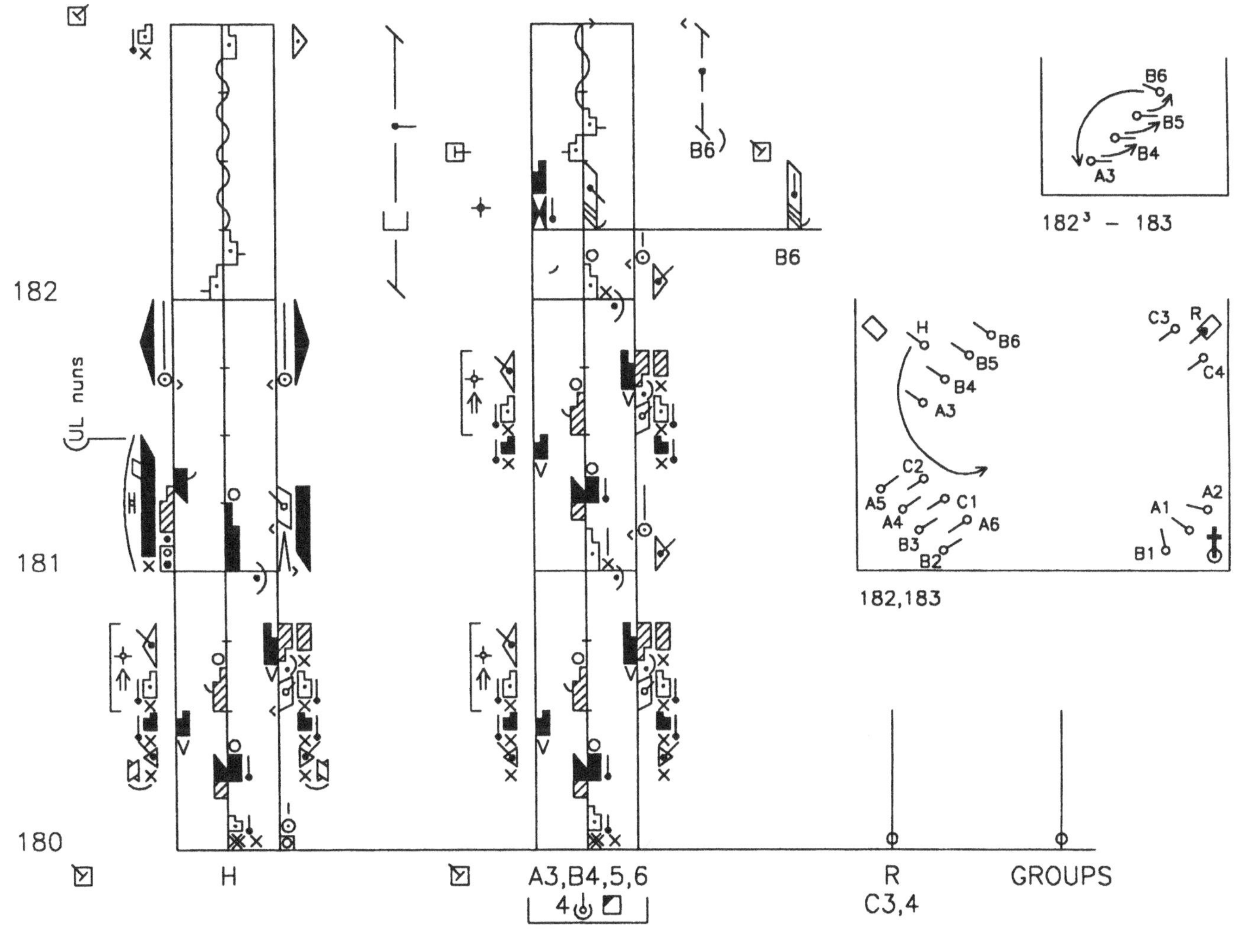

ROBERT LE DIABLE - THE BALLET OF THE NUNS

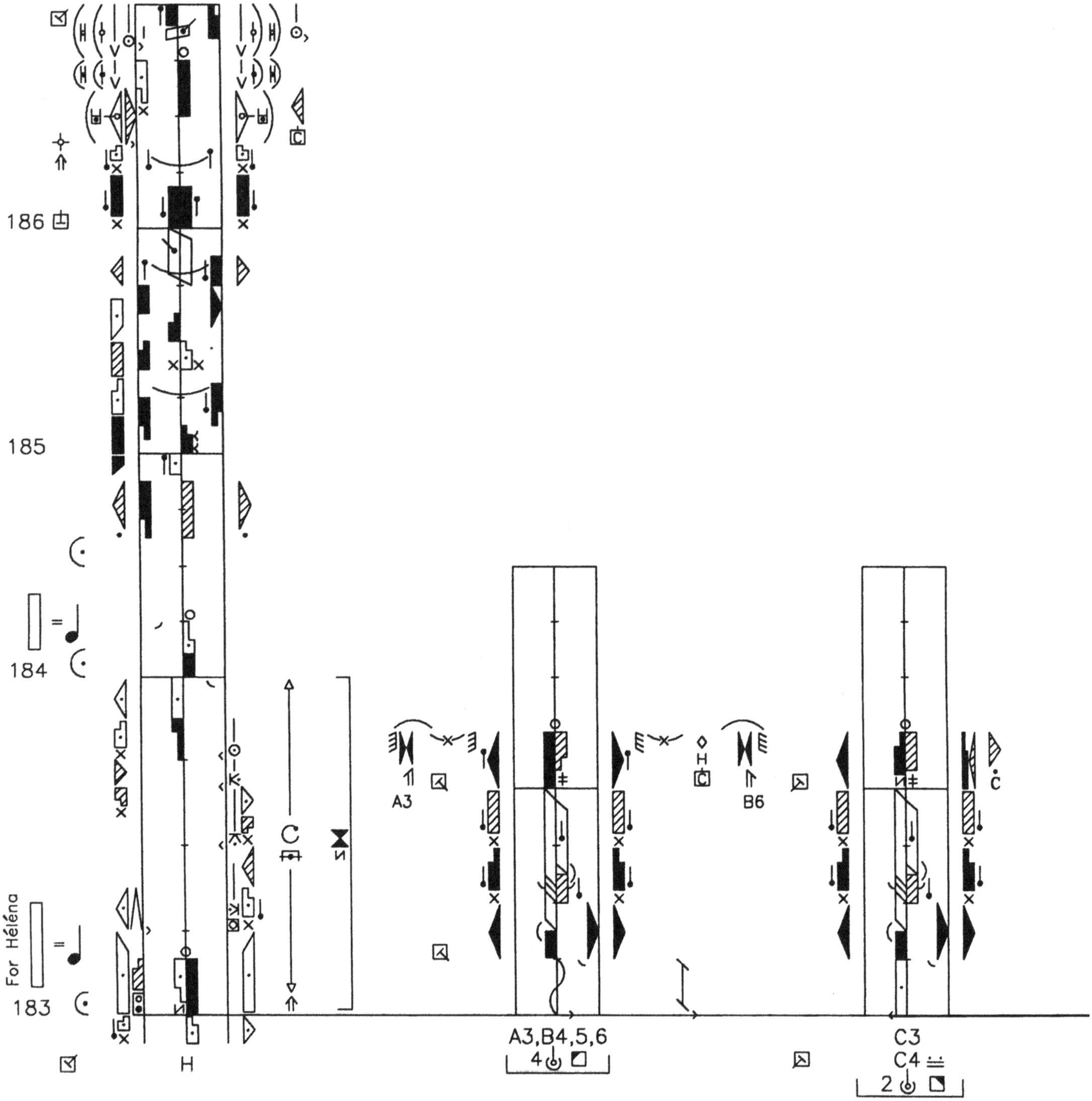

1ᴱᴿ AIR DE BALLET   119

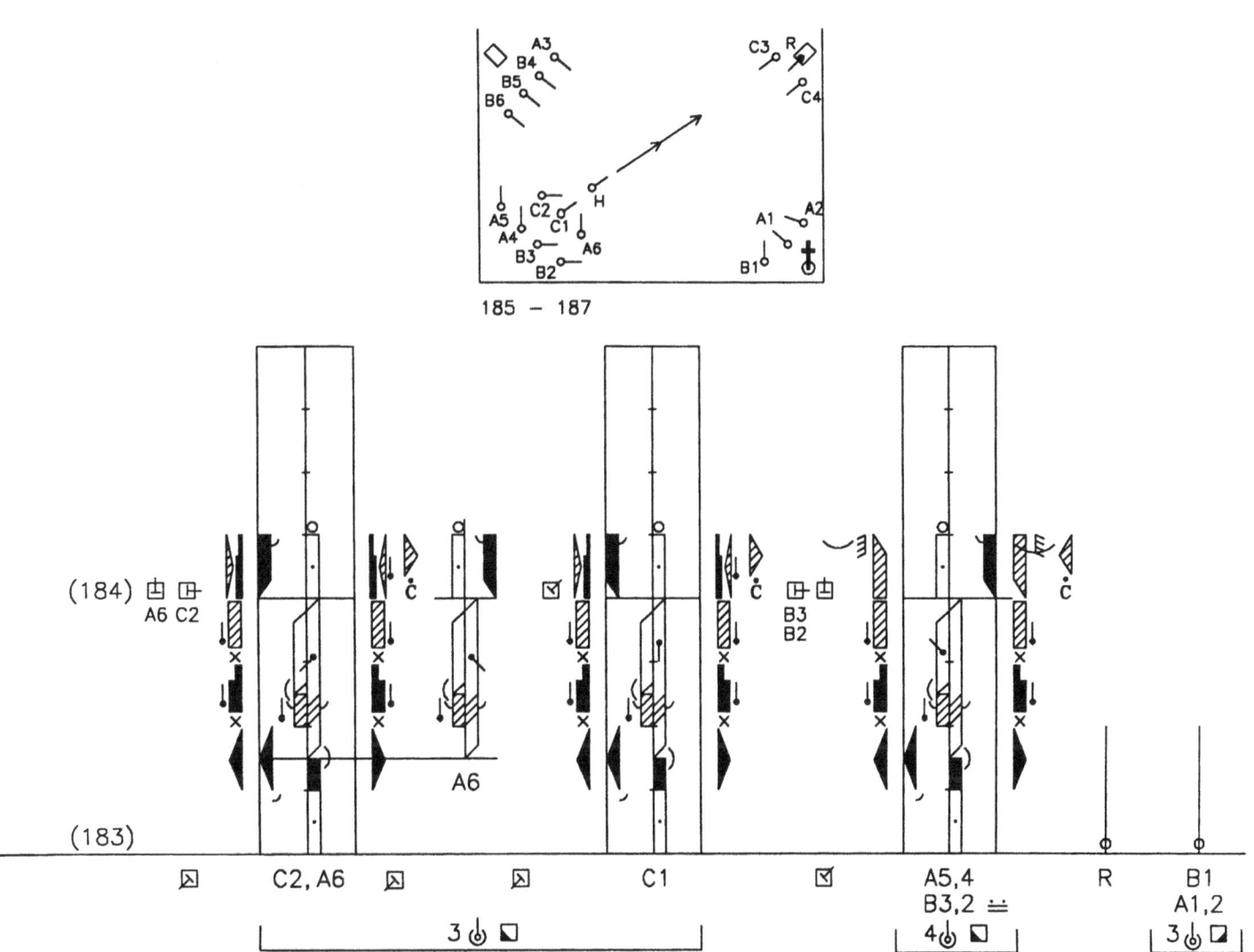

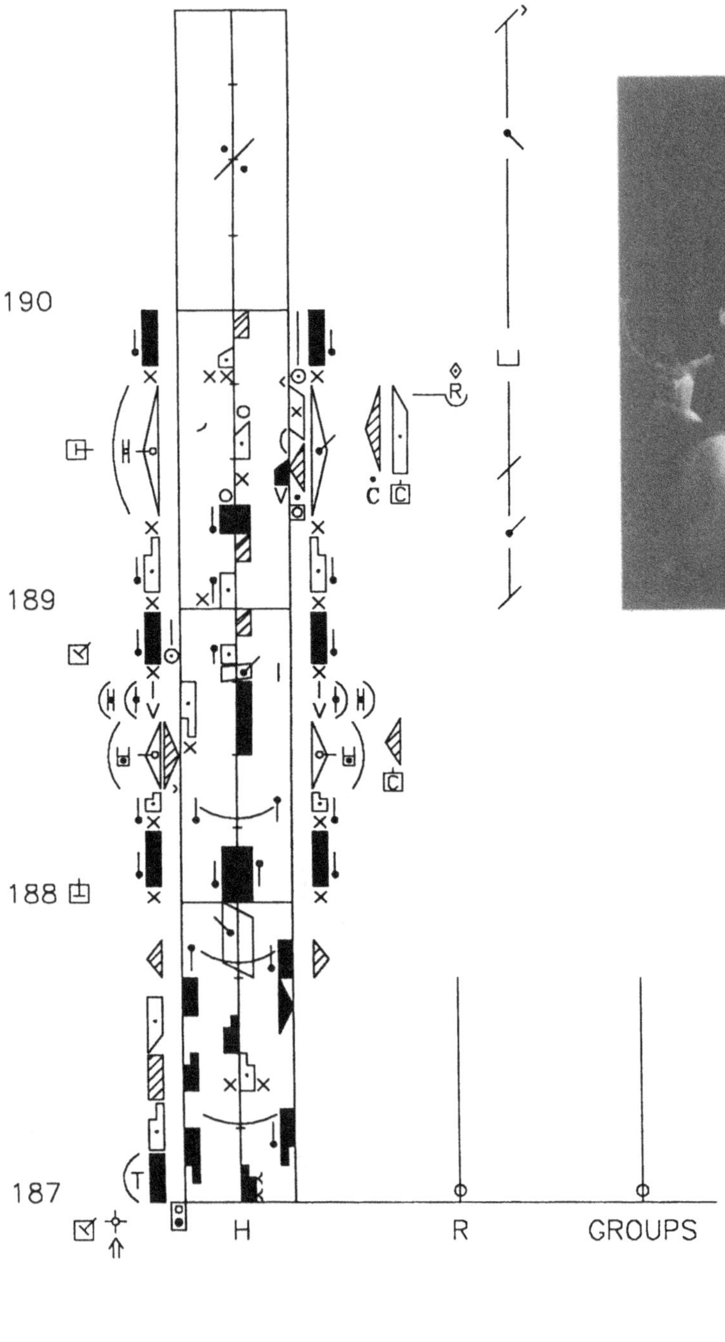

120 ROBERT LE DIABLE - THE BALLET OF THE NUNS

measure 188, count 3

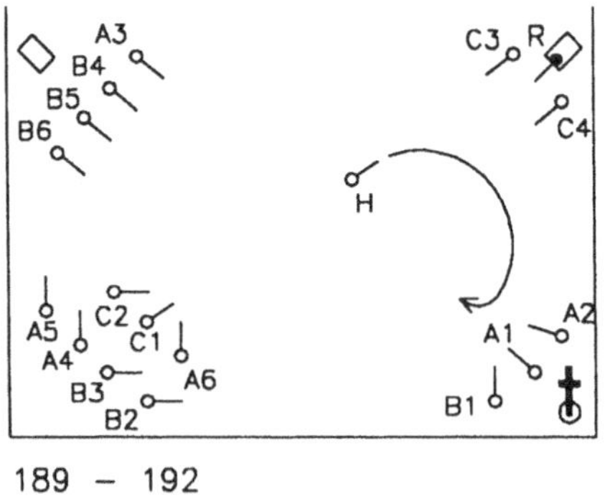

1ᴱᴿ AIR DE BALLET

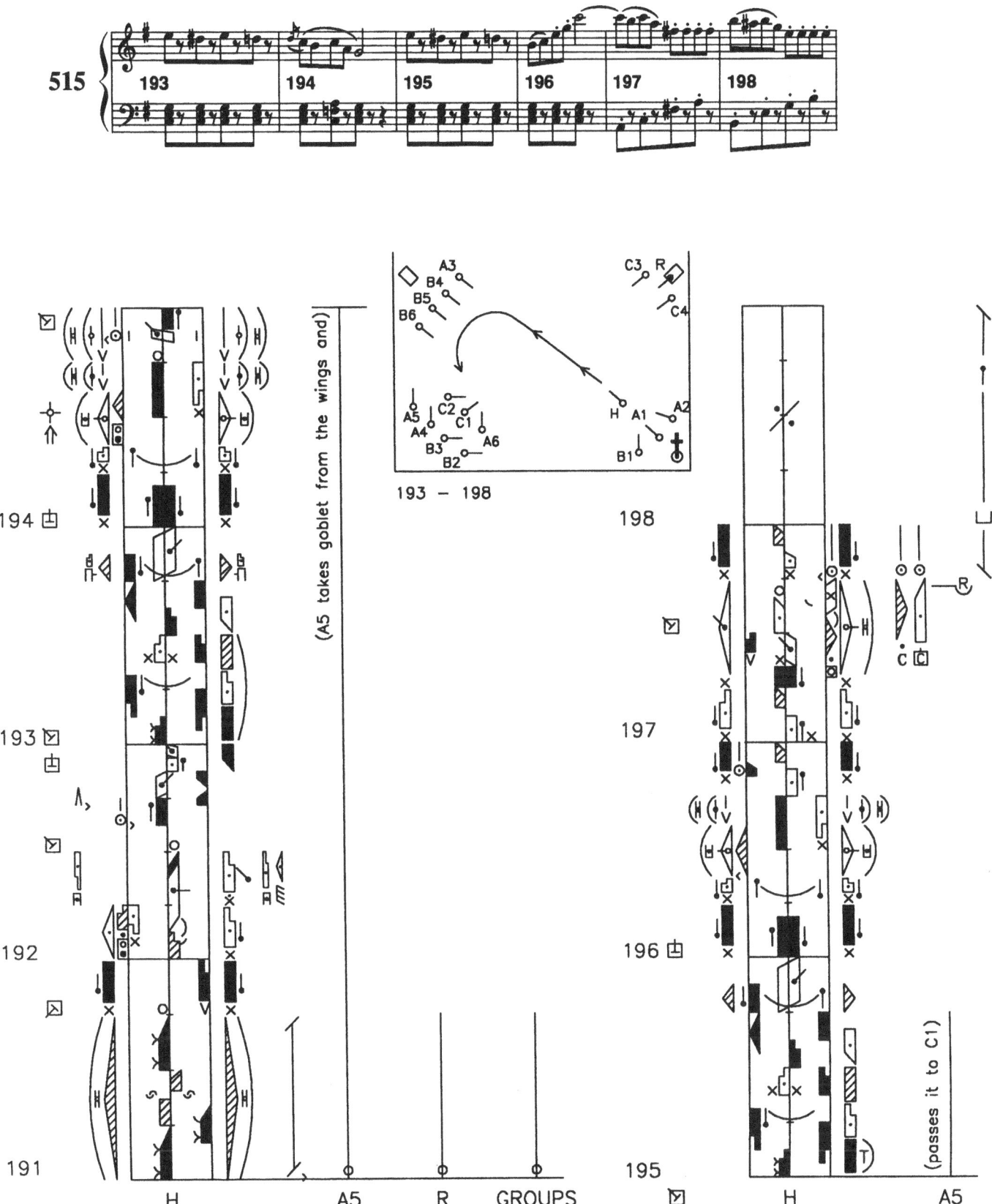

122 ROBERT LE DIABLE - THE BALLET OF THE NUNS

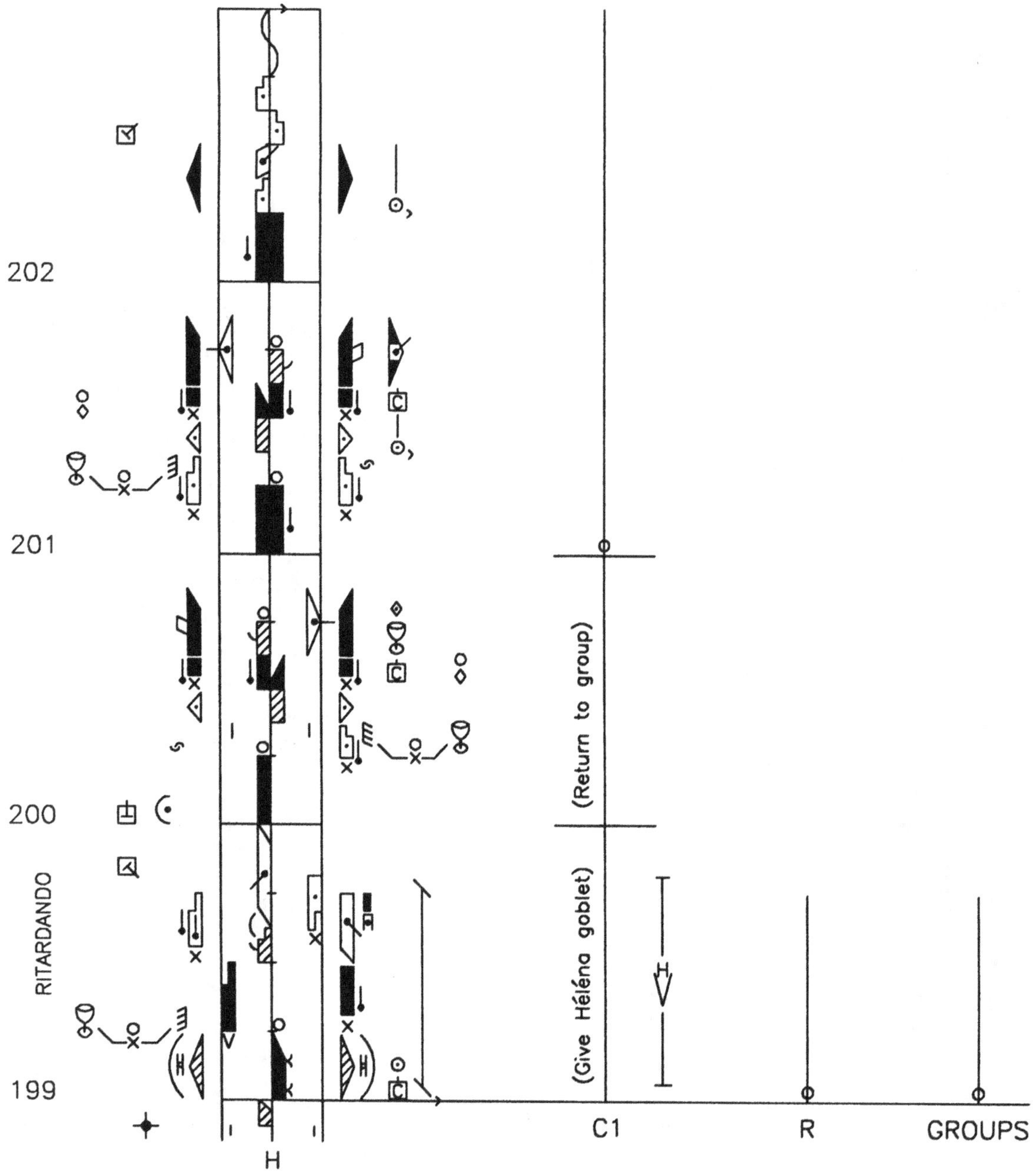

1ᴱᴿ AIR DE BALLET

measure 201

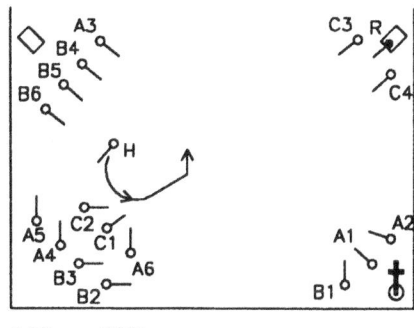

199 – 202

124 ROBERT LE DIABLE - THE BALLET OF THE NUNS

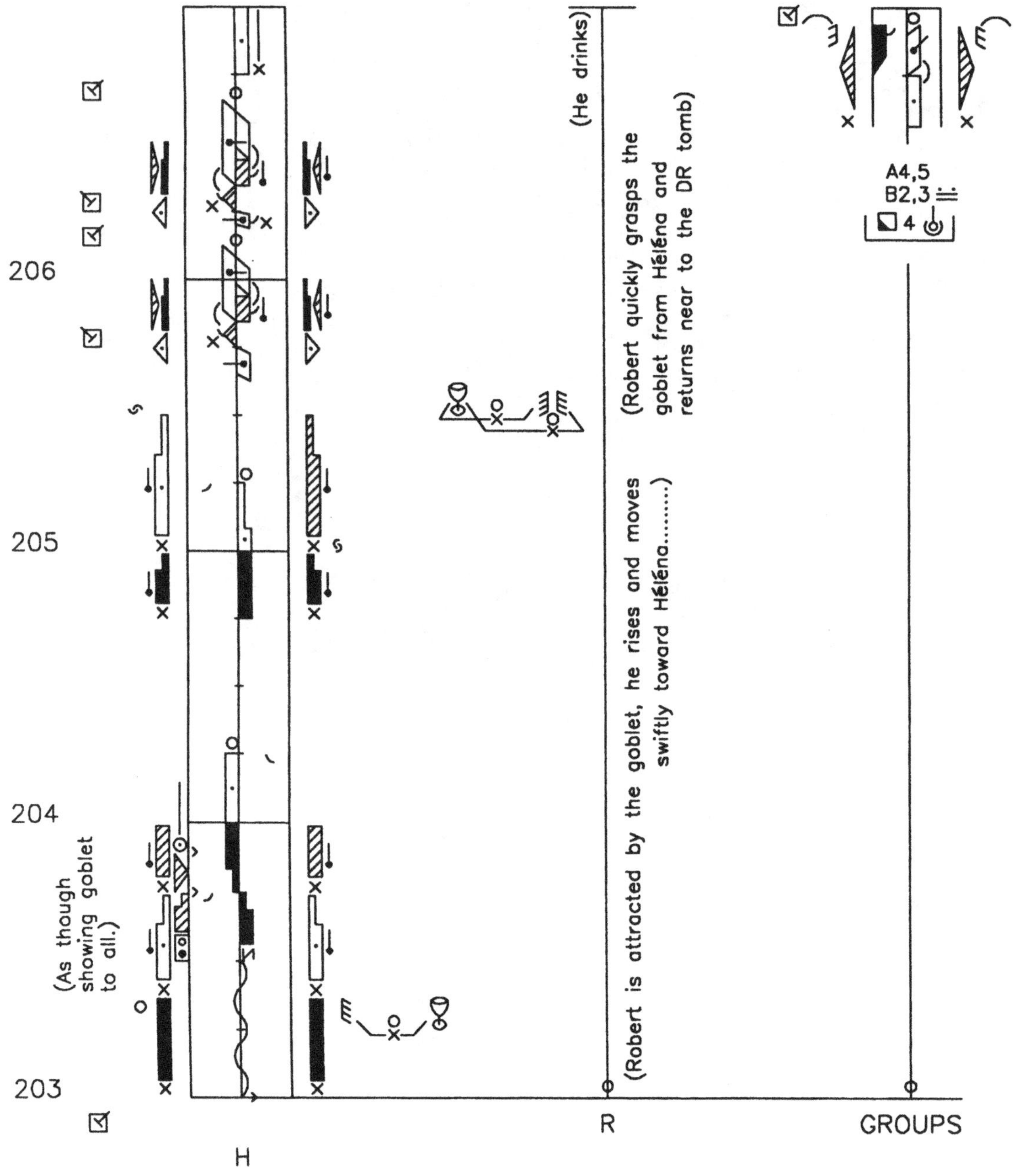

1ᴱᴿ AIR DE BALLET

205⁴, 206

203, 204

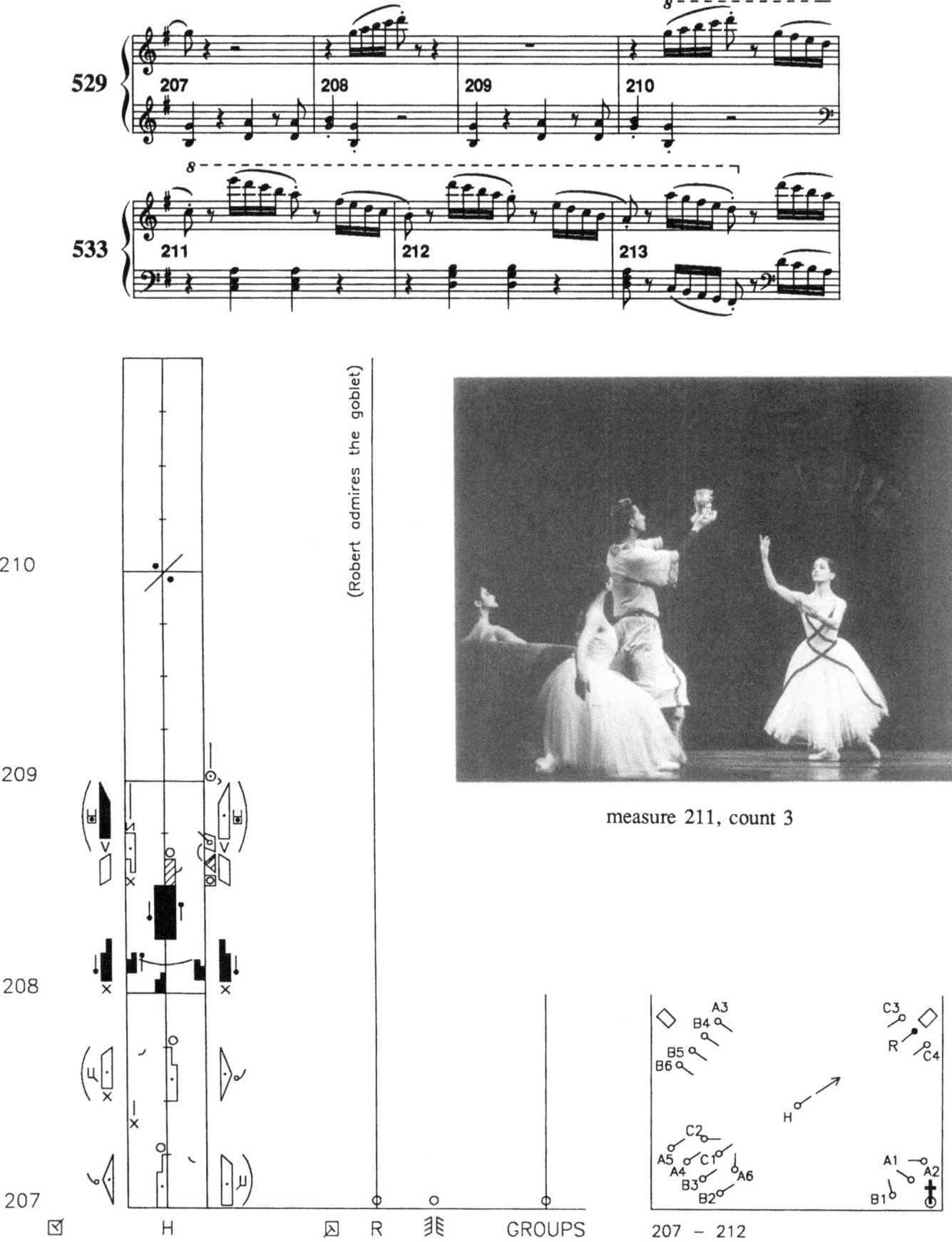

measure 211, count 3

1ᴱᴿ AIR DE BALLET

127

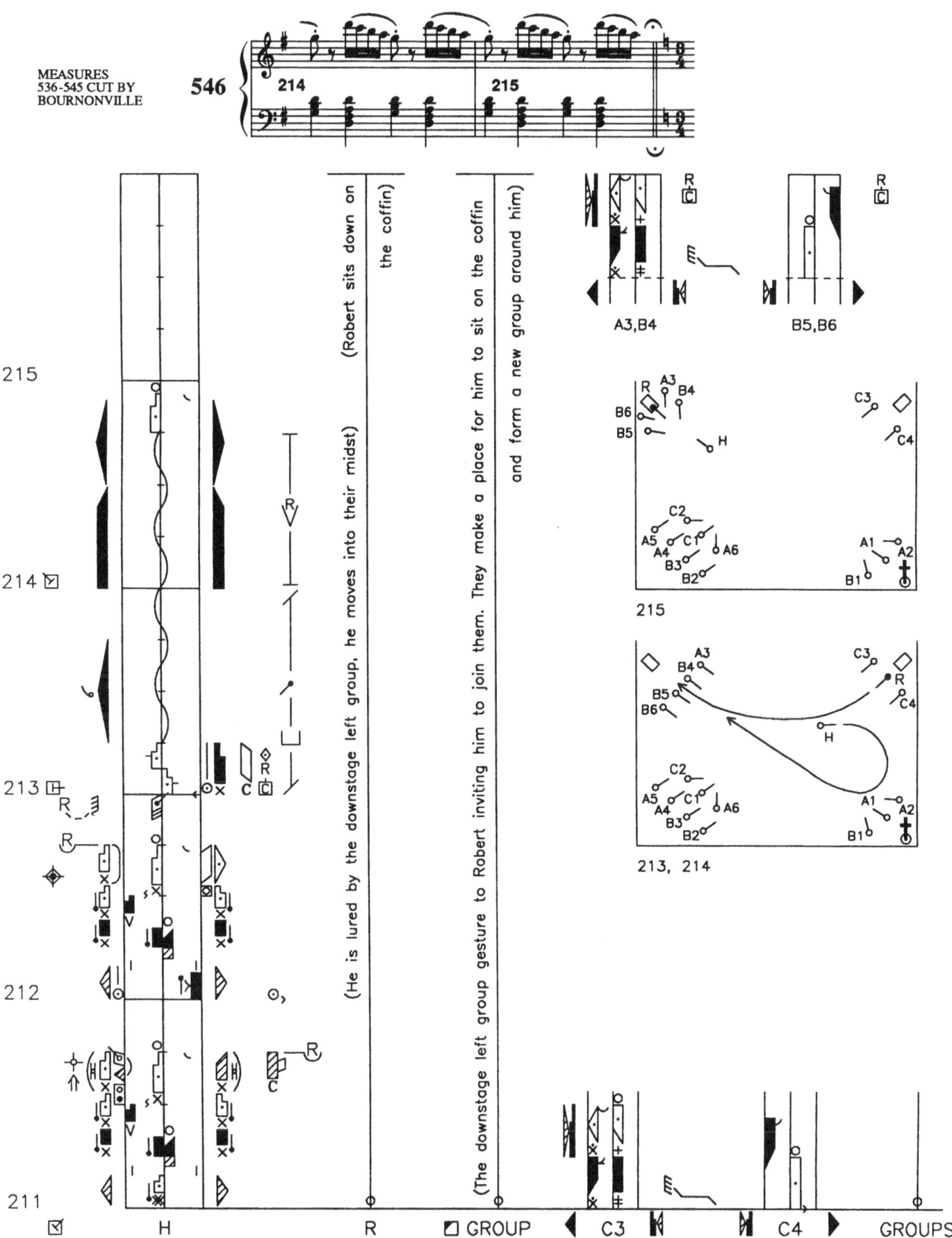

128 ROBERT LE DIABLE - THE BALLET OF THE NUNS

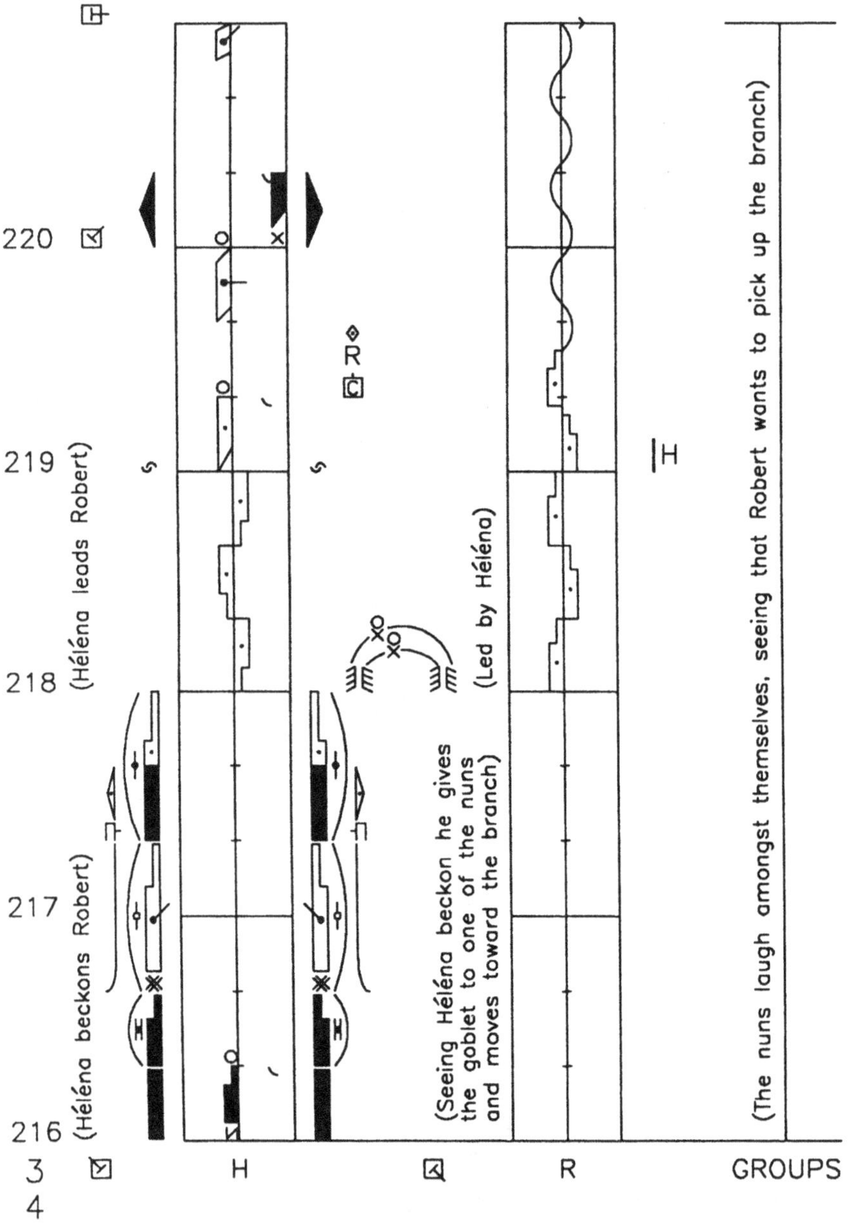

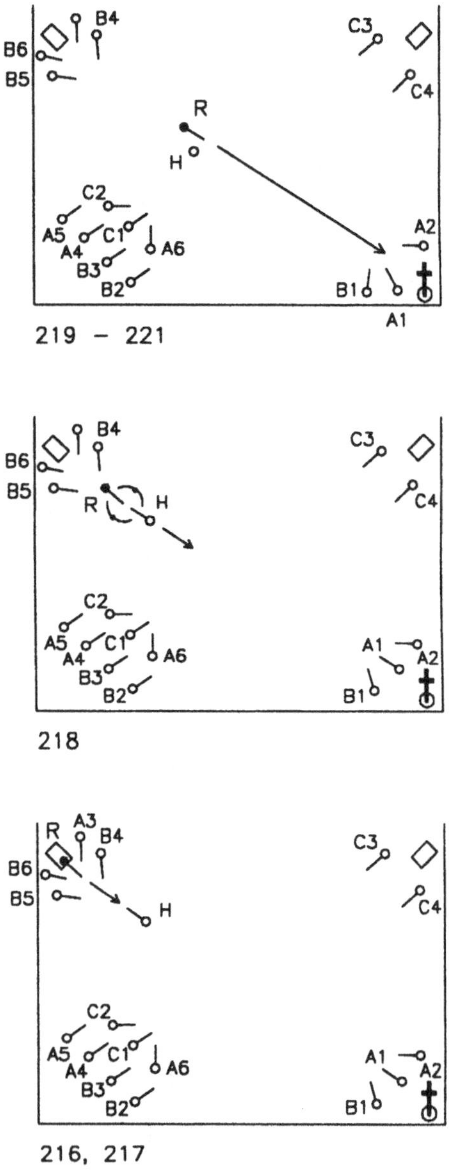

553
221
222
ff
223
224

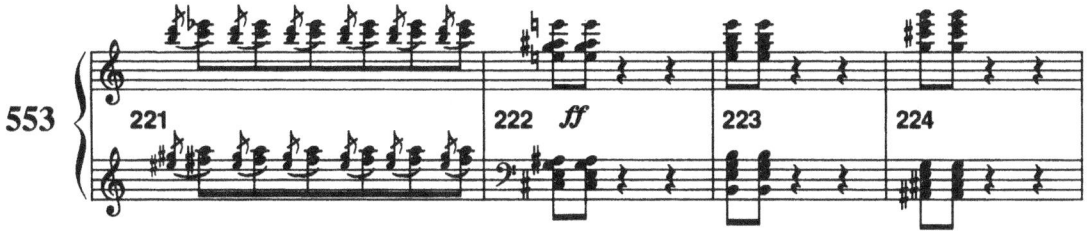

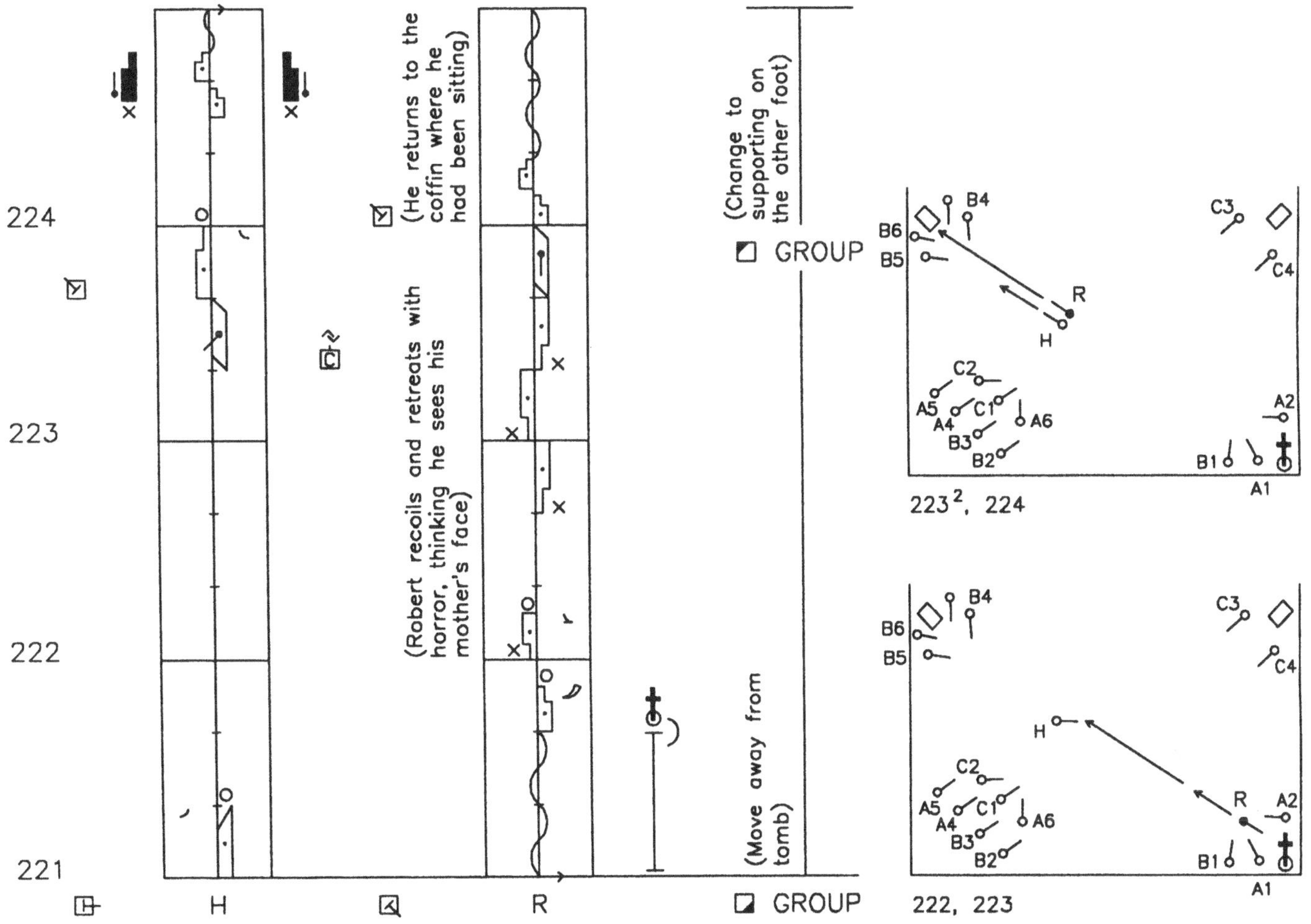
221
222
223
224
H
R
GROUP
GROUP
(Move away from tomb)
(Robert recoils and retreats with horror, thinking he sees his mother's face)
(He returns to the coffin where he had been sitting)
(Change to supporting on the other foot)
B4
B6
B5
C3
C4
R
H
C2
A5
A4
C1
A6
B3
B2
A2
B1
A1
223², 224
B4
B6
B5
C3
C4
H
R
A2
C2
A5
A4
C1
A6
B3
B2
B1
A1
222, 223

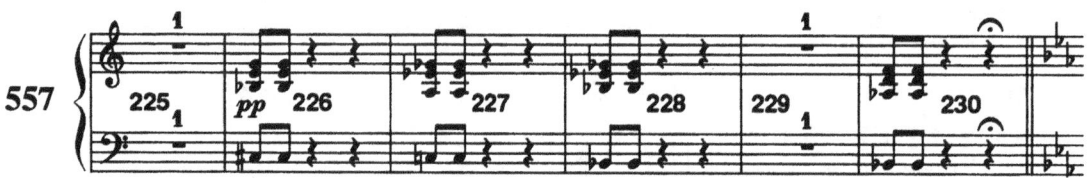

557
225
pp 226
227
228
229
230

2me Air de Ballet
Séduction du jeu

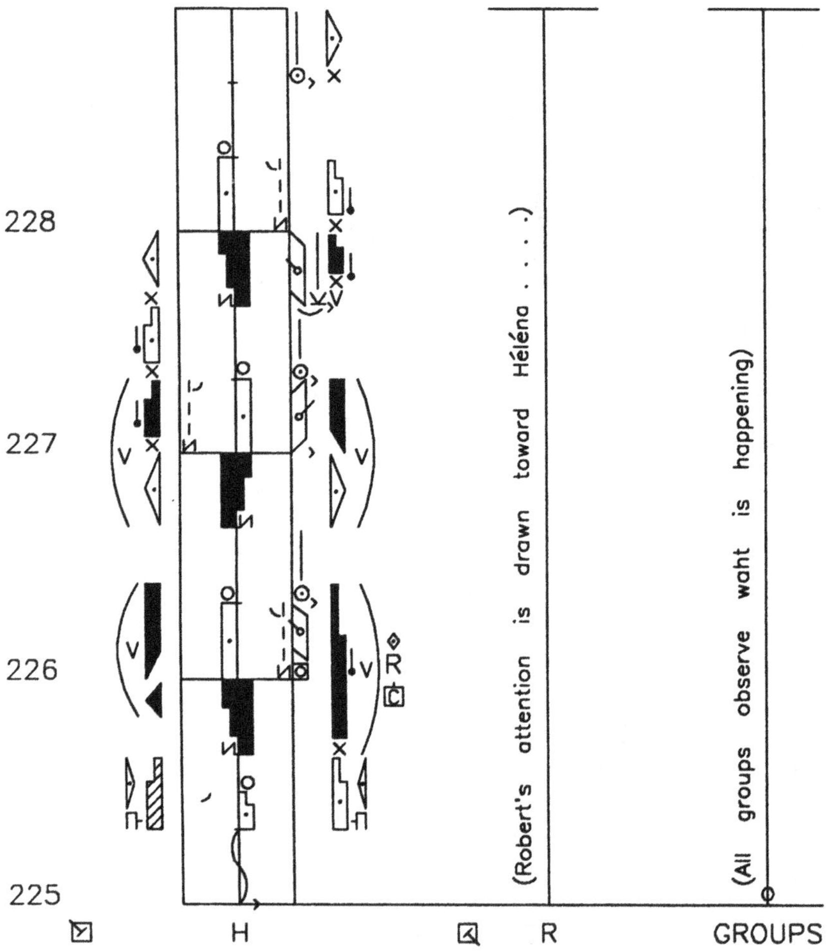

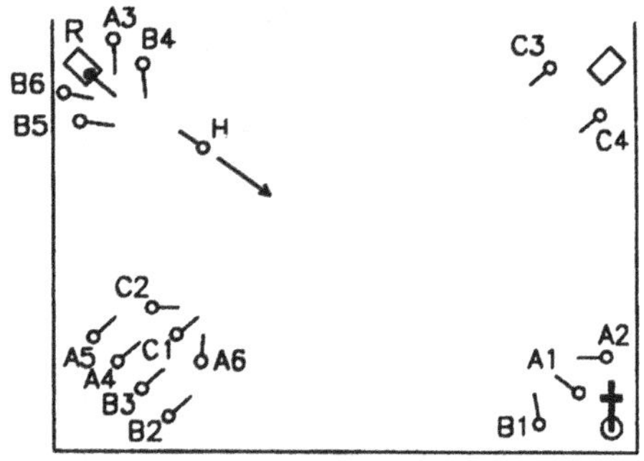

(Robert's attention is drawn toward Héléna . . . .)
(All groups observe waht is happening)
228
227
226
225
H
R
GROUPS

R
A3
B4
B6
B5
H
C3
C4
C2
A5
C1
A6
A4
B3
B2
A1
A2
B1

226 – 230

563
Allegro moderato
231
p
232
dol. e stacc.
233
234

234
233
232
231
230
229
H
R
GROUPS

R
A3
B4
B6
B5
C3
C4
H
C2
A5
A4
C1
A6
B3
B2
A1
A2
B1
233 - 236

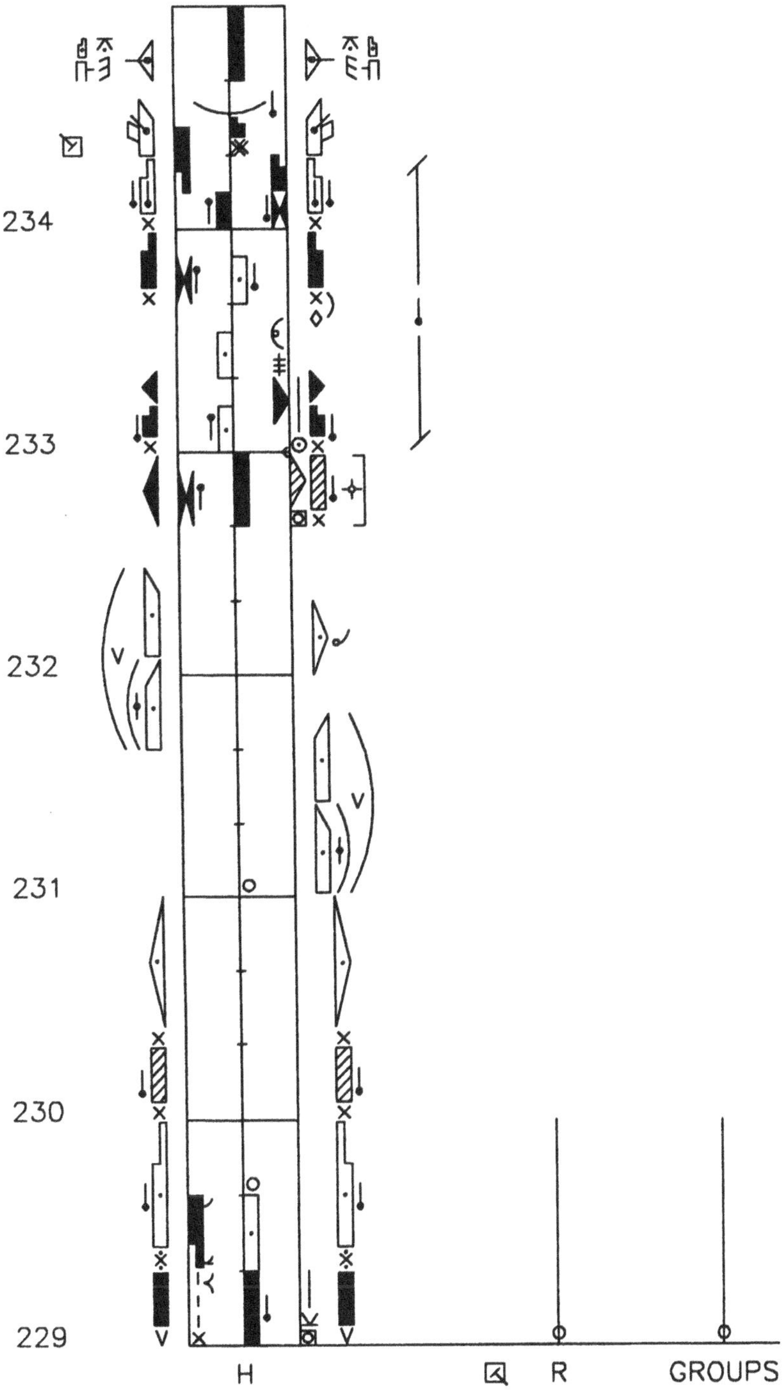

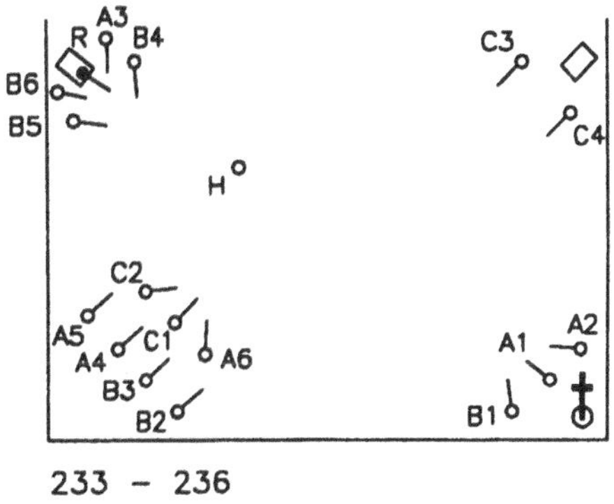

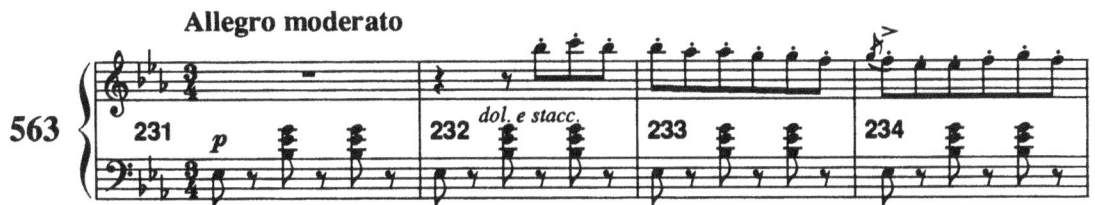

132 ROBERT LE DIABLE - THE BALLET OF THE NUNS

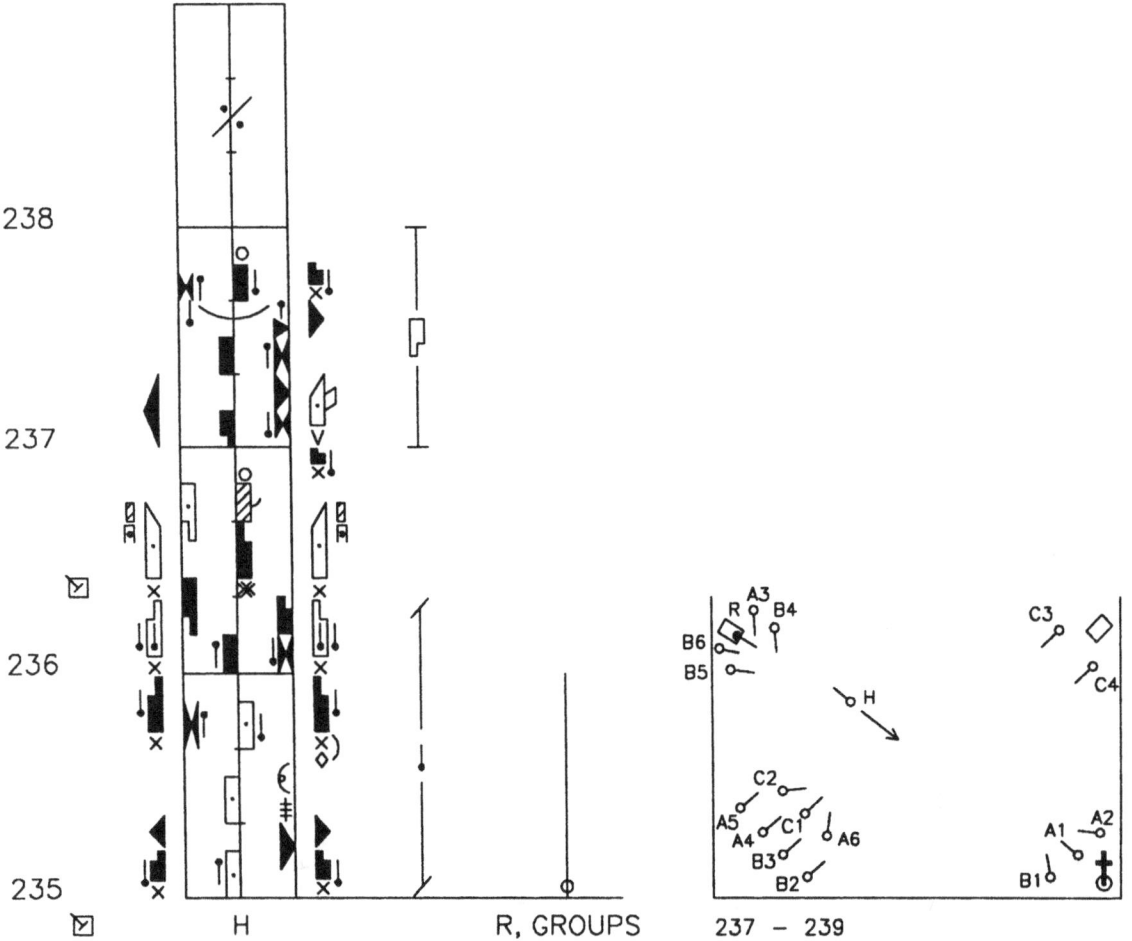

2ᴹᴱ AIR DE BALLET

133

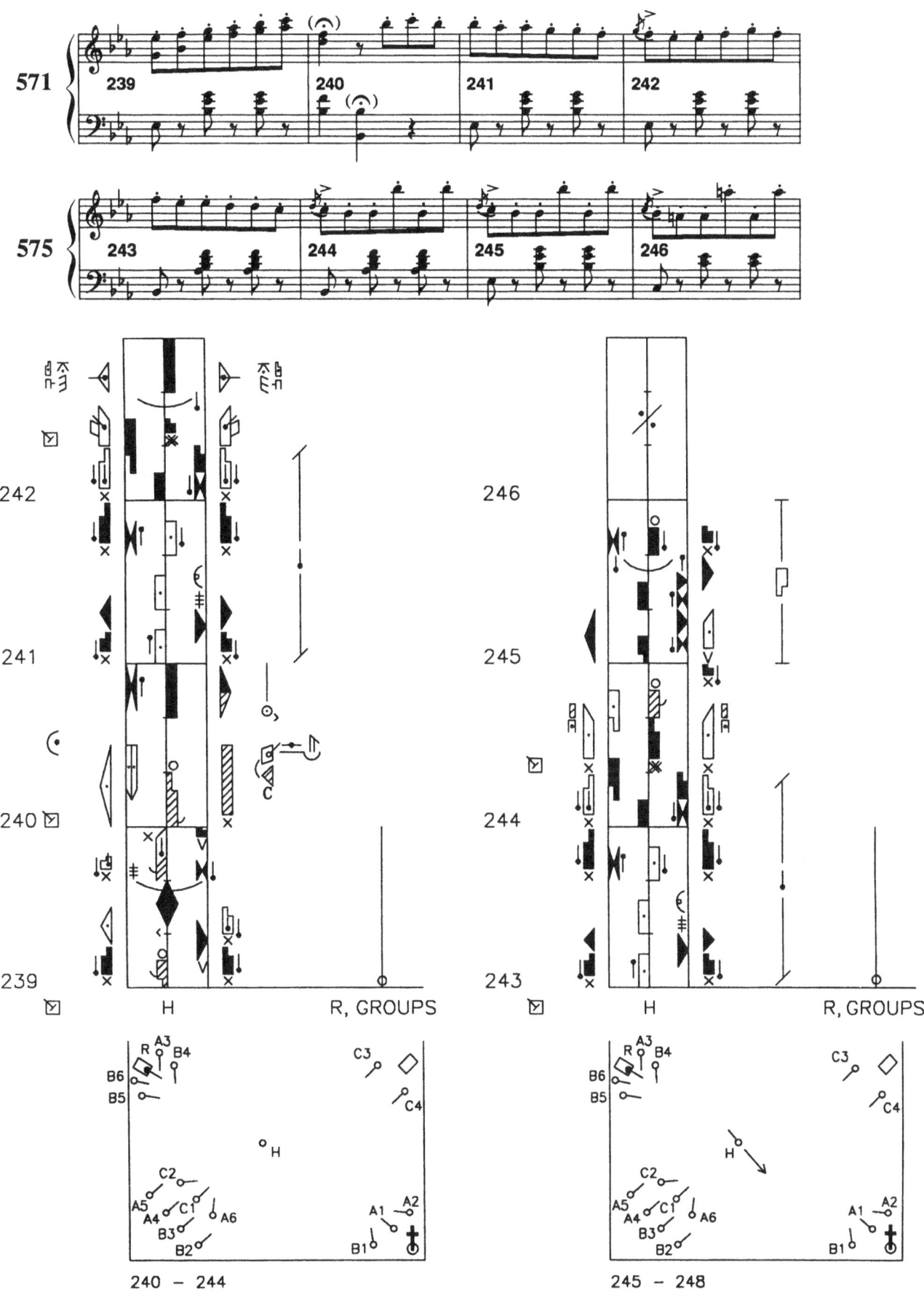

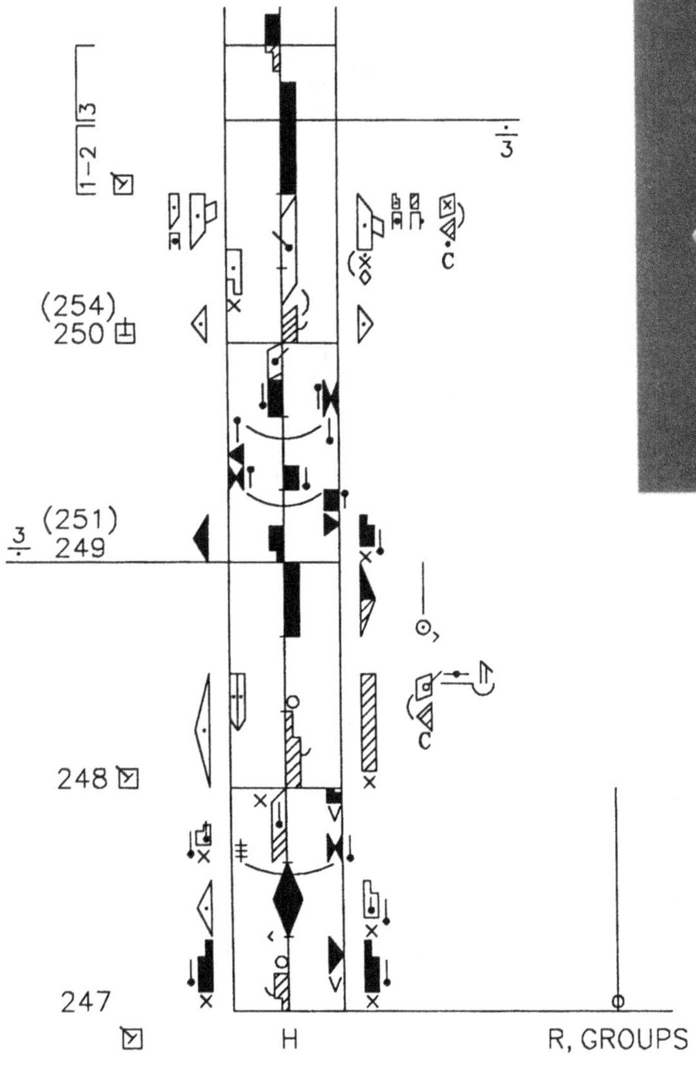

134 ROBERT LE DIABLE - THE BALLET OF THE NUNS

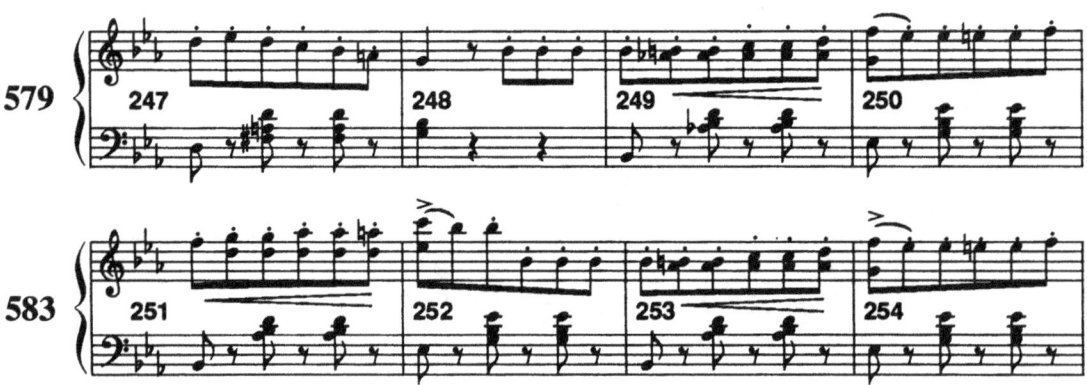

measure 250, count 3

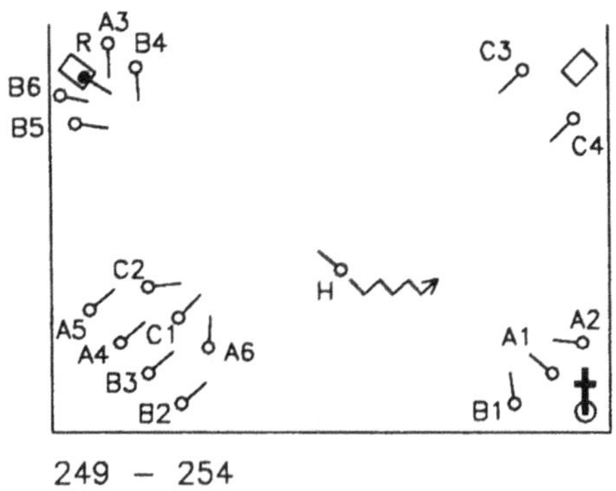

249 – 254

587
255
256
257
258
259

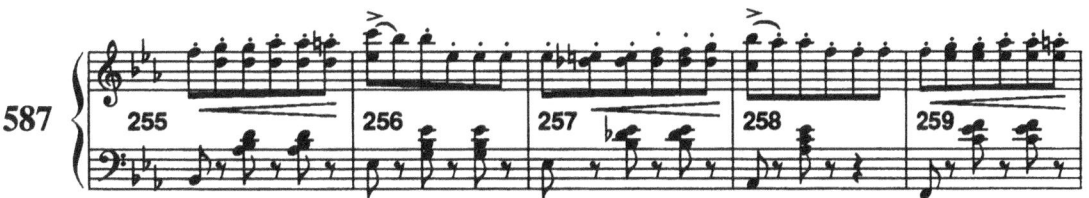

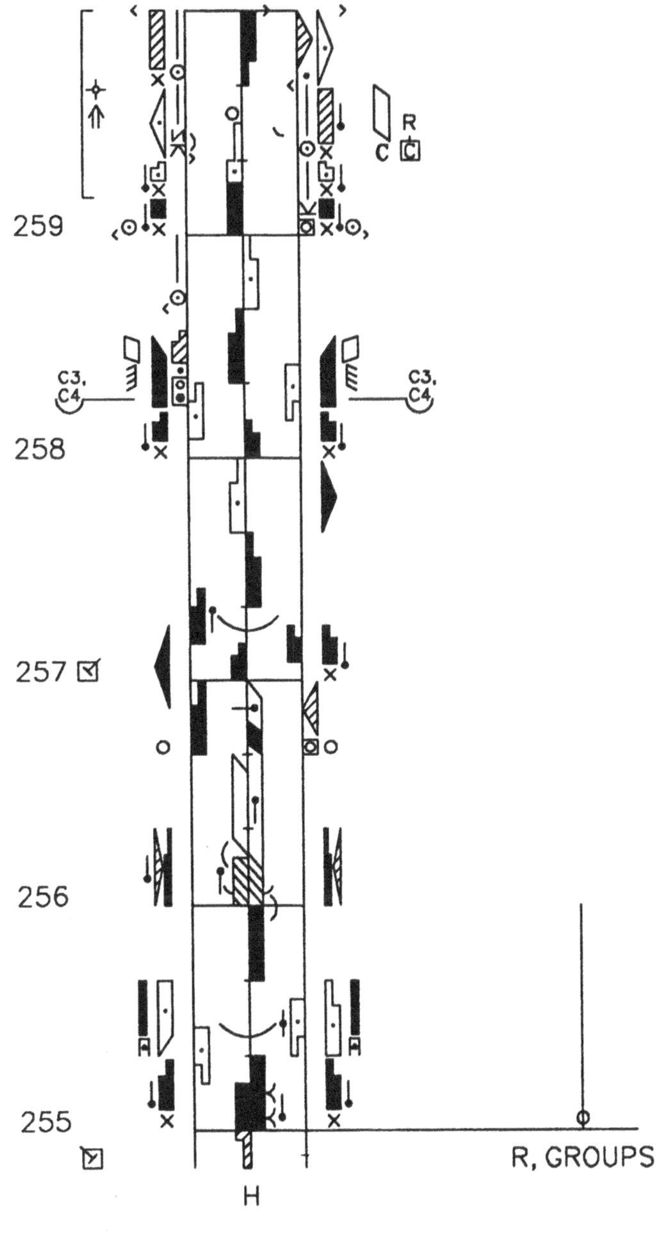
R
C
259
C3,
C4
C3,
C4
258
257
256
255
R, GROUPS
H

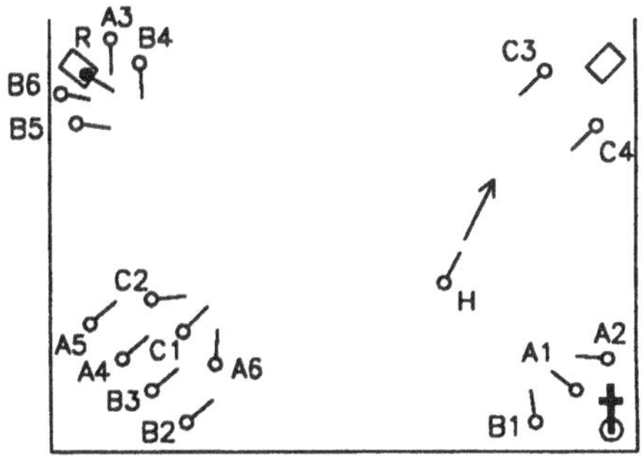
R
A3
B4
B6
B5
C3
C4
C2
H
A5
C1
A6
A4
B3
B2
A1
A2
B1

257, 258

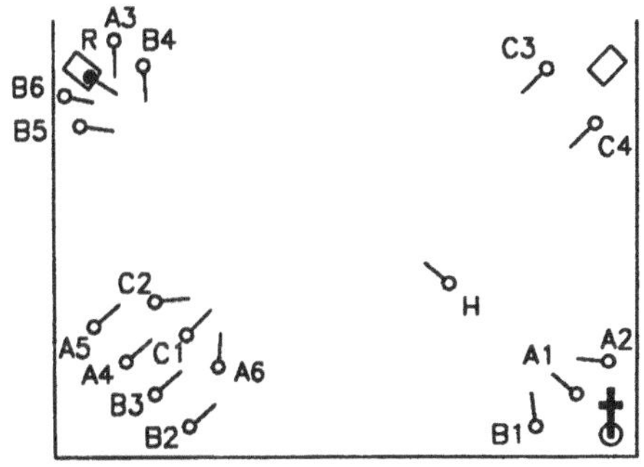
R
A3
B4
B6
B5
C3
C4
C2
H
A5
C1
A6
A4
B3
B2
A1
A2
B1

255

136 ROBERT LE DIABLE - THE BALLET OF THE NUNS

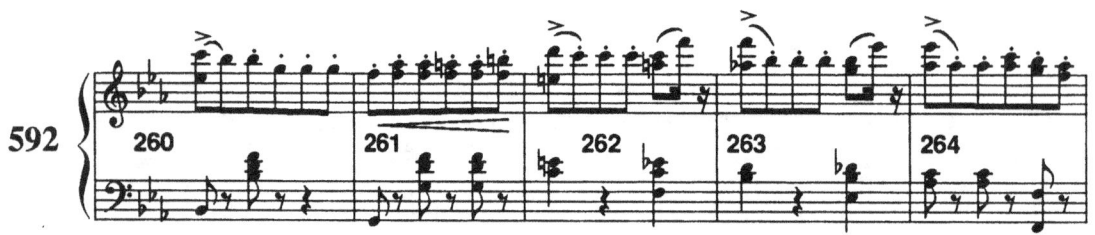

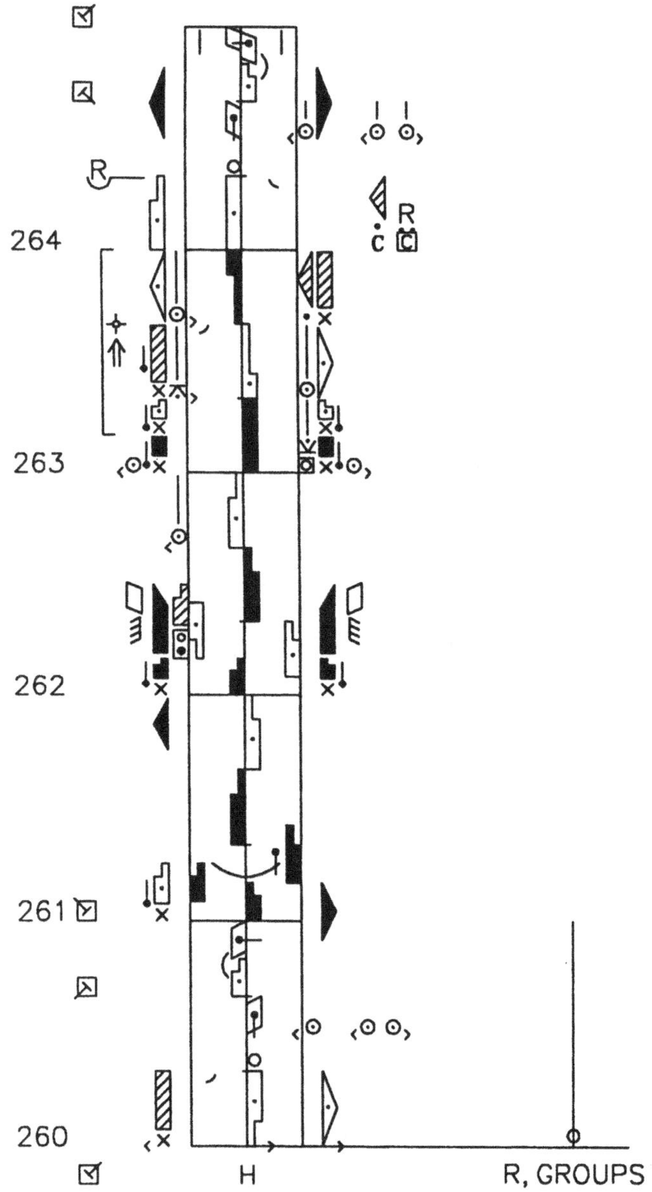

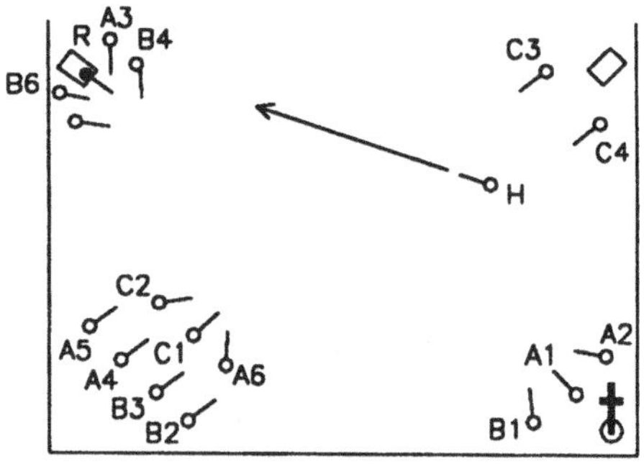

261 – 263

597
265
266
267
268
269
cresc.

269
268
267
266
265
R
C
H
R, GROUPS

R
A3
B4
B6
B5
H
C3
C4
C2
A5
C1
A6
A4
B3
B2
A1
A2
B1
265 – 269

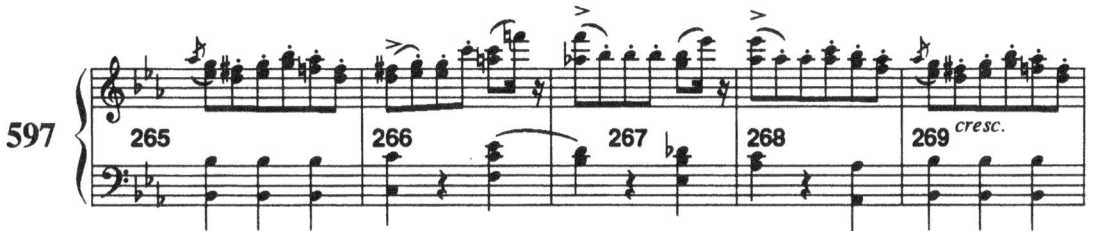

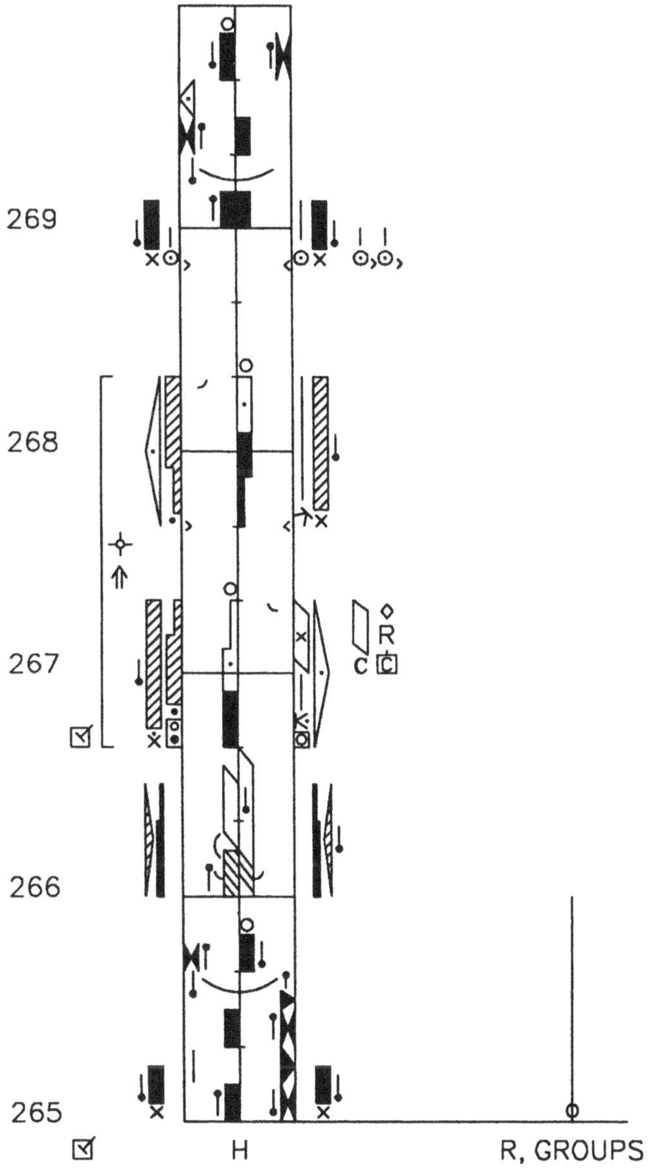

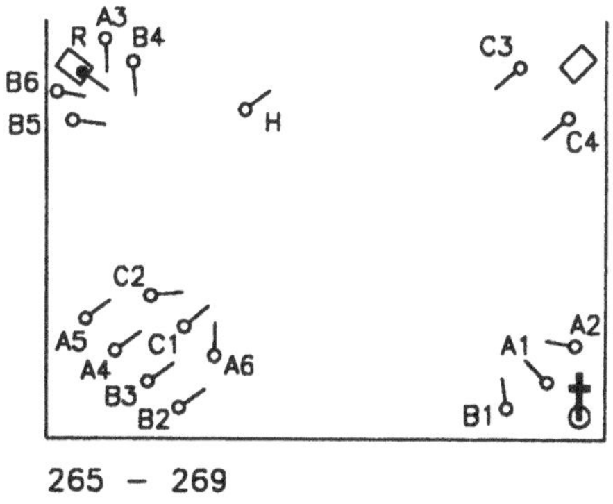

ROBERT LE DIABLE - THE BALLET OF THE NUNS

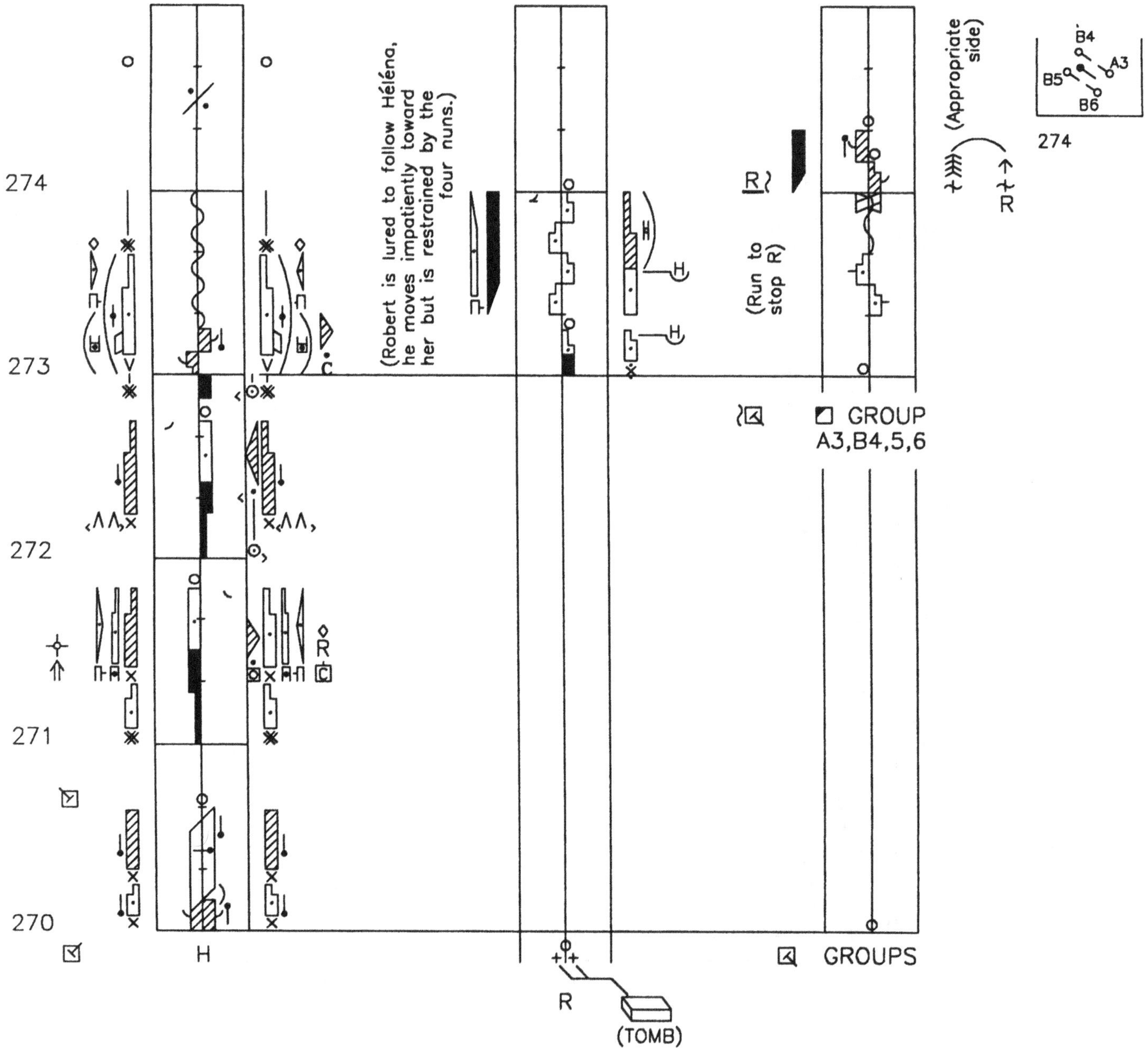

(Robert is lured to follow Héléna, he moves impatiently toward her but is restrained by the four nuns.)

(Run to stop R)

(Appropriate side)

GROUP A3, B4, 5, 6

GROUPS

(TOMB)

2ᴹᴱ AIR DE BALLET

measure 274

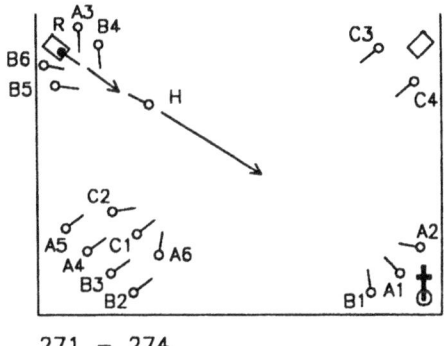

271 – 274

140 ROBERT LE DIABLE - THE BALLET OF THE NUNS

MEASURES 611-662 NOT RECONSTRUCTED

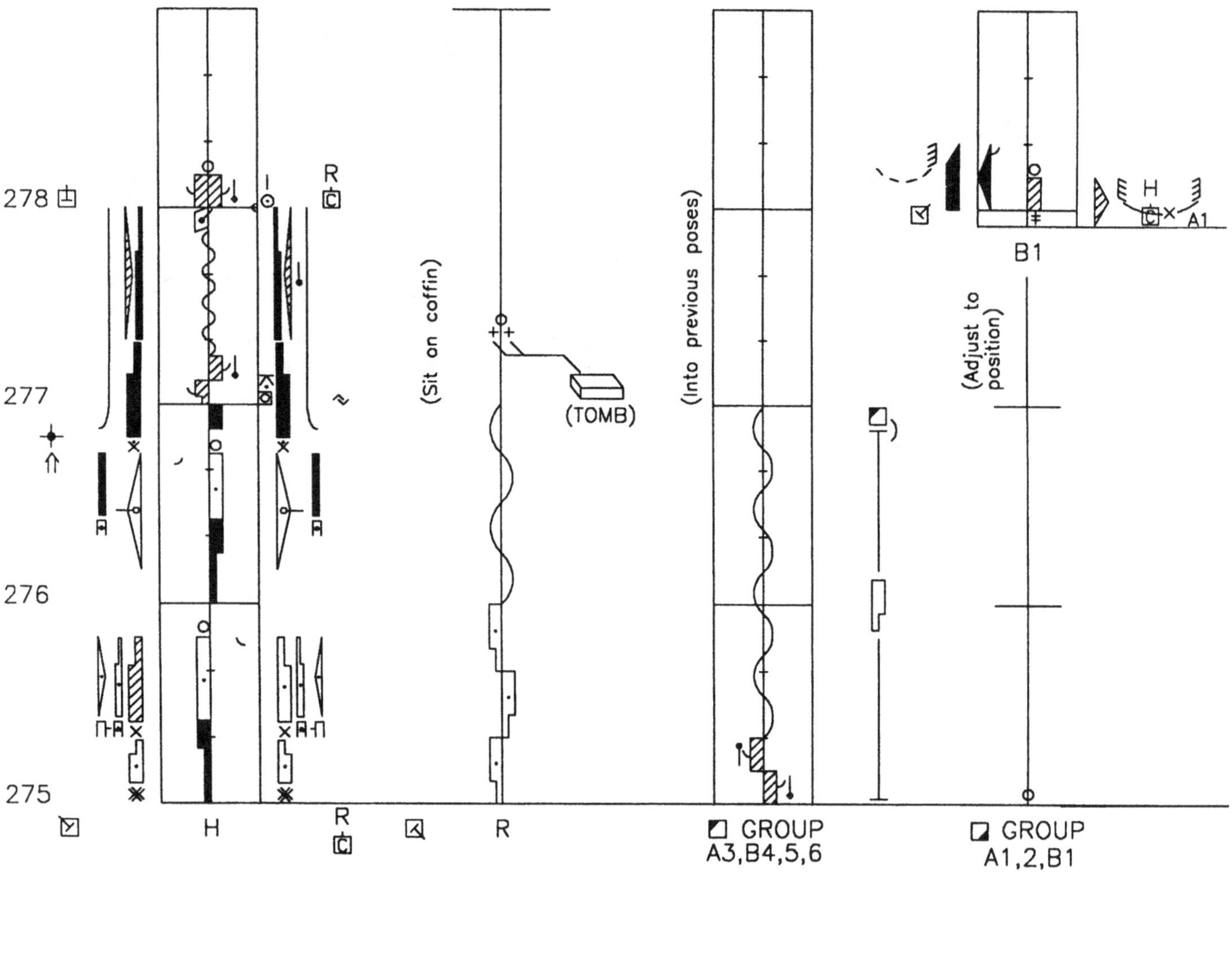

2ᴹᴱ AIR DE BALLET 141

Héléna and upstage right group, measure 278

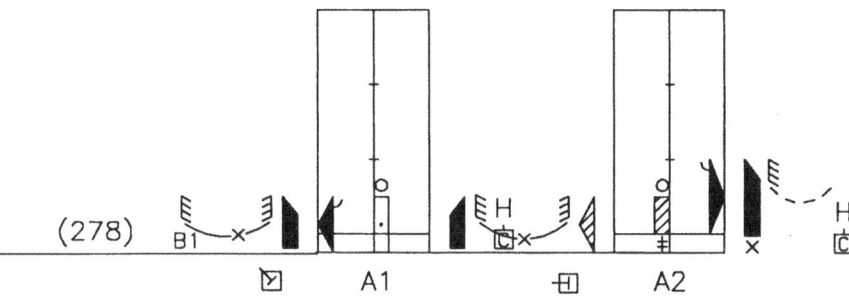

(278)

(277)

(276)

(275) OTHER GROUPS

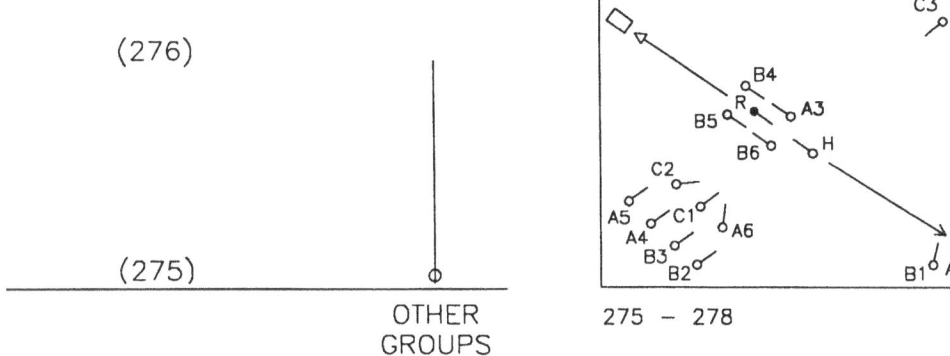

275 – 278

142 ROBERT LE DIABLE - THE BALLET OF THE NUNS

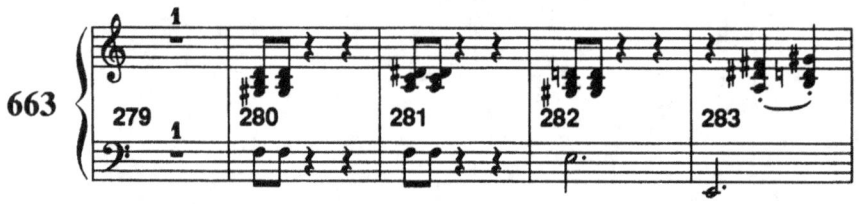

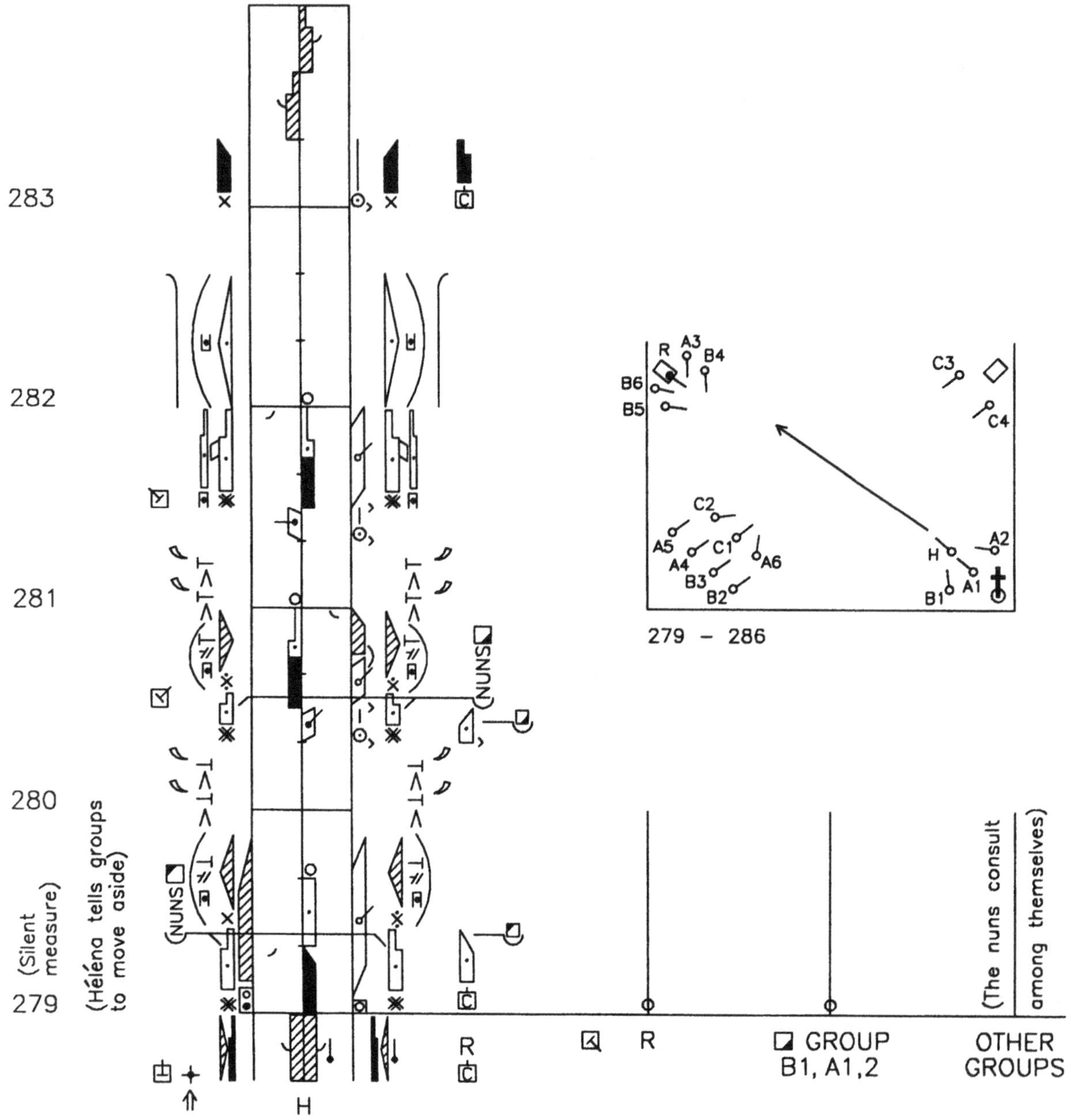

668

284
285
286
287
288
289
290
291
p
dim

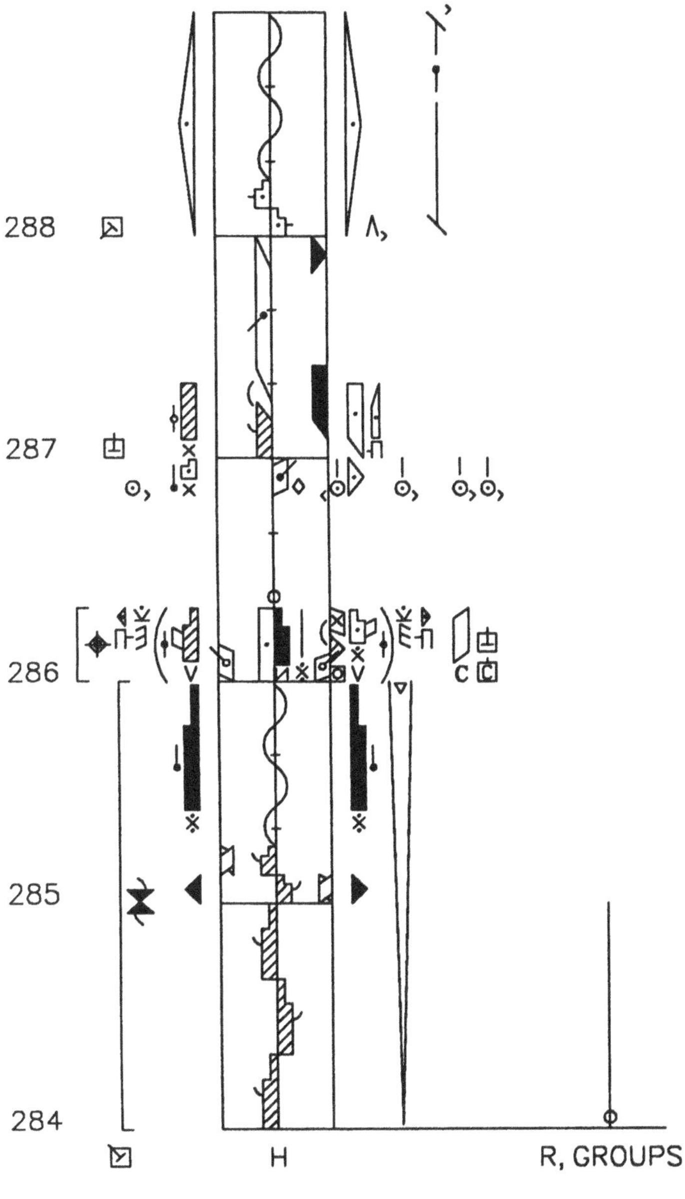
288
287
286
285
284
H
R, GROUPS

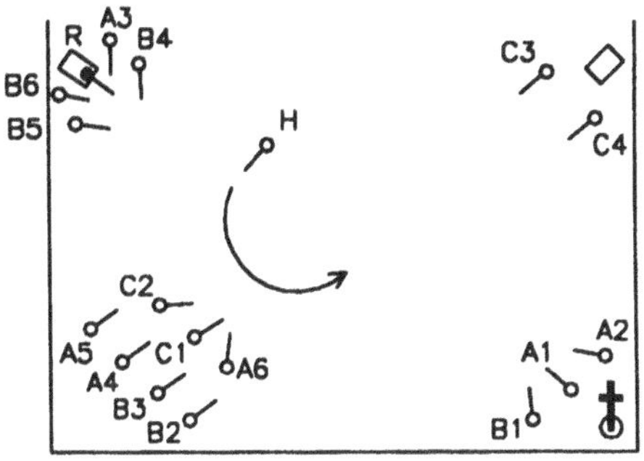
R
A3
B4
B6
B5
H
C3
C4
C2
A5
C1
A6
A4
B3
B2
A1
A2
B1

288, 289

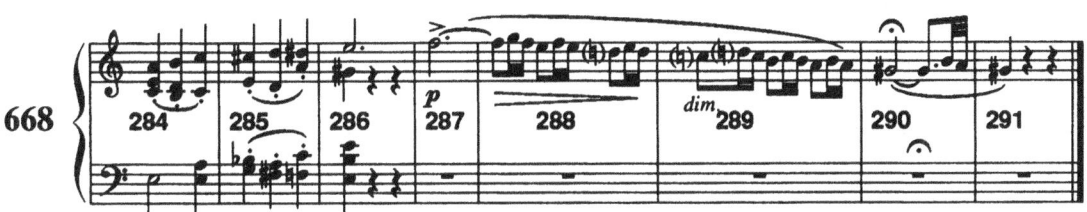

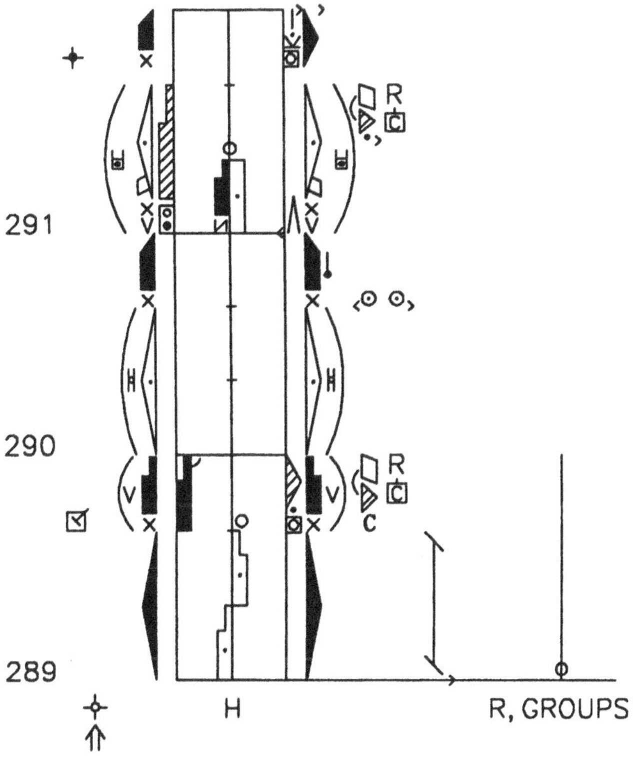
291
290
289
R
C
H
R, GROUPS

3me *Air de Ballet*
Séduction de l'amour
Pas seul d'Héléna

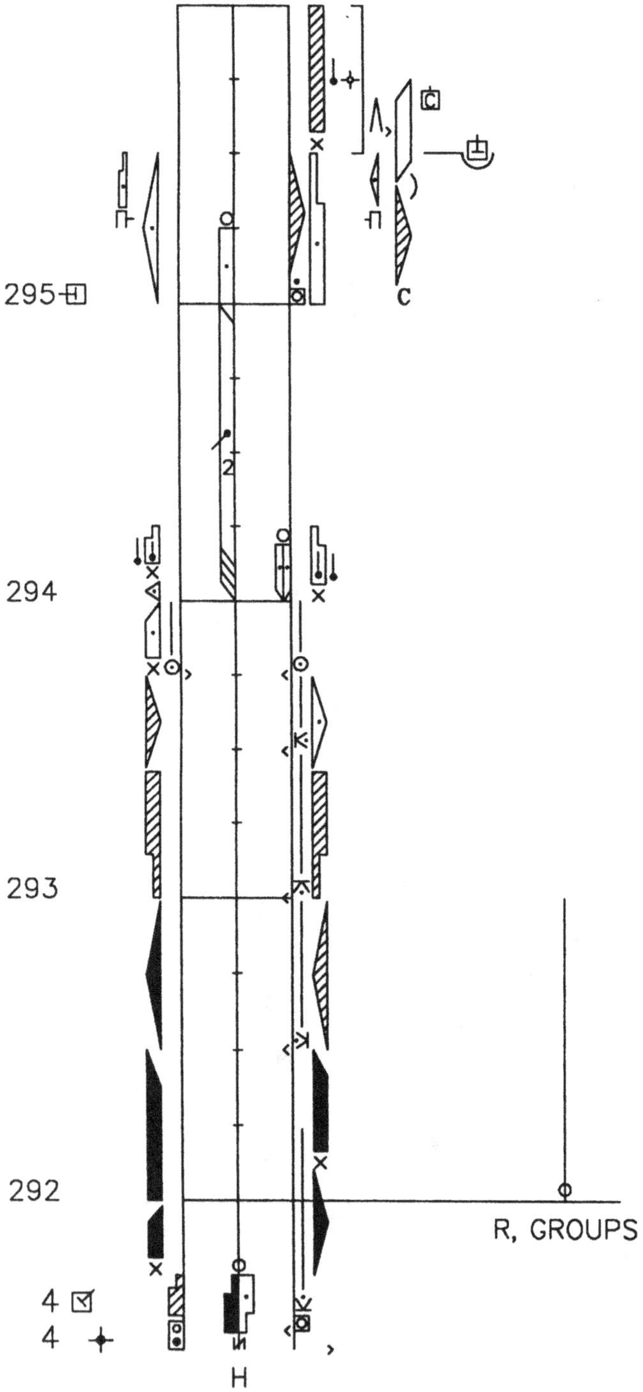

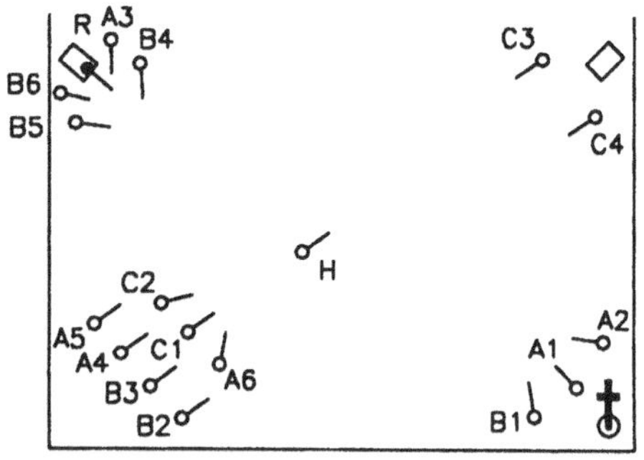

R, GROUPS

292 – 299

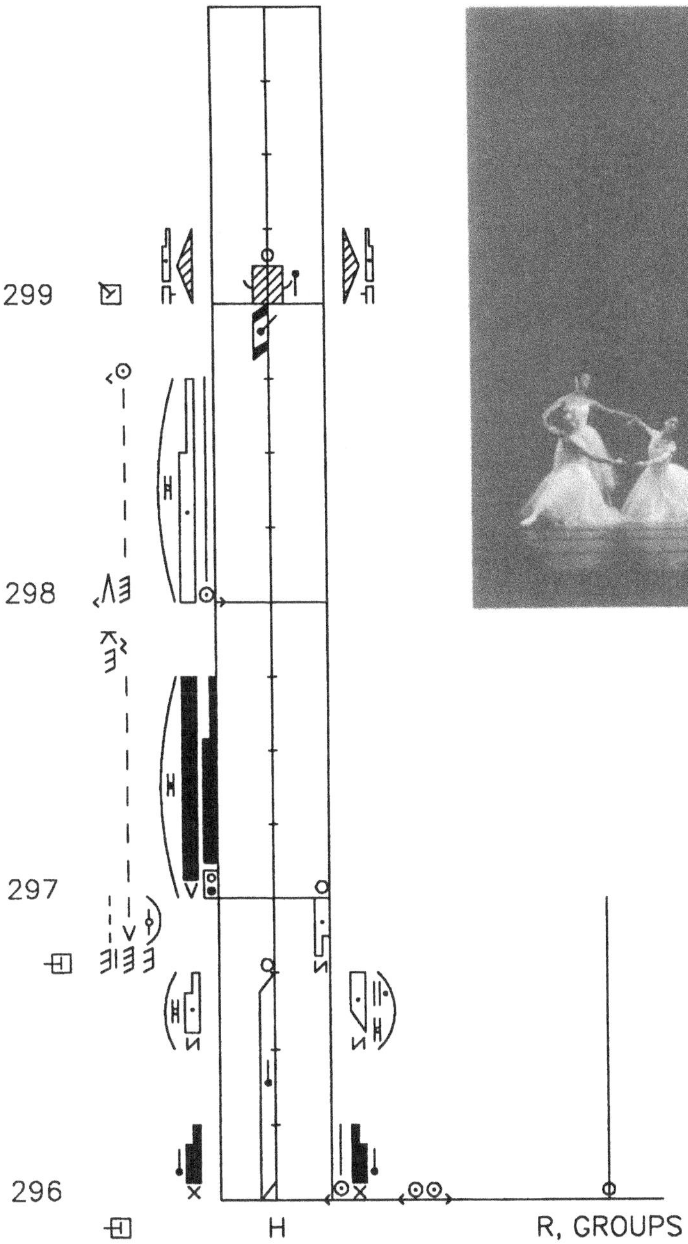

3ᴹᴱ AIR DE BALLET 145

measure 297

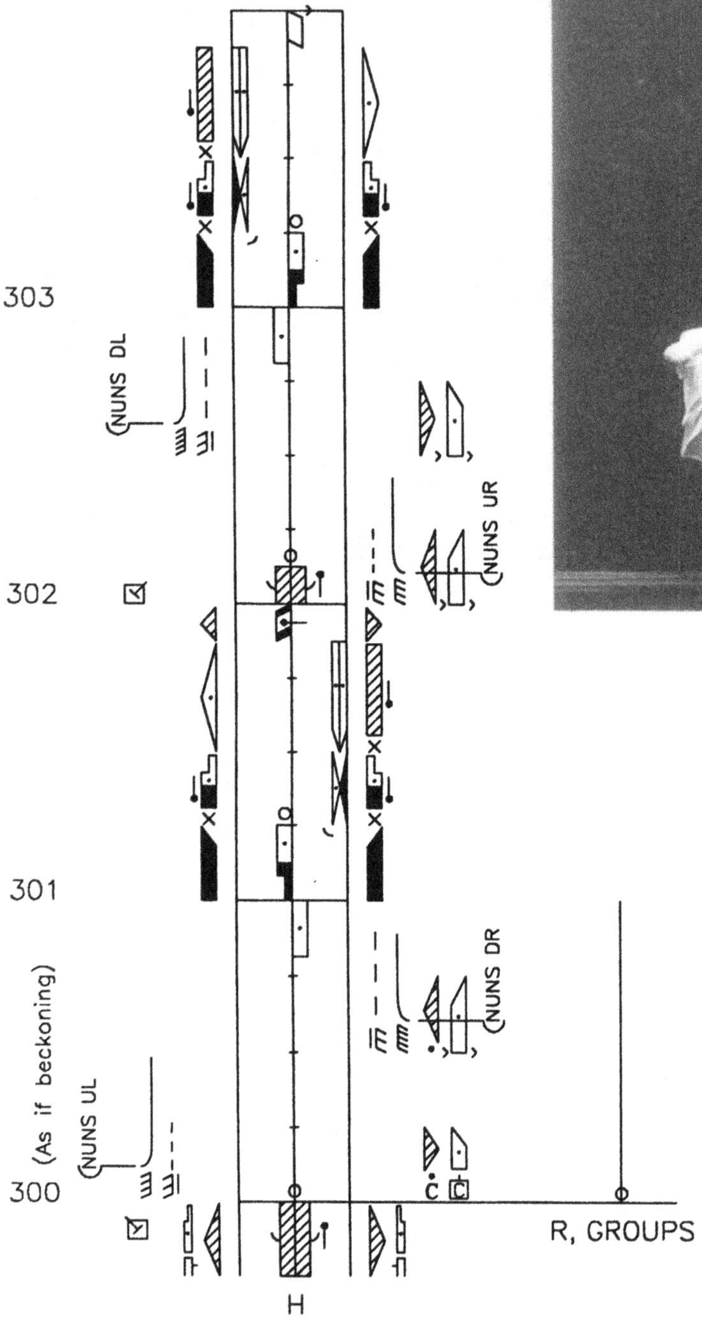

146 ROBERT LE DIABLE - THE BALLET OF THE NUNS

measure 305

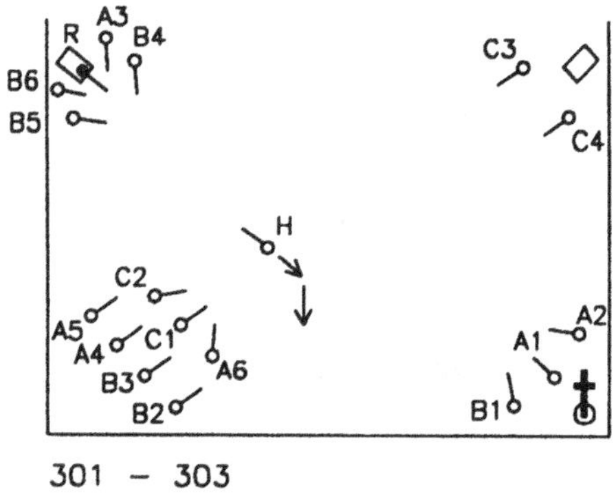

3ᴹᴱ AIR DE BALLET

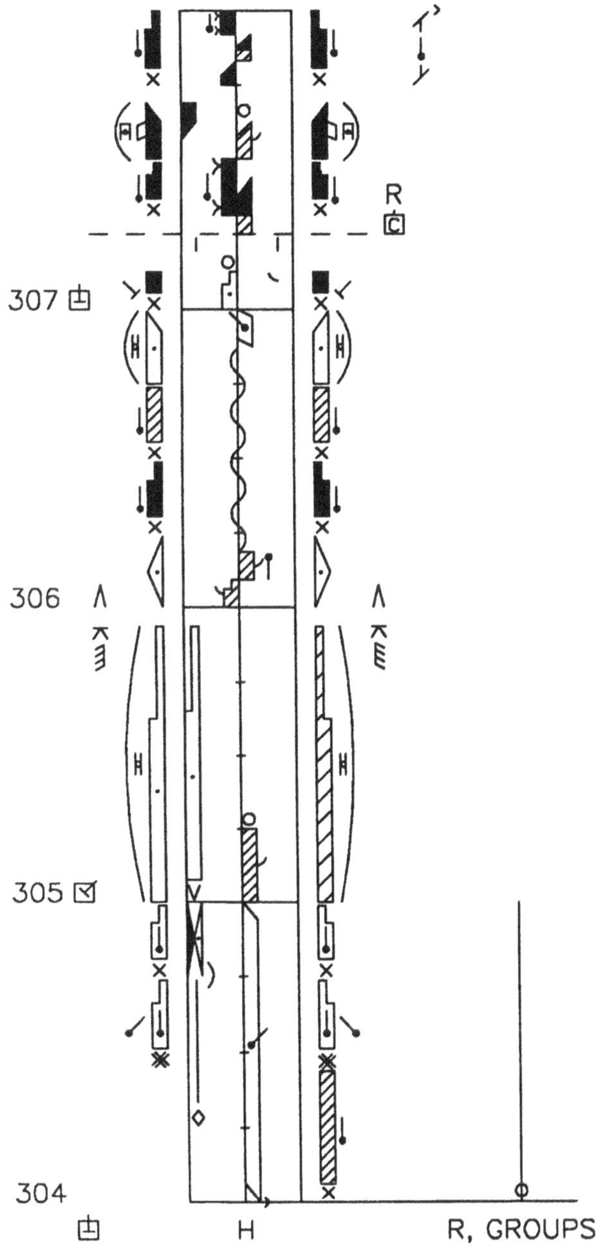

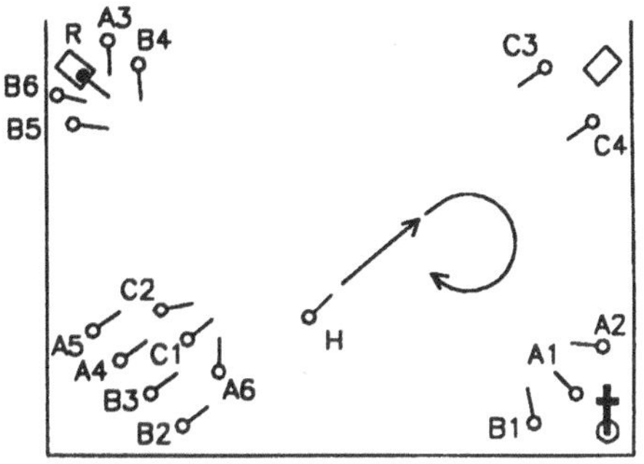

306 – 309¹

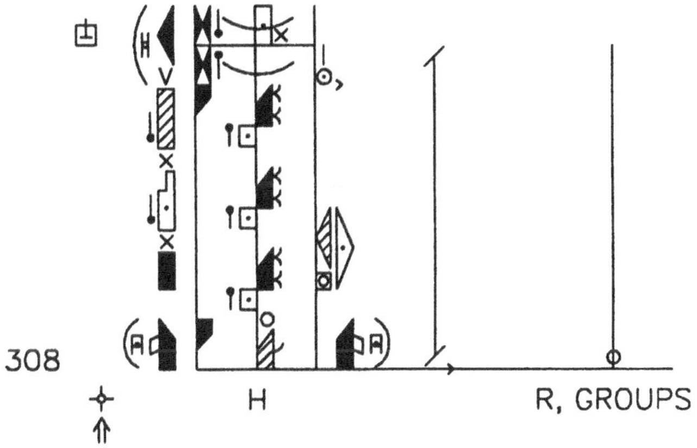

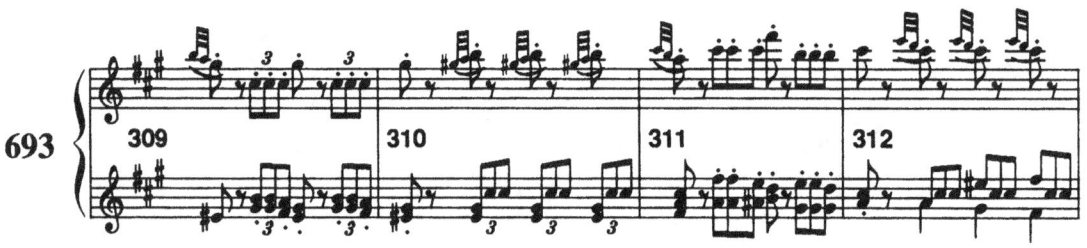

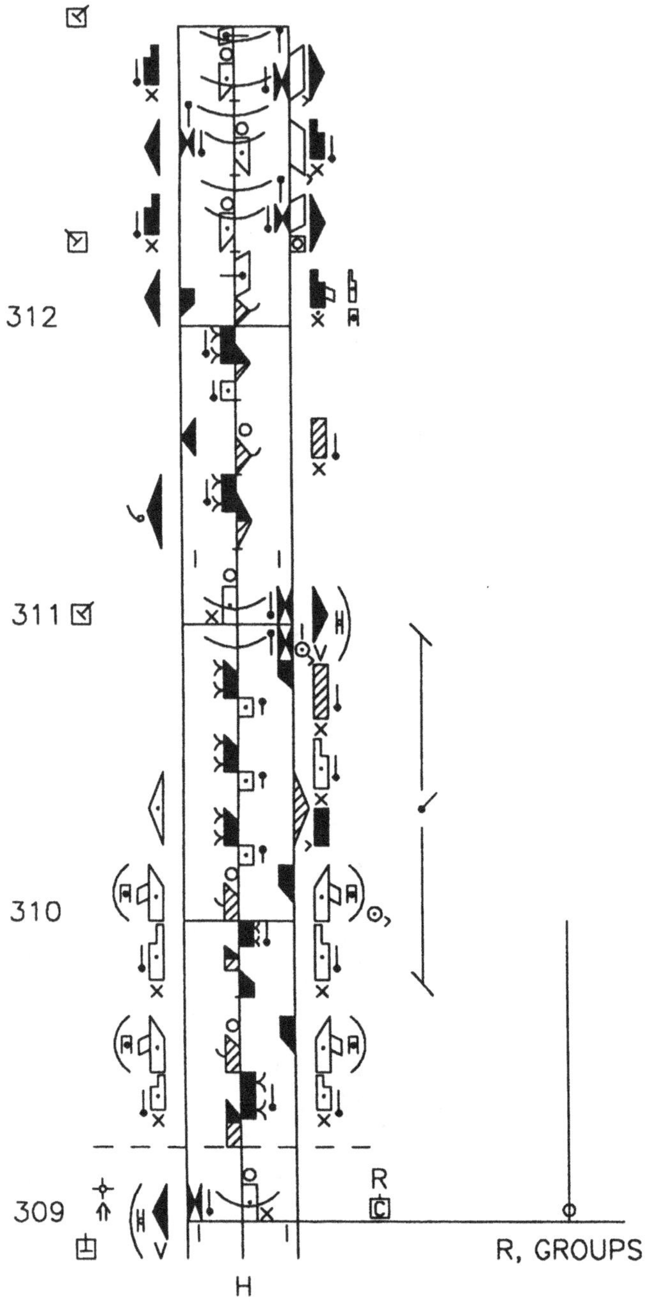

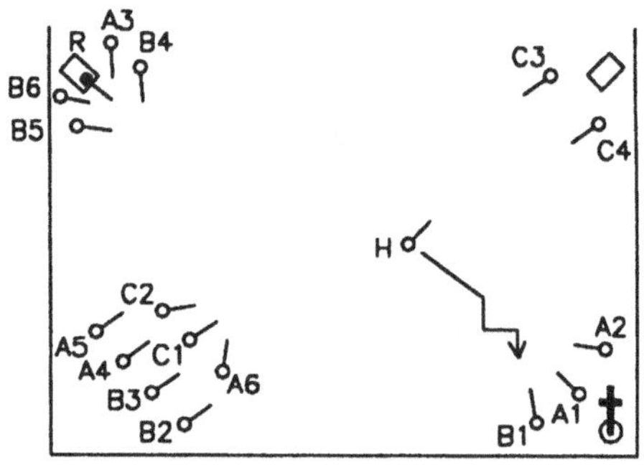

R, GROUPS

311^2, 312

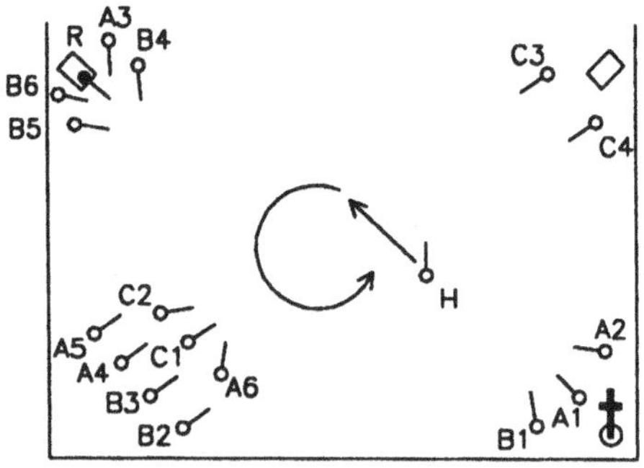

$309^2 - 311^1$

3ᴹᴱ AIR DE BALLET

149

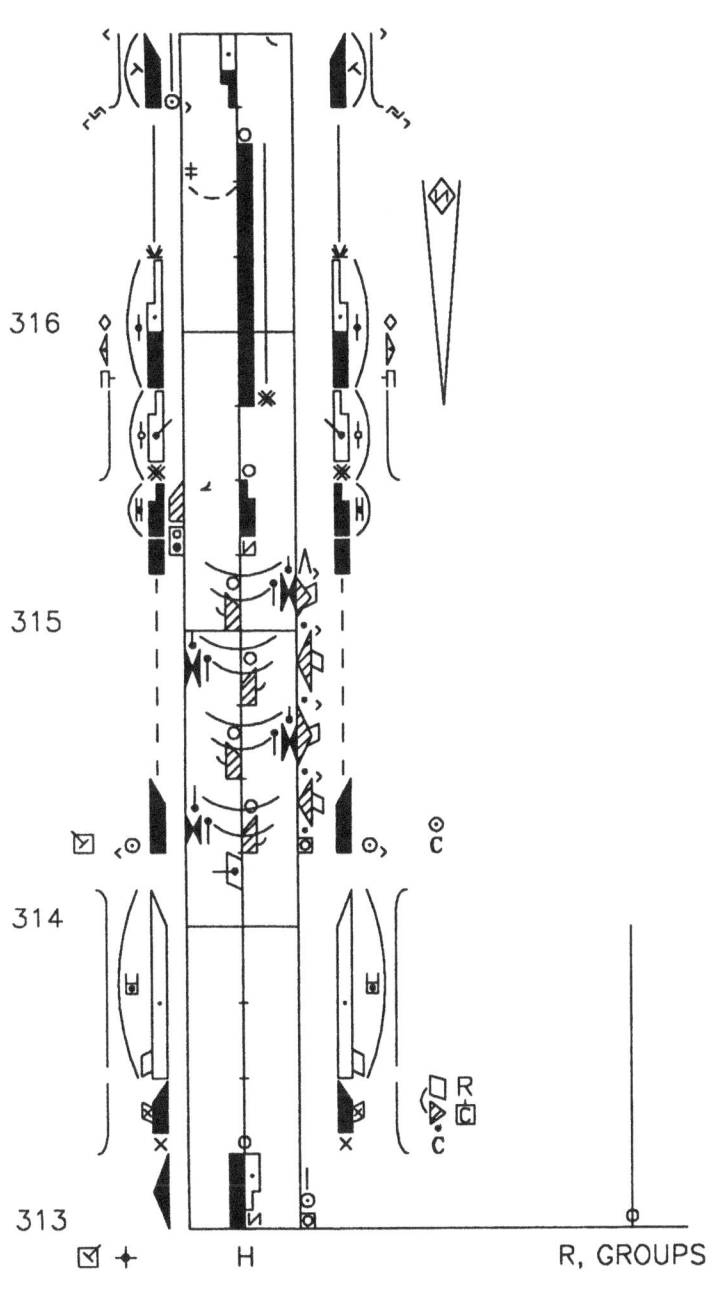

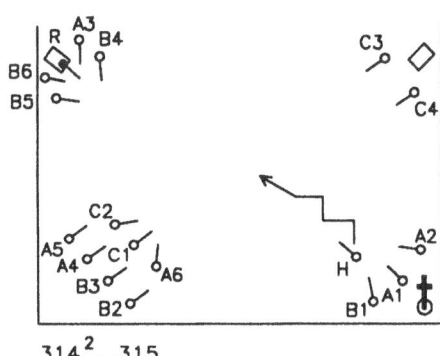

314², 315

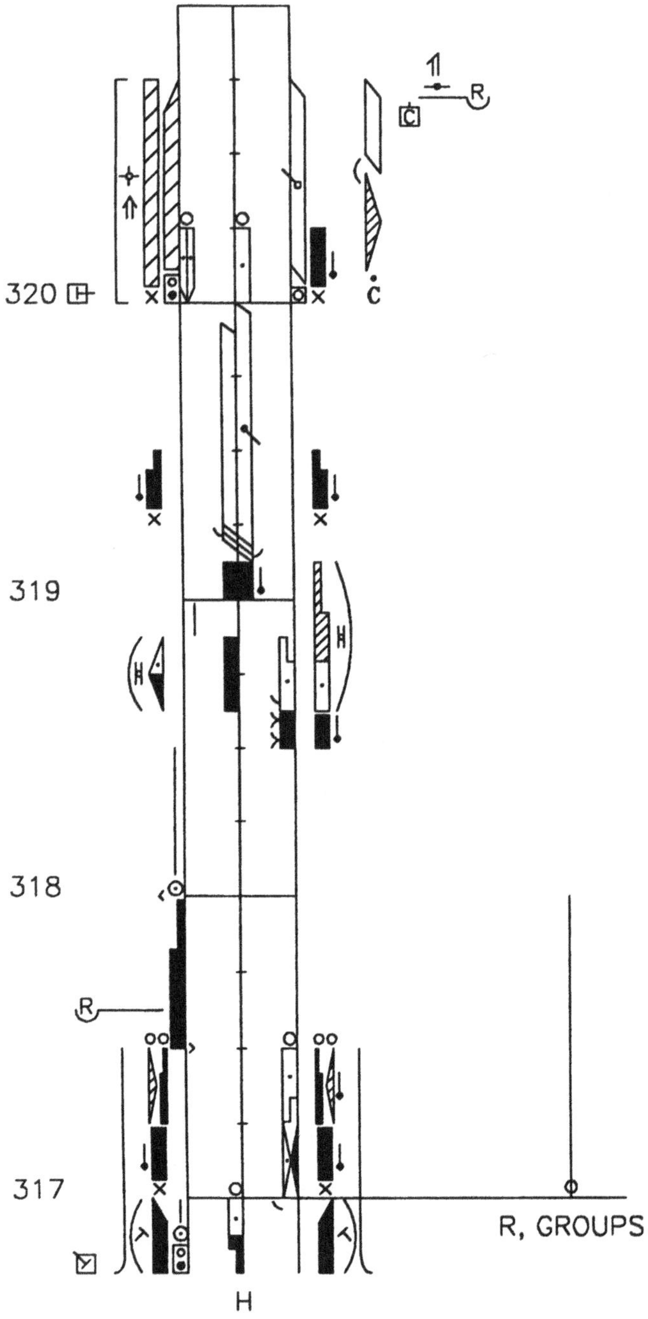

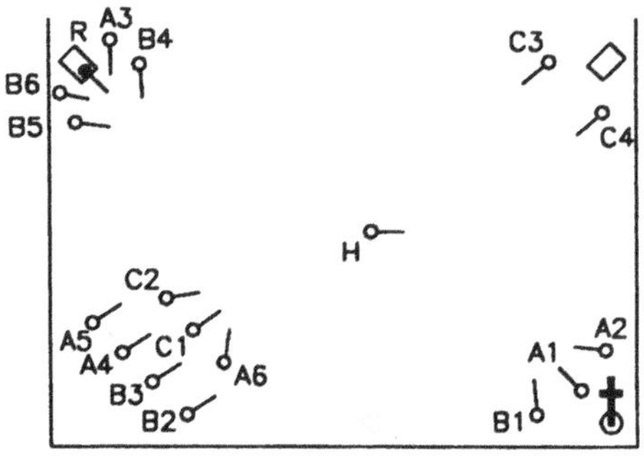

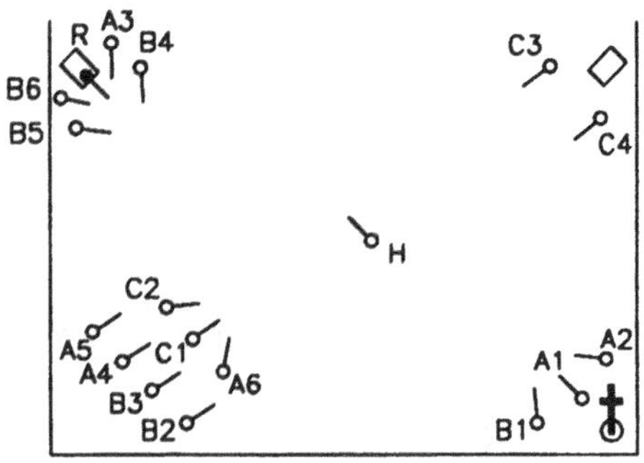

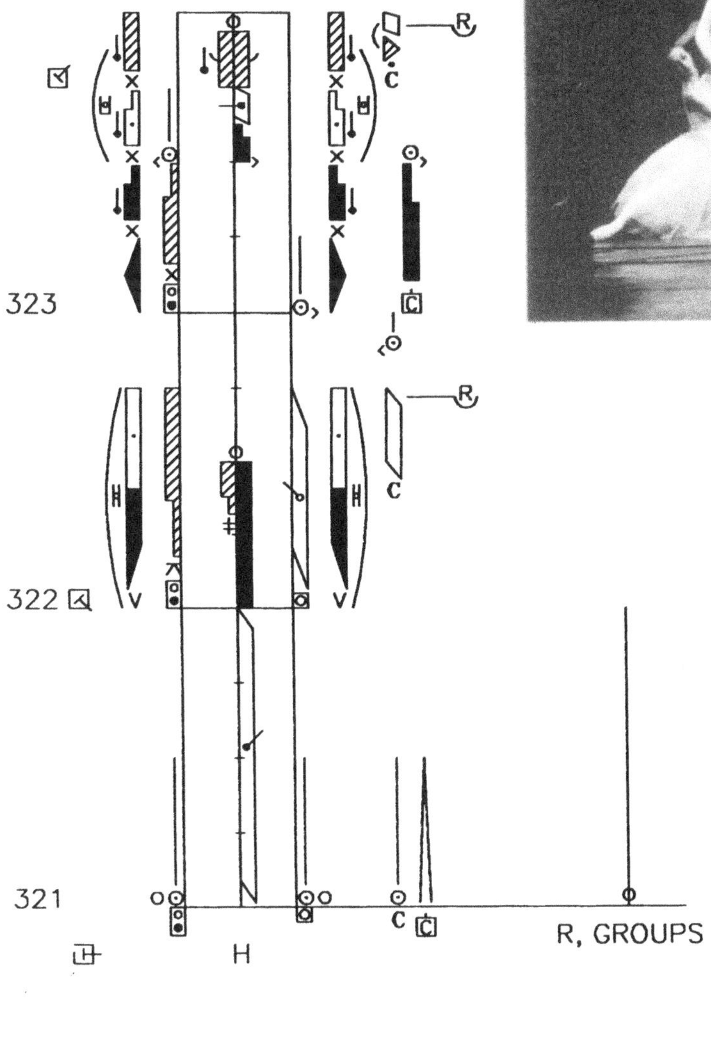

3ᴹᴱ AIR DE BALLET   151

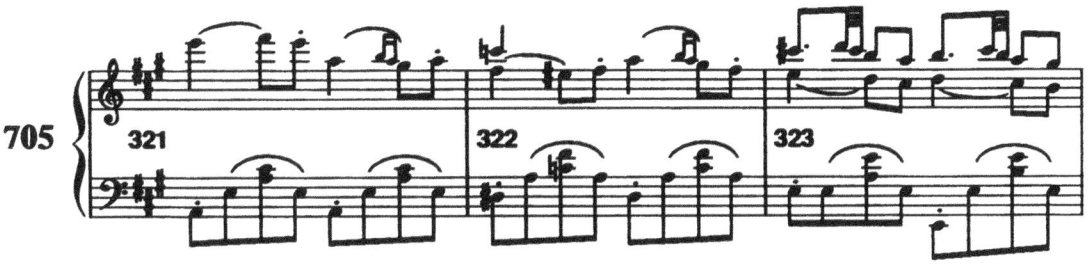

measure 320

R, GROUPS

152 ROBERT LE DIABLE - THE BALLET OF THE NUNS

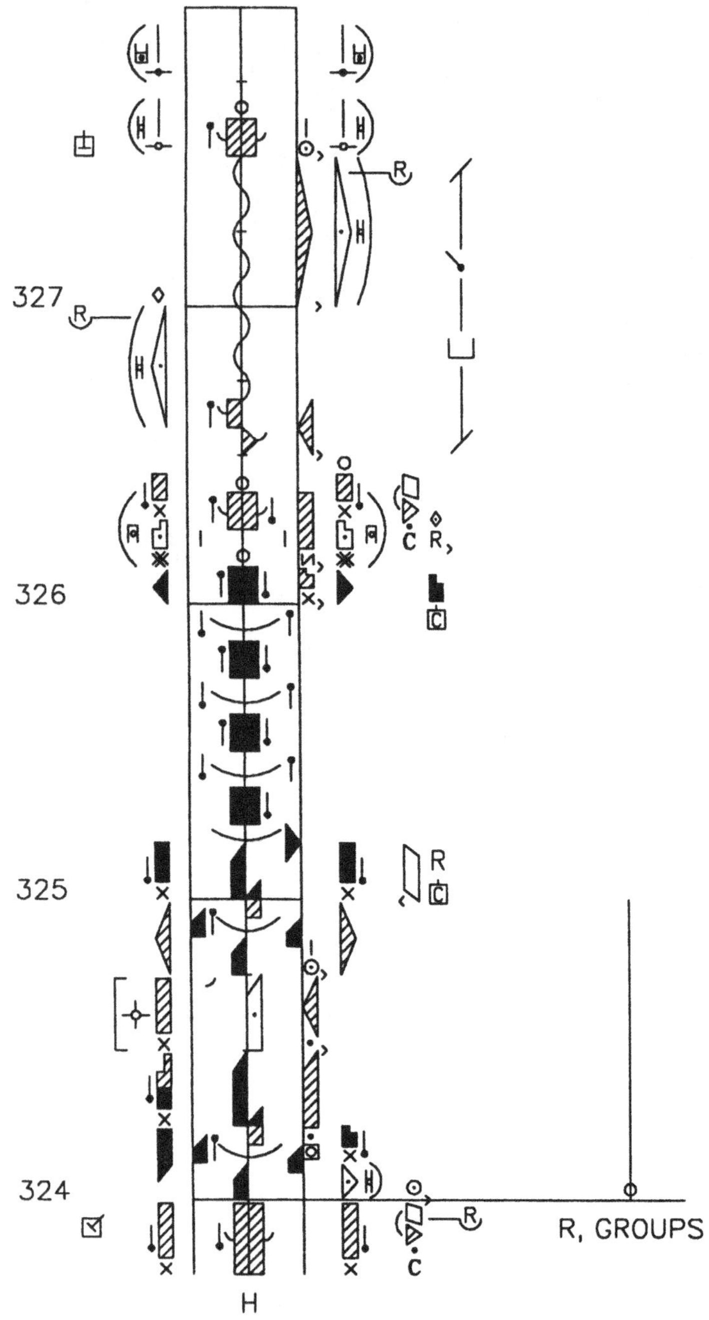

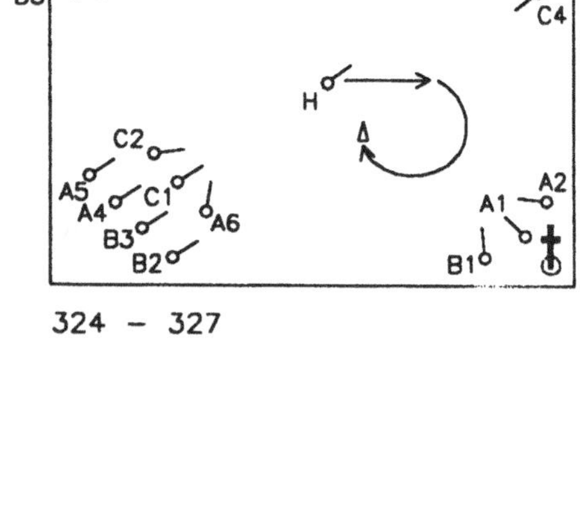

R, GROUPS

324 – 327

712
328
329
330
331

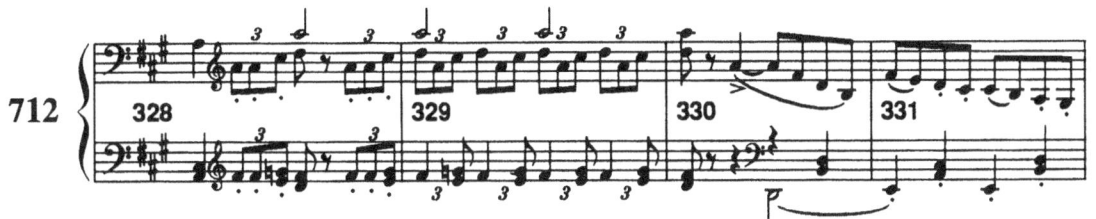

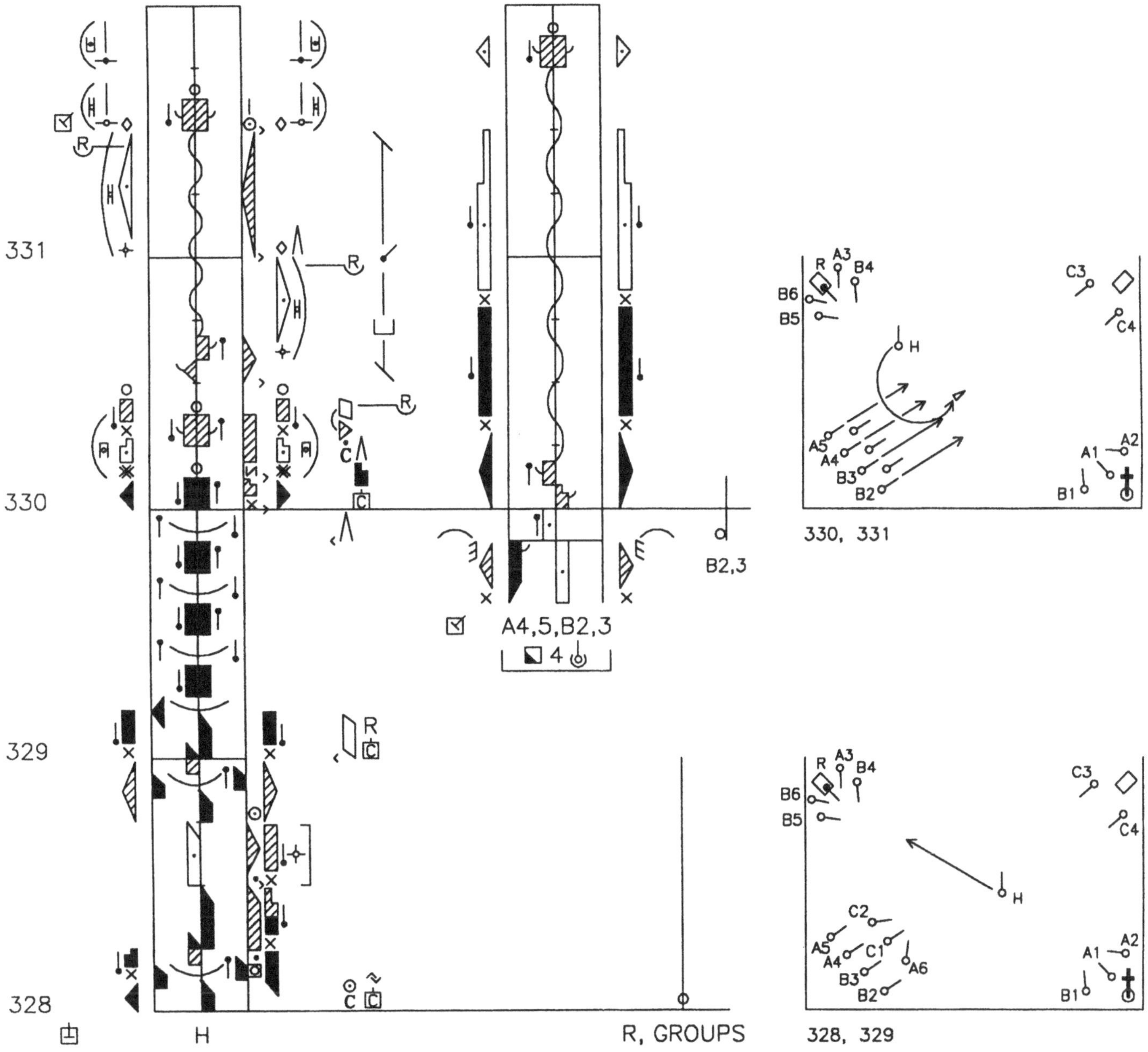
331
330
329
328
H
R, GROUPS
B2,3
A4,5,B2,3
4
330, 331
328, 329
R
C
H
A1
A2
A3
A4
A5
A6
B1
B2
B3
B4
B5
B6
C1
C2
C3
C4

ROBERT LE DIABLE - THE BALLET OF THE NUNS

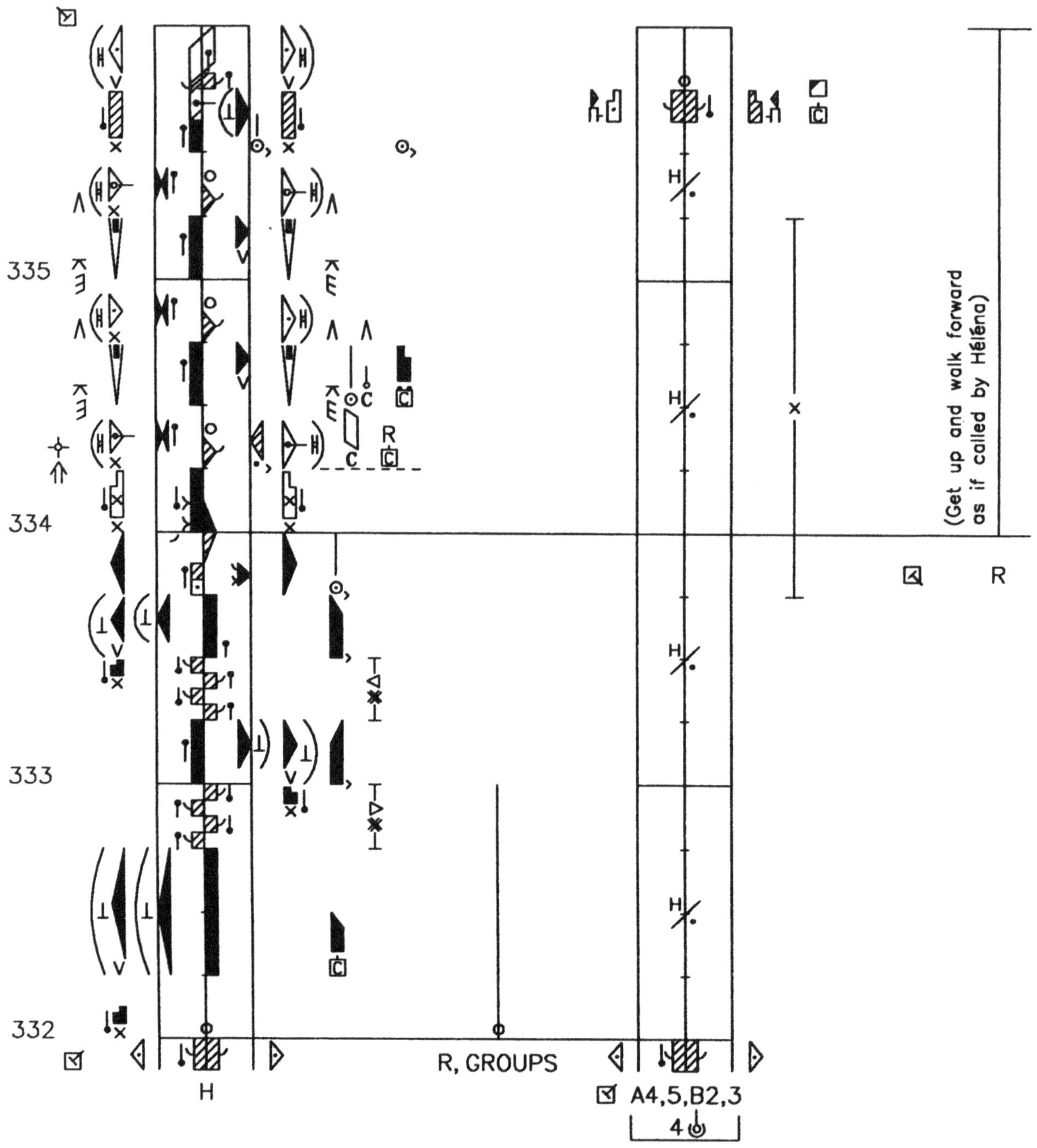

3ᴹᴱ AIR DE BALLET 155

measure 332, counts 2, 3

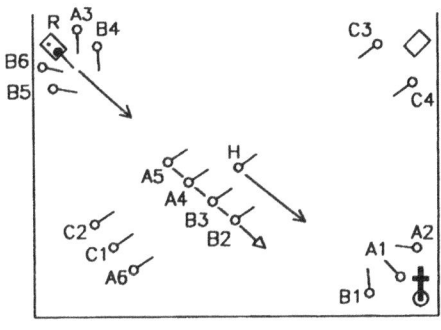

334, 335

156 ROBERT LE DIABLE - THE BALLET OF THE NUNS

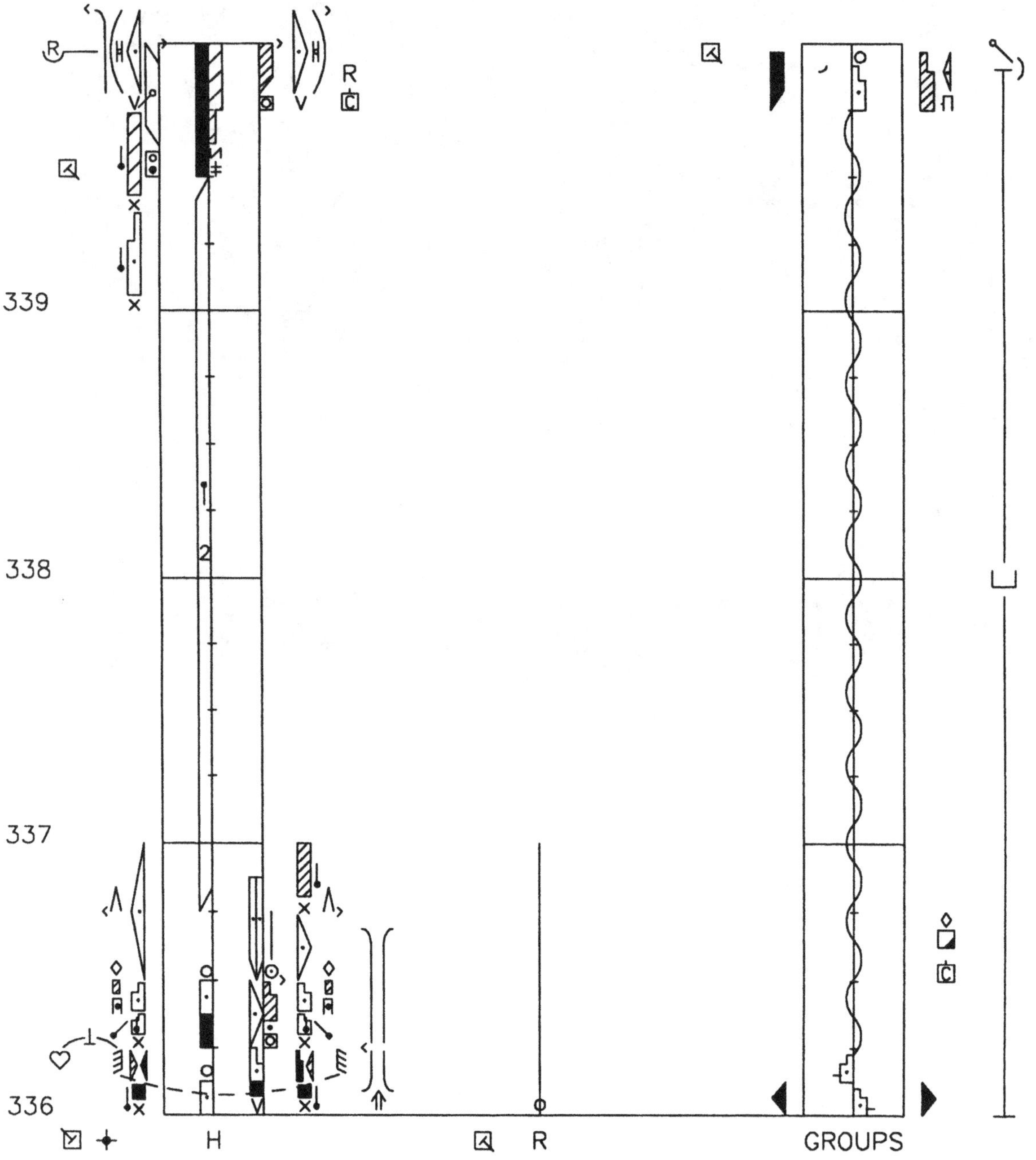

3ME AIR DE BALLET 157

measure 337

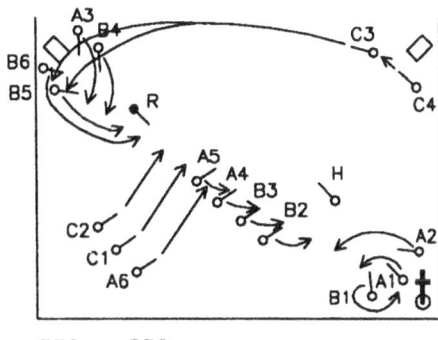

336 – 339

158 ROBERT LE DIABLE - THE BALLET OF THE NUNS

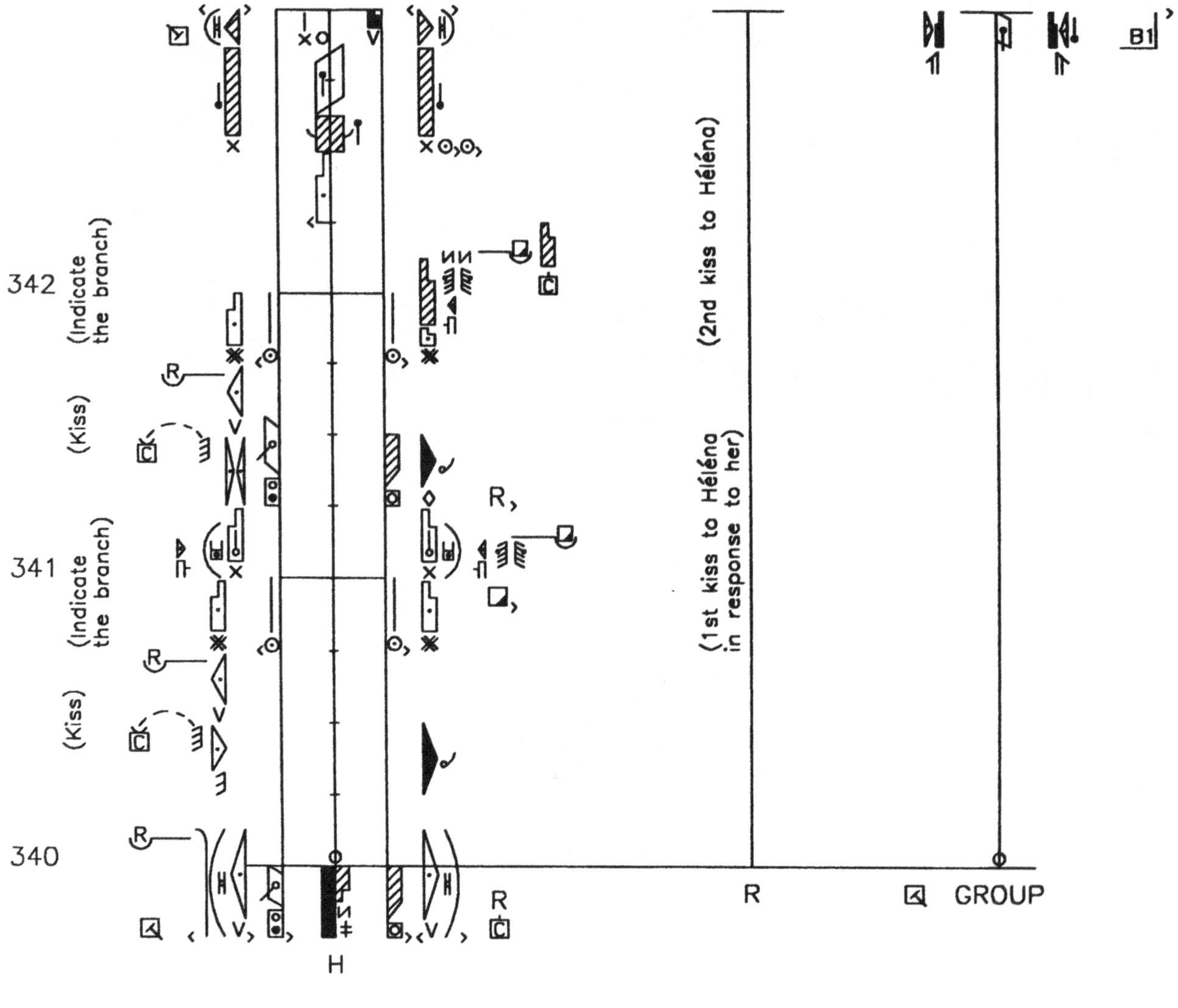

3ᴹᴱ AIR DE BALLET 159

measure 341

measure 340

340 – 342

160 ROBERT LE DIABLE - THE BALLET OF THE NUNS

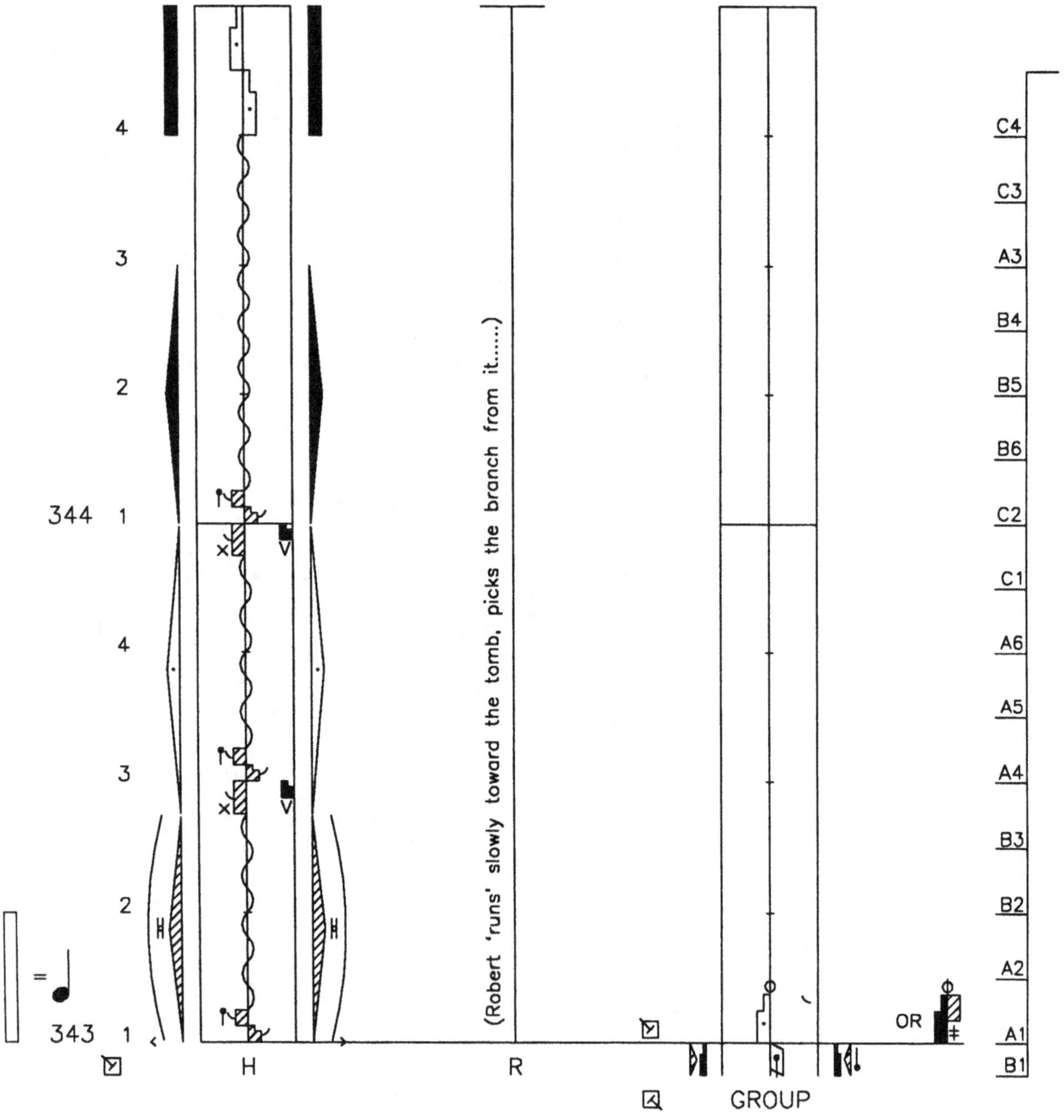

3ᴹᴱ AIR DE BALLET

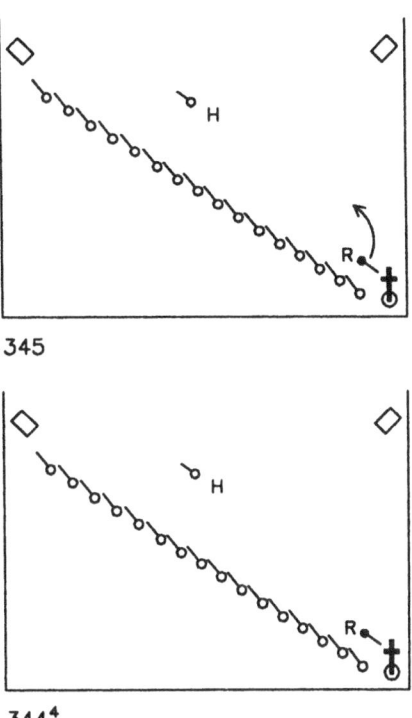

345

344⁴

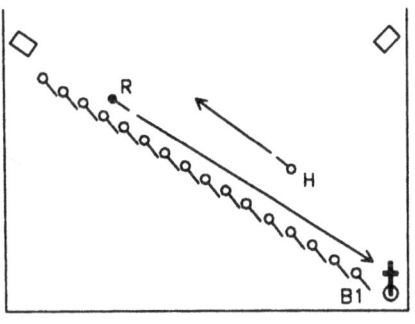

343 — 344 (Turn in canon)

162 ROBERT LE DIABLE - THE BALLET OF THE NUNS

Curtain Falls

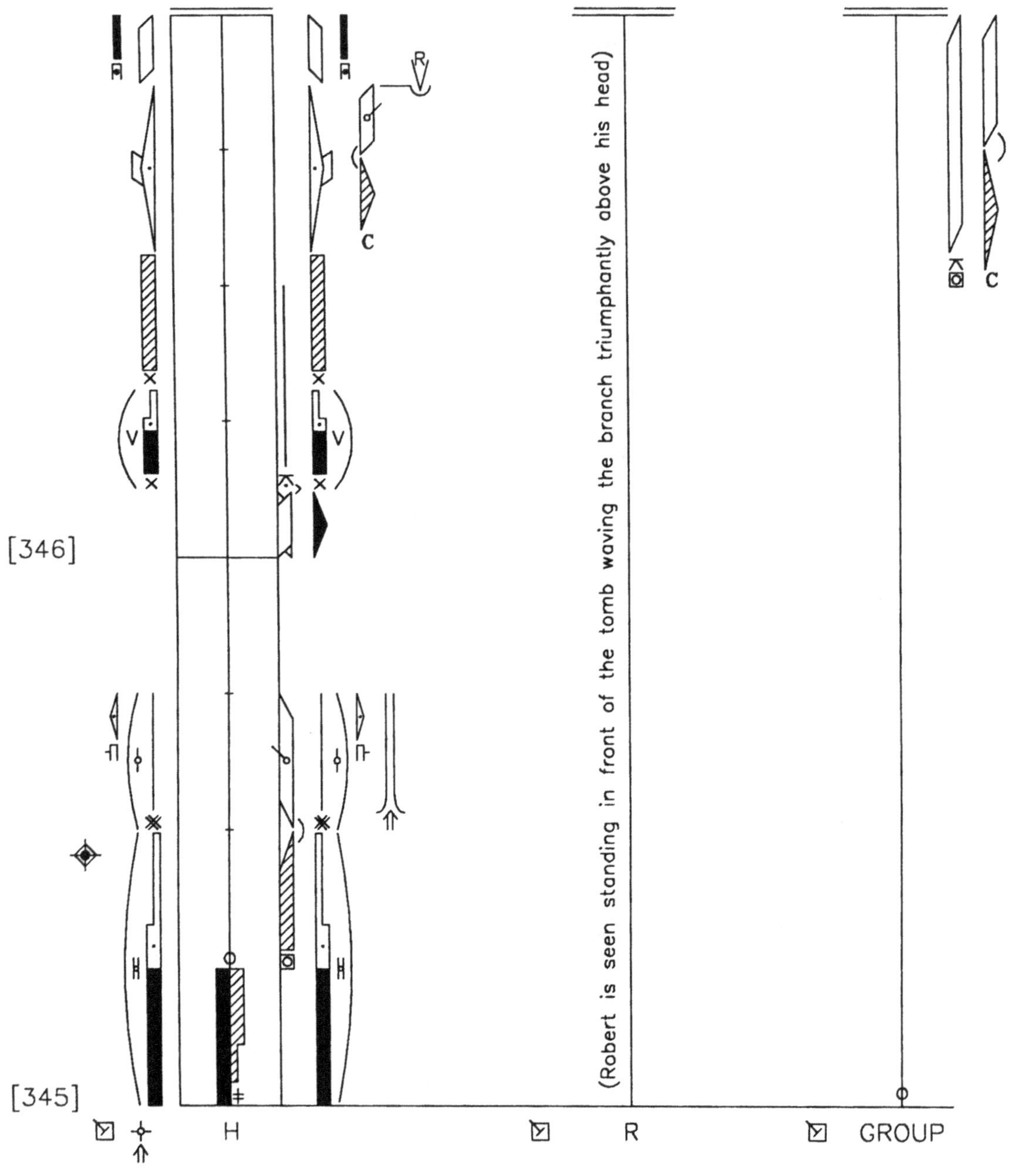

(Robert is seen standing in front of the tomb waving the branch triumphantly above his head)

3ᴹᴱ AIR DE BALLET

measure 346

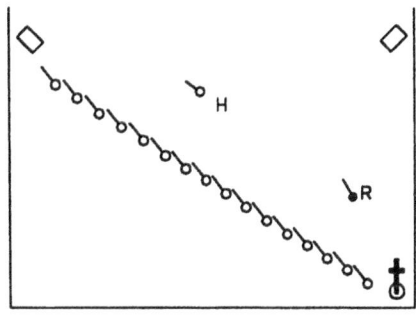

346

APPENDIX A

The Sources

Bournonville's autographed sources for *Robert le Diable*:

Manuscript *mise en scène*. Ms. Autograph. Brown ink 4 pp. (22.5 x 18 cm)
Scene = Arrangement./til/Robert af Normandiet.
Unsigned and undated [Written according to Bournonville's diary most probably between December 1872 and January 1873]
[SSm; Daniel Fryklunds samling no. 145

Production note. Ms. Autograph (partially in another's hand). Black ink. 2 pp. (35.5 x 21.8 cm)
Robert af Normandiet./Bipersonerne/ (1ste Akt.)
Unsigned and undated [c. December 1872]
[DKKkt; F.M. (Ballet)

Other manuscript sources (Copenhagen):

Manuscript libretto. Ms. Autograph (by Th. Overskou). 1 vol. (20.8 x 16.8 cm)
Robert af Normandiet/Opera i 5 Acter/af/Scribe og G. Delavigne/Musiken/af/Meyerbeer./Oversat og indrettet for den danske Skueplads/af/Th: Overskou.
Signed (on the title page): "Th: Overskou.", undated [1833]
[DKKkt; F.M. (Operaer)
This Danish manuscript libretto for Meyerbeer's opera dates from its 1833 Copenhagen première (mounted by Thomas Overskou, with the Act III ballet choreographed by Pierre Larcher). Its text served for all later stagings of this opera in Copenhagen during Bournonville's lifetime. The scene with the Act III ballet (pp. 52-53 and 80-85) reads as follows:

"3.die Act./En vild Egn med Ruinerne af et gammelt Tempel, hvis Söilegang strækker sig i det Fjerne; [...] under Besværgelsen svæver Lygtemænd frem under Portalet, de hoppe omkring et Öieblik, som om de lyttede til den, og forsvinde strax efter paa samme Sted; naar Bertram har endt gaaer han lansomt bort og forsvinder imellem Söilerne. Et klart ildrödt Skjær dæmper Maanens Skin; man seer den grønne Green, som, stærkt belyst, hæver sig blandt de mosbegroede Ruiner i Baggrunden. Onde Aander stige op under Portalet, nogle ere forvandlede til skjønne unge Piger, andre er i deres vilde Skikkelse; flere af de sidste leire sig om det Sted hvor Grenen staaer, andre deeltage i den vilde bacchantiske Dands, hvori de forvandlede Aander udtrykke deres diævelske Glæde. Ved Slutningen af Dandsen udtrykker Musiken Roberts Komme. Alle, de undtagne der bevogte Grenen, skjule sig bag Söilerne/Robert nærmer sig langsomt/og dvælende:/[...]/I det Öieblik da Robert flyer seer han sig omringet af de forvandlede Aander; en af Dem rækker ham et Bæger, men han afslaaer at modtage det; en anden griber Bægeret og søger at forföre ham med tryllende Tillokkelser; han beskuer Aanden, som i yndige Skikkelser omsvæver ham, og griber Bægeret med Henrykkelse; Alle troe at han vil bryde Grenen, de fryde sig ved deres Seier, men han farer forskrækket tilbage. - Aandeme söge nu at henrive ham ved Spil, de bringe Terninger og grupperede om nogle afbrudte Söiler begynde de at spille. Robert er fristet til at deeltage i deres Spil; men snart standser han med Afsky. Nu ville de overvælde hans Sandser ved Elskovs-Tryllerier; de omringe ham med Udtryk af ömhed, og i skjønne bedende Stillinger opmuntre de ham til at afbryde Grenen; hans Öine hvile paa de bedende med Henrykkelse, han kan ikke modstaae, henrevet af Elskov iler han hen og afbryder Grenen; i samme Öieblik omringe alle Aanderne ham i en forvirret Kjede; han baner sig vei imellem dem, svingende Grenen over Hovedet. Det röde Skjær forsvinder, et stærkt Mörke udbreder sig, det afbrydes kun af enkelte korte stærke Lyn=glimt, som belyser den vilde Dands, imedens et underjordisk Chor toner frem af Natten."

Stage director's record. Ms. Autograph (by unknown). Brown ink. 4 pp. (15,5 x 9,6 cm)
Robert af Normandiet/[...]/3 Act/[...]/2 Scene/[the drawing of the stage including several helpful explanatory notes]
Unsigned and undated [c. 1833]
[Private collection (Copenhagen)

Music sources (Copenhagen, 1848-1893):

Printed orchestral score. 5 vol. Act I 220 pp. of which two are blank, Act II 152 pp. of which one is blank, Act III 238 pp. of which two are blank, 170 pp. of which two are blank, Act V 109 pp. of which one is blank (32 x 25 cm with minor variants)
ROBERT LE DIABLE/Opéra en 5 Actes
Paris, M. Schlesinger, pl. no. 1155 [1831]
[DKKk; U 6 (KTA 303)]
This printed orchestral score was used for all performances of *Robert le Diable* in Copenhagen from its 1833 première there and throughout Bournonville's lifetime. It contains several conductor's notes and metronome markings (written in black ink) indicating the exact tempi of the three solo variations performed by the abbess Héléna in the Act III *divertissement* (score no. 16), and the tempo of the final *Choeur dansé*.

Répétiteur's copy. Ms. Copy by an unknown hand. Brown ink. 1 vol. 24 pp. (32.5 x 25.5 cm with minor variants)
Répétiteur Partie af/Robert af Normandiet/1848-/51A/A303/Repetiteur Parti/til/Robert fra Normandiet/af Meyerbeer/[...]/2.den Akt/[...]/3. die Akt
Unsigned and dated (by Bournonville on the front cover): "1848. -"
[DKKk; MA ms 3065 (KTA 303 (1))]
This répétiteur's copy clearly dates from the 1833 Copenhagen première of *Robert le Diable*, but was (according to Bournonville's later dating on the front cover) also used for his 1848 restaging of Meyerbeer's opera. It contains the music for the Act II *Choeur Dansé* (score no. 7), and the complete *divertissement* and *Choeur Dansé* in Act III (score no. 16). Bournonville's choreographic notes (written in brown ink) are included for the Act II *Choeur dansé* while his autographed pencilled notes describe the choreography of the Act III *divertissement*. These notes are almost certainly written in connection with his 1848 staging of Meyerbeer's opera, while his other pencilled autographed choreographic numbers (nos. "1-16" and "1-9", written into the music for the Act III *divertissement*) seem to refer to a later, not yet traced separate notation of the ballet (most probably made for his staging of this *divertissement* at Vienna's Kärnthnerthor Theatre with Juliette Price on July 23, 1855).

Répétiteur's copy. Ms. Copy by an unknown hand. Brown ink. 1 vol. 20 pp. of which one is blank (33.6 x 24.9 cm with minor variants)
168/Repetiteurpartier/til/1. Robert af Normandiet/[...]/89/[...]/Repetiteurparti/til/ Robert af Normandiet
Unsigned and undated [1863]
[DKKk; MA ms 2920 (1) (KTA 303 (2))]
This répétiteur's copy dates from the restaging of Meyerbeer's opera in Copenhagen on November 8, 1863 (then mounted by the French dancer and choreographer, Gustave Carey). This dating can be deduced from the fact that the music is included in a volume containing the répétiteur's copies for two other works (entitled *"En Nat mellem Fjeldene"* and *"Divertissement Dansant"*, the latter by Carey) which were premièred at Copenhagen's Royal Theatre on April 11, 1863, and November 7, 1862 respectively.
The volume was clearly re-used by Bournonville for his later restaging of *Robert af Normandiet* in 1873 and contains his autographed choreographic numbers and notes (written in brown ink) describing nearly all of the Act III *divertissement*. They were (according to his diary) written between October 2, 1872 and January 5, 1873 and also include the name of the ballerina who performed the part of the abbess Héléna during this period (Marie Westberg).
Printed piano score. 1 vol. 370 pp. (27 x 19 cm)

ROBERT LE DIABLE/Opéra en 5 actes par G Meyerbeer./Robert der Teufel/OPER IN 5 ACTEN VON SCRIBE/Deutsch von Th. Hell/Music von G MEYERBEER./Vollständiger Clavierauszug/mit deutschem und französischem Text/VON G. PIXIS.
Berlin, Schlesinger (Rob. Lienau), pl. no. S. 6656 [c. 1873]
[DKKk; KTA 303 (Instruktørpartier)
This printed piano score was used by the director (Bournonville) when mounting Meyerbeer's opera in Copenhagen in 1873. It contains several pencilled notes indicating the cuts and the omissions made that year throughout the opera.

Répétiteur's copy. Ms. Copy by an unknown hand. Brown ink. 1. vol. 20 pp. of which one is blank (34.7 x 26 cm)
A 303/Emil Hansen/Repetiteurparti/til/Robert af Normandiet.
Unsigned and undated [1893]
[DKKk; MA ms 3066 (KTA 303 (3))
This répétiteur's copy clearly dates from the 1893 restaging of Meyerbeer's opera in Copenhagen by Emil Hansen, whose autographed pencilled signature is written on the title page. It contains Hansen's complete transcription of Bournonville's notes in the earlier repetiteur's copy used for his 1873 Copenhagen production of *Robert af Normandiet*. Moreover, Hansen himself inserted several pencilled notes in this volume that explain in further detail Bournonville's technical terms.

Parts. Ms. Copy. 41 + 13 vol.
4 vl I, 4 vl II, 2 vla, 4 vlc e cb, fl picc, fl 1/2, ob 1/2, cor ingl, cl 1/2, fag 1/2, cor 1/2/3/4, tr 1/2/3/4, trb 1/2/3, tuba, timp, gr cassa, piatti, tri e gong, arpa. On stage: conductor's part, stage manager's part, fl, ob, cor 1/2/3, trb 1/2/3, gr cassa, piatti, tri e gong. 82 vocal parts.
Unsigned and undated [1833]
[DKKk; KTA 303
This set of parts was used for all performances of *Robert af Normandiet* in Copenhagen since its 1833 première there and throughout Bournonville's lifetime.

Music sources (Vienna 1855):

Orchestral score. Ms. Copy. Black and brown ink. 1 vol. 632 pp. (30.9 x 24.6 with minor variations)
Robert der Teufel/Partitur/3. Akt.
Unsigned and undated [c. 1833]
[AWn; O. A. 1341
According to the numerous conductor's notes (written with pencil, and red and black crayon) this score was used for all performances of Meyerbeer's opera at Vienna's Kärnthnerthor Theatre between August 31, 1833 and January 25, 1870. It clearly is made up of several manuscript copies dating from different periods and places since some sections are given with French titles, while others include either German or Italian headings.
Conductor's notes on pp. 200r-316r indicate several later omissions and cuts in the Act III *divertissement* as follows:

(1) *"Recit.vo et Evocation"*, Molto moderato in 4/4 time (69 meas.). Meas. 13-25 are here omitted.
(2) *"Procession der Nonnen"*, Andante sostenuto in 3/4 time (54 meas.). No omissions indicated here.
(3) *"Recitativo"* in C time (25 meas.). No omissions indicated here.
(4) *"Bachanale"*, Allegro con moto in 4/4 time (alla breve) (300 meas.). Meas. 13-55, 86-89, 122-123, 127-131, 139-

144, 155-156 were first omitted, but became (according to conductor's notes reading "Gilt") reinstated at a later stage.
(5) Without title, *Allegro vivace* in 6/8 time (65 meas.). A pencilled metronome marking here indicates the tempo with a dotted crochet equal to "76". According to conductor's notes a general pause ("halten/Pause") was inserted in this movement between meas. 40 and 41.
(6) *"Recitativo"*, *Andante* in C time (53 meas.). No omissions indicated here.
(7) Without title and indication of tempo, in C time (alla breve) [=1st solo variation for Héléna] (33 meas.). This movement proceeds into a *poco meno* section in 4/4 time (16 meas.) that holds a pencilled metronome marking indicating the tempo with a crochet being equal to "104". It continues into a "Tempo I" section in 4/4 time (*alla breve*, 25 meas.) after which the whole movement ends with a section in 3/4 (14 meas.) of which the first nine bars were omitted.
(8) *"IIme Air de Ballet"*, *Un peu moins vite*, *Moderato assai* in 3/4 time (113 meas.). No omissions indicated here.
(9) *"II [i.e. III] Air Ballet"* (54 meas.). No omissions are indicated here except for the very first bar, which was shortened at a later stage thereby containing only the upbeat.
(10) *"Tanz mit Chor"*, *Allegro vivace*, *All.o* in 4/4 time (*alla breve*) (69 meas.). Meas. 59-62 are here omitted.

Printed piano vocal score. 1 vol. 462 pp. (26.6 x 18.2 cm)
Roberto/Il Diavolo/ Opéra en 5 Actes [...] avec Paroles/ Italiennes et Allemandes
Paris, Brandus & Cie, pl. no. B. & C.ie 5284 [c. 1846]
[AWn; O. A. 1945

No répétiteur's copy and set of parts dating from the 1855 performances of *Robert der Teufel* in Vienna have yet been traced.

Printed sources (Vienna):

Printed libretto. 1 vol. 42 pp. (17.1 x 11.4 cm)
Robert der Teufel./Grosse romantische Oper in fünf Akten
Wien, A. Pichler's Witwe & Sohn, 1854.
[AWn; 987.6680 - A M. TB
The décor and the *divertissement* in Act III (scene 7) is described in this libretto (pp. 30-31) as:

"Verwandlung. Die Bühne zeigt den innern Theil einer in Ruinen zerfallenen Burg mit einem Kirchhofe. Die Gegend ist vom Mond erhellt. Auf einer Statue erblckt man einem Kirchhofe. Die Gegend ist vom Mond erhellt. Auf einer Statue erblickt man einem grünen Zweig. [...] Tanz [...] Robert will entfliehen, wird aber von phantastischen Gestalten durch Tanz verleitet, den Zweig zu brechen. er widersteht lange, unterliegt aber am Ende, er bricht den Zweig, schwingt ihn durch unterliegt aber am Ende, er bricht den Zweig, schwingt ihn durch die luft, und eilt ab."

At the Vienna restaging of *Robert der Teufel* on January 3, 1854 the ballet in Act III was choreographed and mounted by Paul Taglioni, with the part of the abbess Héléna being danced by Marie Taglioni the younger.

Library Sigla

[AWn: Öesterreichischer Nationalbibliothek, Wien.
[DKKk: Det kongelige Bibliotek, København.
[DKKkt: Det kongelige Teaters Bibliotek og Arkiv, København.
[SSm: Musikmuseet, Stockholm.

APPENDIX B

Giacomo Meyerbeer's Notes in his Musical Drafts

A complete transcription of Giacomo Meyerbeer's autographed notes in his musical drafts for the ballet in Act III of *Robert le Diable* (Paris, c. August-November 1831; FPo, call no. Rés. A. 500 a. 2 (p)).

Meyerbeer's notes in the musical drafts for the ballet in *Robert le Diable*, in which Héléna is called by her original name of Lea, read as follows:

[Bertram:] Nuns, do you hear me, nuns arise
The Will o'the wisps fly on to the tombs.
The tombs open. Procession of the nuns.
[...] (The stage becomes lit)
Bacchanal
The women espy Robert, and remain immobile.
The nuns see Robert from afar and hide
Entrance of Robert who does not see the nuns = Recitatif: He wishes to pluck the branch, but recoils in fright (last verse of Recitatif)
[...] The nuns raise their cups to him, and alternatively drink and invite him to drink.
Robert refuses to drink: Lea reproaches the nuns for their risqué manners: This is the way to behave, she seems to be telling them as she approaches Robert whom she excites: Robert appears to be struck by her charms, and looks at her with rapture.
Lea invites Robert to drink
Robert drinks: the nuns dance around him and show him the branch (*) If Mr. Taglioni finds this passage too long, what is between the two (*) can be deleted
(*) Silence
Robert slowly approaches the branch: the nuns laugh among themselves Robert recoils in terror
The nuns consult among themselves:
Lea and the nuns try to make Robert follow in their footsteps, & by dancing lead him to the place where they gamble
The nuns gamble
Robert slowly goes towards the branch: the nuns laugh among themselves.
Robert recoils in terror
Lea says to Robert: wretched Knight, is this your courage? You make me [word illegible]! I shall go and pluck the branch for you: but after that, no, for I despise you.
Robert seems to reply: Stop: I am determined to pluck it: it was the memory of my mother that terrified me: but let me recover from my distress: Lea makes Robert sit by her side and summons her companions.
Lea and her suite surround Robert, continually forming groups about him
M.lle Montessu and her suite then seize hold of Robert and dance around him.
(M.lle Taglioni) (M.lle Montessu) (M.lle Taglioni) (M.lle Montessu)
(Robert) (M.lle Taglioni) Groups around Robert & Lea during this dialogue (M.lle Montessu) (M.lle Taglioni)
Carried away little by little by these groups Robert has arrived at the foot of the statue without noticing it
Robert, his passion inflamed to a state of delirium by the foregoing scenes, gives a sign that he is about to pluck the branch
Robert plucks the branch Thunder: Transformation
The Statue of the Saint shatters.
(Chorus) (triumphant dance around Robert)
#[...]#
The curtain falls.
If this passage is too long, Mr. Taglioni can cut what is between the two signs #

APPENDIX C

Examples of Bournonville's Dance Notations

Example 1.   Page 5 of Violin Rehearsal Score I which includes the opening measures of the *Bacchanale*. Note Bournonville's indication of "dansé par L: F. James-" at the top right. Only a little dance instruction is given here as the *corps de ballet* is merely entering for the *Bacchanale*.

APPENDIX C

Bournonville Notations

Example 2. Page 9 of the Violin Rehearsal Score II showing the first solo section in 6/8 meter, danced by Héléna (measure 113 onward).

Bournonville Notations

Example 3. Page 12 of the Violin Rehearsal Score III showing Héléna's first solo variation, the so-called "*Séduction par l'ivresse*" (measure 168 onward). At the start can be seen Emil Hansen's additional pencilled notes, clarifying details of the choreography originally notated by Bournonville.

APPENDIX D

August Bournonville's and Emil Hansen's Production Notes

A comparative transcription of the production notes by August Bournonville and Emil Hansen in the three répétiteur's copies for the Act III ballet of *Robert af Normandiet* (Copenhagen, 1848-1893). For the deciphering of Bournonville's abbreviations and steno-choreographic signs *see* Knud Arne Jürgensen and Ann Hutchinson Guest: *The Bournonville Heritage* (Dance Books, London, 1990).

Violin Rehearsal Score I (1833, 1848, 1855) (Bournonville's production-notes 1848, 1855)		Violin Rehearsal Score II (1873) (Bournonville's production-notes 1873)		Violin Rehearsal Score III (1893) (Emil Hansen's production-notes 1893)	
Bars:	Nr. 16 Finale dansé par L:F.James -	Bars:		Bars:	
1 - 148	[omitted]	1 - 54	[omitted]	1 - 54	[omitted]
		55 - 69	[end of Bertram's recitative]	55 - 84	[notes as in Violin Rehearsal Score II]
		70 - 72	[Procession of the Nuns]		
		73 - 76	1.ste Ligkiste D.S. [1st coffin Stage left]		
		77 - 80	2.den Ligkiste K.S. [2nd coffin Stage right]		
		81 - 84	3.die Baggrund [3rd (coffin) in the background]		
		85	4.de Baggrund [4th (coffin) in the background]	85 - 92	4.de Baggrund Gongon [gong]
		86 - 123	5.	93 - 114	Processionen begynder her [The procession begins here]
				115 - 122	Gongon

Violin Rehearsal Score I (1833, 1848, 1855)	Violin Rehearsal Score II (1873)	Violin Rehearsal Score III (1893)
		123 Gongon *Lagnerne trækkes ned og Kisterne lukkes igjen. [The shrouds are drawn down and the coffins close again]
	124 - 148 [omitted]	124 - 148 [omitted]
149 - 156 1. les dames arrivent	149 - 152 1. De löbe frem, dreje sig omkring [They run forward and run around each other]	149 - 191 [notes as in Violin Rehearsal Score II]
	153 - 156 spörge hinanden "Hvor ere vi ?" [ask each other "Where are we ?"]	
157 - 160 2. (Interrogations)	157 - 160 2. De föle Pulsslaget - Hovedet - Hjertet. [They feel the pulse beat - The head - The heart]	
161 - 168 3.	161 - 164 3. De omfavne hinanden - til Höire og Venstre [They embrace each other - to the right and the left]	
	165 - 168 tager hinanden i Haanden (Tre og Tre), [take each others hands (three and three)] gaae frem og löfte Armene jublende. [walk forward and raise their arms exultantly.]	
169 - 191 4.	169 - 172 4. De fire fra Kisterne vise deres Hvilested [The four from the coffins point to their graves]	
	173 - 191 De andre fra Lemmen pege mod Jordens Dyb. [The others from the trapdoor point towards the depth of the earth]	
175 - 190 [cut by Bournonville]	175 - 190 [cut by Bournonville]	175 - 190 [cut by Hansen]
192 - 203 5. (4 Damer)	192 - 198 5. Alle. "Vi ere her !" [All: "We are here!"]	192 - 198 [notes as in Violin Rehearsal Score II]
194 - 197 [cut by Bournonville]	194 - 197 [cut by Bournonville]	194 - 197 [cut by Hansen]

APPENDIX D 175

Violin Rehearsal Score I (1833, 1848, 1855)	Violin Rehearsal Score II (1873)	Violin Rehearsal Score III (1893)
	199 - 200 Gravene hade og trodse vi! [The graves we hate and defy!]	199 - 203 [notes as in Violin Rehearsal Score II]
	201 - 202 Lader os nyde Livet! [Let us enjoy life!]	
	203 (De stille sig til Dands rundt fra D.S.) [They position themselves to dance in a circle from Stage left]	
204 - 211 6. (Danse)	204 - 207 6. Temps - levés med höire og venstre Fod [with right and left foot] gl - à 3 p.. failli, 3 soubresaults en Att:	204 - 207 6. Temps - levés med h og v fod gl à 3 p. failli 3 soubresaults en tournant
	208 - 211 Bis de la phrase - terminez p.d.bq & attitude. (De fire förste damer i front) [The four first ladies in front]	208 211 [notes as in Rehearsal Score II]
212 - 214 7. (Ballet) les premières arrivent en av...	212 - 213 7. De 4 Förste [The 4 first ladies] 4 p.de course	212 - 213 7. De 4 Første 4 pas de course vF hF vF
	214 - 215 cp ÷ echappé ♪ & relevé ♂	214 - 215 cp ÷ echappé and relevé ♂ flere Toure [many turns] ↑↑ v o h ↑↑
215 - 220 (Tour de mains)	216 - 217 det samme opad - traversere med de 4 Andre: [the same upstage - change place with the 4 others:] Tour de mains	216 - 236 [notes as in Violin Rehearsal Score II]
	218 - 221 De bagerste traversere til Siderne med samme Trin [Those farthest back change place to the sides with the same steps]	
221 - 224 8.	222 - 225 8. det samme Trin for Alle i Kreds, sluttet i tre Linier [the same step for all in a circle finished in three lines xxxxxx xxxxx xxxx]	

Violin Rehearsal Score I
(1833, 1848, 1855)

225 - 228   9. (4 Damer) les dames: Temps levés & c -

229 - 230   10. Groupes

231 - 233   bis -

234 - 235   (les premières)

236   les Groupes se deployent

237 - 276   [cut by Bournonville]

277 - 290   11. p.d.course....

291 - 294   12. en rond

295 - 325   [cut by Bournonville]

Violin Rehearsal Score II
(1873)

226 - 229   9. Temps - levés til modsatte Sider [to opposite sides], gl - cp. Jt ⏵ & p.b.b. ⁔ & ⁔ ⏵.

230 - 231   10. Gruppe. [group]

232 - 233   Gruppe.

234   Gruppe.

235 -   De Fire Förste opløse Gruppen og dandse: [The four first ladies dissolve the group and dance:]

237 - 276   [cut by Bournonville]

277 - 278   11. Trois p.d.course - ballonné - Jt

279 - 280   cp ⁔ gl. à - 3 - pas, Jt ⏵ & p.d.b...

281 - 282   Pas de course, Ballonné - Jt.

283 - 286   2 Attitudes à reculons, relevé ⊕ Cabriole.

287 - 290   Bis de la phrase

291 - 294   12. de træde tilbage og byde Taushed. [they travel back and order silence]

295 - 325   [cut by Bournonville]

Violin Rehearsal Score III
(1893)

237 - 276   [cut by Hansen]

277 - 294   [notes as in Violin Rehearsal Score II]

295 - 325   [cut by Hansen]

APPENDIX D

Violin Rehearsal Score I (1833, 1848, 1855)

326 - 329 13. (Ballet) arriver en diagonale aux genoux l'une après l'autre.

330 - 331 14.

332 - 339 en rond

340 - 343 15. en traversant

344 - 351 grande chaîne serpentée....

352 - 359 16. (1.) (Solo) (Frk. Juliette [Price])

Violin Rehearsal Score II (1873)

326 - 327 13. Alle give Hænderne [All take hands] Allemande = Att. -

328 - 329 faillis en tournant sur place,

330 - 331 14. tournoyez - toutes.   xxxxxx xxxxx xxx

332 - 333 3 p.d.course ✓, gl. à 3 p. - failli - Att.

334 - 335 contretemps - course & Jt ↻

336 - 339 Bis

340 - 341 15. Temps - levé & cp - Jt ↻ - (à gauche)

342 - 343 Bis (à droite) & formez la chaîne

344 - 345 Gl. - Jt. &c. -

346 - 349 & course pour arriver

350 - 351 en diagonale   knælende [kneeling]

352 - 353 16. Westberg. (K.S) [Stage right] Assemblé - Att. battm, jt ‿ - jt ⌣ - & (Jt - p.l.jb.)

354 - 355 chassé ∴ sissonne, gl & Jt en remontant:

356 - 357 Bis du comm.

358 - 359 jt ∴ - pir - renversée, cp ‿ - & p.d.bq.

Violin Rehearsal Score III (1893)

326 - 327 13. (Ballet) Alle give Hænderne Allemande: Att. -

328 - 329 faillis en tournant sur place/4 temps levé rundt til Plads i Linier [4 temps levé turning around and into lines]

330 - 331 tournoyez toutes/   xxxxxx xxxxx xxx alle rundt paa Stedet ↑↑ [all turn around sur la place]

332 - 333 14. 3 p.d.course ✓ gl à 3 p. failli - Att.

334 - 335 contretemps & Jt ↻ til h/jt ent. til h

336 - 339 Bis til v

340 - 341 15. Temps - levé & cp - Jt (à gauche)/2 temps levé til v 2 jt rundt til v

342 - 363 [notes as in Violin Rehearsal Score II]

Violin Rehearsal Score I (1833, 1848, 1855)	Violin Rehearsal Score II (1873)	Violin Rehearsal Score III (1893)
360 - 367 2.	360 - 363 17. Hun befaler Søstrene at holde Fest [She commands the sisters to have a celebration]	
	364 - 367 De rejse sig og dandse omkring hende med faillis imedens hun gjör Pirouette - Att: ♪ . [They arise and dance around her with faillis while she does Pirouette - Att: ♪]	364 - 367 De rejse sig og danse omkring hende med faillis medens hun gjör pirr. Att. hF op
368 - 371 3.	368 - 369 18. W[estberg]. Brisé: Bt ⌣ Att & p.d.b. ⌣ & ⌢	368 - 369 18. W[estberg]. Brisé - Bt ⌣ Att & p.d.b. & ⌢ - [a] brissé til h og Ass for hojt springende Att hF vF bag ⎯⎯⎯⎯ jt hF for jt p.d.b. rundt til h 2 jt vF løs bag og hF løs bag. [b] brissé til h battu foran hF - Att vF op bag.
370 - 371 Bis à gauche		
372 - 374 4.	372 - 375 Cp - Jt ♫ cp - Jt ♫ & arabesque	372 - 375 Cp - Jt ♫ cp hF bag ent tournant til v hF bag ⎯⎯⎯⎯⎯⎯⎯⎯⎯⎯⎯⎯⎯⎯⎯⎯⎯⎯⎯⎯ Jt ♫ & Arabesque entournant til v pir til v hF op bag
375 - 379 5.	376 - 379 19. Tournez à l'attitude (Le demi-cercle ballancé)	376 - 379 [notes as in Violin Rehearsal II]
380 - 383 6.	380 - 381 20. W[estberg]. p.d.b. ⌣ & ⌢ , Gl. à 3 p. en rem: & battu.	380 - 381 20. W[estberg]. p.d.b. ⌣ & ⌢ , vF bag opad til h - hF foëtté bag Gl à 3 p. en rem: & battu gl à 3 pas, battu vF bag i Att
	382 - 383 Bis de la phrase	382 - 283 [notes as in Violin Rehearsal II]
384 - 399 [cut by Bournonville]	384 - 399 [cut by Bournonville]	384 - 399 [cut by Hansen]

APPENDIX D   179

Violin Rehearsal Score I (1833, 1848, 1855)	Violin Rehearsal Score II (1873)	Violin Rehearsal Score III (1893)
400 - 405 7.	400 - 401 assemblé ⌣ & Entr 3, relevez ⌣ 6.	400 - 401 Assemblé ⌣, 2 Entr. 3. relevez ↑↑ ⌣ 6 vF bag hF for rundt til v ⇑⇑
	402 - 403 Bis	402 - 403 [notes as in Violin Rehearsal Score II]
	404 gl - à 3 p entr 5 ∴	404 Gl à 3 p til h ⌐ entr: 5 ∴ hF for cr fremad vF bag
	405 bis	405 - 417 [notes as in Violin Rehearsal Score II]
406 - 409 8.	406 - 407 cp⌣ p.d.bq en remontant, 2 fois.	
	408 - 409 pirouette sur le coudepied. - - Arrêt !	
410 - 417 9.	410 - 413 Hun fører Robert fra D.S. og befaler Søstrene at bortfjerne sig. [She leads Robert from Stage left and commands the sisters to withdraw]	
	414 - 417 Halvcirklen fra flöiene følger Abedissen ad D.S. Baggrund. [The semicircle from the wings follows the Abess along the background of Stage left.]	
418 - 462 [not reconstructed]	418 - 462 [not reconstructed]	418 - 462 [not reconstructed]
463 - 470 [end of Robert's recitative]	463 - 470 [end of Robert's recitative]	463 - 470 [end of Robert's recitative]
471 - 478 Elle s'avance vers lui	471 - 472 damen fra D.S. (med Kande og Bæger) [the lady form Stage left (with jug and cup)] 1. Deux pas - marchés, cp. brisé - att.	471 - 472 Damen fra D.S. (med Kande og Bæger) Soyer og Kornerup Reumert Robert × 1. Deux pas marchés til h, cp brissé-att:ef vF hF vF bag
	473 - 474 Bis	473 - 478 [notes as in Violin Rehearsal Score II]

Violin Rehearsal Score I (1833, 1848, 1855)	Violin Rehearsal Score II (1873)	Violin Rehearsal Score III (1893)
	475 - 478 gl. cp ∕ gl. cp ∕ course autour de Robert Groupe (K.S.)	
479 - 497 [cut by Bournonville]	479 - 497 [cut by Bournonville]	479 - 497 [cut by Hansen]
498 - 504 de l'autre [côté]	498 - 506 2. den samme Phrase gjentages af fire Andre. - Resten kommer hurtig ind og stiller sig i Midten omkring Abedissen [the same phrase repeated by four other. - The others enter quickly and take their positions in the center around the Abess.]	498 - 535 [notes as in the Rehearsal Score II]
505 - 506 poco ralent: P.d.bras	507 - 508 3. Robert K.S. [Stage right] W[estberg]. Solo: Contretemps btm - assemblé s.l.cpd. Att - allongée	
507 - 525 à tempo (danse)	509 - 510 Bis............	
	511 - 514 gl - cp> gl - cp> 2 gl - en renv: Att ↷ en renv.	
	515 - 520 Bis de toute la phrase	
	522 - 526 4. Cp Gl - degagé ↶ Cp Gl. degagé ↶ course autour de Robert Att derrière lui.... groupe devant lui (sur genou).	
526 - 528 Elle l'appelle au jeu .. -	527 - 528 cp ↶ relevé ⊕ cp ↶ relevé ⊙	
529 - 547 (1. er pas)	529 - 530 5. Hun tager Bægeret fra Höire, giver det til Venstre. [She takes the cup from right and hands it to the left.]	

APPENDIX D

Violin Rehearsal Score I (1833, 1848, 1855)	Violin Rehearsal Score II (1873)	Violin Rehearsal Score III (1893)
	531 - 535 Kvinden fra Höire skjænker til Venstre - (Alt i Grupper) [The Woman from right pours to the left - (everything done in groups)]	
536 - 545 [cut by Bournonville]	536 - 545 [cut by Bournonville]	536 - 545 [cut by Hansen]
548 - 553 Il s'arrache du jeu	546 - 547 Hun byder ham at drikke (Gruppe) [She invites him to drink (Group)]	546 - 580 [notes as in Violin Rehearsal Score II]
	548 - 551 6. Robert griber Bægeret og kaster det til Höire, idet han selv gaaer over til Venstre. [Robert grabs the cup and throws it to the right while he walks across the stage to the left.]	
	552 - 553 Abedissen vredes men dölger sin Harme. [The Abess becomes angry but conceals her ire.]	
554 - 556 on lui presente à boire	554 - 562 Søstrene vinke ad Robert for at vise Abedissen. [The Sisters signal to Robert to draw his attention to the Abess.]	
557 Groupe		
558 - 560 il refuse &veut s'enfuir. -		
561 on l'arrête		
562 - 563 (le voile)		
564 Solo.	563 - 564 7. Westberg (Solo)	
565 - 572 jetés Perrot. - jt. lancé cp. battu	565 - 566 cp ⟶ r.dj jt ⌒ jt ⟵ jt ⟵ jt ⟶ Bt ⟍ ...	

Violin Rehearsal Score I (1833, 1848, 1855)	Violin Rehearsal Score II (1873)	Violin Rehearsal Score III (1893)
	567 - 568 Bis.............relevé ⌐	
	569 cp ⌢ ft. brisé ⌐	
	570 Bis	
	571 - 572 Echappé - pir s.l.cpd. Att ⌐ :	
573 - 646 [crossed out]	573 - 580 Bis de toute la phrase	
573 - 580 bis. -		
581 - 588 cp. jeté entr. 3 & Att renv. - 3 fois	581 - 590 & Cp ⌢ jt ⌢ brisé ⌉ Att ⌐ en remontant. 3 fois.	581 - 584 [indication for a repetition of these 4 bars]
589 - 592 cp. brisé jt lancé 2 posés - en av. & en arr, & relevé en 4.ieme	591 - 592 Cp brisé ⌢ Jt - lancé & coupé ⌐ penché (à gauche)	589 - 602 [notes as in Violin Rehearsal Score II]
593 - 597 bis de l'autre [côté]	593 - 594 Bis (à droite)	
	595 - 602 cp. ft. jt ⌐ - pirouette - renversée, cp ⌢ & p.d.bg.	
598 - 602 encore..... entr. à 3 jt & retournez	598 - 601 [omitted]	598 - 601 [omitted]
603 - 606 Coupées à rebours & p.d.b. -	603 - 606 2. Hun vinker ad Søstrene, der omringe hende i en lokkende Gruppe. [She motions to the sisters, who surround her in an alluring Group.]	603 - 644 [notes as in Violin Rehearsal Score II]
607 - 610 2.me. fois -	607 - 610 Robert gaaer atter overtil K.S. [Robert returns to Stage right]	

APPENDIX D

Violin Rehearsal Score I (1833, 1848, 1855)	Violin Rehearsal Score II (1873)	Violin Rehearsal Score III (1893)
611 - 652 (les autres)	611 - 623 Søstrene flokke sig om Kisten D.S. og spille Terninger. Abedissen viser dem til Robert. [The sisters crowd around the coffin Stage left and play with dice. The Abess points them out to Robert]	
	624 - 629 Robert lokkes over til Spillet (D.S.) [Robert is lured to the game (Stage left)]	
	630 - 633 han spiller med Søstrene [he plays dice with the Sisters]	
	634 - 635 de fire stille sig i Midten. [the four [first ladies] take place in the center]	
	636 - 638 Abedissen opfordrer dem til dands - medens hun selv spiller med Robert. [The Abess invites them to dance - while she herself plays dice with Robert.]	
	639 - 640 de fire [the four]: Entr 3. jt ⌒ jt ⟶ Jt ⟩ & Battu.	
	641 - 642 Bis.	
	643 - 644 cp - renv: ft & Jt. 3 fois	
	645 - 652 [cut by Bournonville]	645 - 652 [cut by Hansen]
653 elle finit à genoux	653 - 675 - arrettez !	653 - 683 [notes as in Violin Rehearsal Score II]
654 - 657 Robert étourdi, se réveille & veut s'en aller		
657 - 675 [replaced in 1833 production by a cello cadence]		
658 - 662 on lui ferme les issues		

Violin Rehearsal Score I (1833, 1848, 1855)	Violin Rehearsal Score II (1873)	Violin Rehearsal Score III (1893)
663 - 665 Groupe		
666 - 675 il s'arrache des bras de la séduction.		
676 - 678 P.d bras -	676 - 677 Port de bras	
679 - Att.	678 - 679 Pirouette = Att. ♪ (2 Bras)	
680 - 682 retournez - Att penchée	680 Tournez ↷	
683 & Groupe	681 - 683 arabesque - pliée. - relevé ☉	
684 - 686 à droite & à gauche	684 - 685 2 Vink [2 Waves] cp - att. à reculons.	684 - 685 2 Vink [2 Waves] cp: Att à reculon [sic] til Robert ? [to Robert ?]
687 - 690 promenade - developpé... & p.d.b.	686 - 687 Bis -	686 - 694 [notes as in Violin Rehearsal Score II]
691 - 707 [originally cut (in 1833?)]	688 - 690 P.d.bras ↷ - Developpé ✓ p.d.b. - & Groupe	
691 - 692 gl. attitude bis	691 - 692 Cp - gl - att. Bis - chassé ∸ cp - btm. ↷	
693 - 695 gl. en remontant 2 fois 3.me	693 - 694 Bis à gauche	
696 - 697 cp. btms. - Att: suppliante	695 - 696 cp ∸ gl. - att en rem. 2 fois - cp. btm ♩	695 - 696 cp ∸ gl - Att en rem: 2 fois cp. btm ✓
	697 - Att suppliante	697 ♩ 69 Att: supplecante [sic] (bedende) [entreating]

Violin Rehearsal Score I
(1833, 1848, 1855)

698 - 700   bis - encore

701 - 707   Att: penchée - tournez assemblé soutenu promenade - à genoux & p.d.b. -

708 - 711   cp. brisé - att: bis - assemblé entr à 4 cp. - p.d.b. -

712 - 715   bis -

715 - 719   p.d.b. degagées. 3 Att: en rem. -

720 - 728   r.d. jambes retournez (à genoux) avancez vers lui - & Att: finale fin -

729 - 741   Robert:

Violin Rehearsal Score II
(1873)

698   cp. - btm ↑

699 - 700   Att. suppliante

701 - 702   Cp. - penchée ↘ à deux Bras. -

703 - 704   Assemblé - soutenu ⌒ .. Att - à la lyre.

705 - 707   tournez & terminez à genou - relevé ☉ & Groupe.

708 - 728   [no notes]

729 - 737   Robert föres hen til Moderens Grav, de vise ham den fortryllende Gren, [Robert is led to the Mother's grave, they show him the enchanted bough]

Violin Rehearsal Score III
(1893)

698   cp. btm ↘

699 - 700   Att suppliante [sic]

701 - 707   [notes as in Violin Rehearsal Score II]

708 - 711   brisé cp > bis - Ass ent. 4 - relevé, ☉ & p.d.b.

712 - 715   Bis à gauche

716 - 717   p.d.b. ⌣ 3 fois

718 - 719   Att: enlevées en rem:

720   R.d.j.

721 - 726   Tournez & terminez à genou......

727   tournez s.l.p. & arriver vers lui

728   Att: supplecante [sic] finale
         Emil Hansen
         Robert

729 - 760   [notes as in Violin Rehearsal Score II]

Violin Rehearsal Score I (1833, 1848, 1855)	Violin Rehearsal Score II (1873)	Violin Rehearsal Score III (1893)
	738 - 740 som han efter nogen Vaklen griber [which he grabs after some hesitation]	
	741 - 744 Han gaaer frem og Nonnerne omringe ham i vild Glæde [He advances and the Nuns surround him with wild delight]	
742 - 744 (le rameau)		
745 - 752 les dames l'entournent	745 - 752 de dandse rundt om ham. - [they dance around him. -]	
753 - 756 elles lui menacent	753 - 760 Han bryder igjennem og iler ud K.S. medens Nonnerne gaae fremad triumpherende [He breaks through and rushes off at Stage right while the Nuns advance triumphantly]	
757 - 776 (1.er pas)	761 - 768 Dæmonerne fra D.S. omringe Nonnerne der samle sig forskrækkede i Midten - De rive dem særskildt til sig. [The Demons from Stage left surround the Nuns, who gather terrified in the center - they [the demons] tug them apart one at a time.]	761 - 795 Dæmonerne fra D.S. omringe Nonnerne der samle sig forskrækkede i midten - De rive dem særskildt til sig.
	769 - 795 kaste dem fra den ene Arm i den Anden svinge dem truende rundt og danne en vild Kjæde der slutter med en dæmonisk Gruppe oplyst af röde Flammer. [they toss them from one embrace to another, swing them menacingly around and perform a wild chain dance, which ends in a demonic group illuminated by red flames]	hver Dæmon har 2 Nonner. [each Demon has 2 nuns.]
777 - 780 gl. relevé gl. relevé bis 4.ième		
781 - 795 bis à l'autre [côté] - & -att: finales....		

APPENDIX E

The Original Danish and French Texts

This appendix contains the original versions of the French and Danish texts quoted.

Page 6:
"Le décor change et représente le cloître aux voûtes sombres et profondes, le caveau sépulchral des nonnes de Sainte-Rosalie. La décoration musicale change aussi: les trombones et l'ophicléide sonnet è l'unisson; leur voix solennelle et funèbre annonce l'arrivée de Bertam; un concert de violoncelles et de bassons unit son harmonie triste et sévère au récitatif obligé chanté par cet esprit de ténèbre. Cette invocation est de la plus grande beauté:

Pour une heure, quittez vitre lit funéraire;
Nonnes, relevez-vous!

Et les nonnes, obéissant au pouvoir discrétionnaire de leur président, se relèvent et reprennent peu è peu une existence éphémère, et, comme le diable ne leur rend pas la faculté de parler, dans la crainte qu'il ne leur prît fantaisie de nous raconter leurs vies, elles restent silencieuses et laissent à l'orchestre le soin de peindre leurs sentimens, de donner une seconde interprétation à leurs gestes en s'unissant à leur pantomine expressive. Le chant instrumental frappe seul l'oreille pendant cette longue et belle scène, et son charme, ses images pittoresques, ses couleurs variées, ses détails pleins d'esprit et de vigueur de sentiment font sur l'âme une sensation profonde. Le prestige de la musique vient accroître dans une progression immense le prestige de la décoration et les séduction de la pantomine.

Les nonnes se relèvent, et les bassons seuls font entendre un chant dont la mélodie ascendante suit le mouvement des statues qui décrivent lentement un quart de cercle pour arriver à la position perpendiculaire. Le *pizzicato* des contrebasses, les trombones en sourdine suivent la route mystérieuse que les bassons ont tracée. L'orchestre s'anime peu à peu par l'entrée succesive de tous les instrumens; le ton mineur, qui a regné pendant tout le tems de cette opération galvanique et fantastique, est remplacé tout à coup par un ensemble éclatante en *ut majeur*, et le bécarre posé sur le *mi* signale aux moins intelligens la vitalité de ces dames, et nous avertit qu'elles sont de nouveau des femmes du monde. Les nonnes savent qu'elles n'ont que cinquante-neuf minutes de congé; elles n'en sont pas plus tristes, et s'empressent de profiter du bon temps que messire Lucifer veut bien leur accorder. Ces joyeuses soeurs commencent par ôter leur voiles et leur longues robes, elles ne gardent qu'une légère tunique. Chacune court à son cellier y prendre coupes et flacons; ce cellier, c'est leur tombeau; le viin doit être frais. Elles avalent à longs traits le vin de Chypre ou de Val-de-Pegnas pour se rafraîchir la bouche, où les araignées ont peut-être tissu des toiles: cela donne du coeur à la danse, et les voilà pirouettant comme des toupies, dansant des rondes et la farandoule, se démenant comme des possédés. Cette galope, sur un six-huit en *ré mineur*, avec acompagnement de triangle, et dont l'effet est entraînant, et toutes ces joyeusetés se passent nécessairement dans la nuit du sépulcre.." [signed "X.X.X."]

Page 8:
7.8.1831: "Le 7. j'ai été entendre chez Mayer Beer la musique qu'il a composé pour les danses de Robert le Diable"
20.8: "Le 20 j'ai été chez Mayer Beer il m'a fait entendre la musique de la scène de seduction des nonnes de R le D destinée à ma fille, cette musique est charmante"
6.10: "Le 6. 1.er répétition de la scène des nonnes"
15.10: "Le 15 j'ai présenté à ma fille [...] Mayer Beer"
22.10: "répétition de la scène des nonnes avec les costumes cela n'a pas marché comme je l'aurai voulu, j'ai commencé l'entrée de Robert (Nourrit)"
31.10: "commencé avec ma fille la scène de séduction."
6.11: "6 répétition des nonnes avec Nourrit, Marie a pleuré parce que la répétition l'avait trop fatiguer [sic]"
21.11: "21 novembre 1.er représentation de Robert de Diable [...] Au changement de la grotte au cloître, le rideau nuage, qui monte pendant que se fait le changement du décors, les cordes qui le tenassit [sic] ce rideaux [sic] rejoint été accrochée en croix se sont brissée, et toute la toile est tombé sur le tombeau ou était couché ma fille, qui heureusement s'était sauvée[...]"

"J'ose espérer, Monsieur, de votre équité et de l'intérêt que vous portez aux auteurs qu'à partir de Lundi vous ne donnez plus "Robert" sans Melle Taglioni. Comme dans ma conviction particulière je crois Mlle Taglioni indispensable pour le succès complet de cet ouvrage, j'y tiens de coeur et d'âme et j'y insiste d'autant plus que le règlement et mon traité m'y autorisent formellement."

Page 13:
30.12.1847, 4.1, 5.1, and 6.1.1848: "Prøve paa Robert"
7.1: "Prøve paa Robert fra 10 til 2 ½"
17.1: "Prøve med Övelse paa Robert"
18.1: "Dands i Robert. Operaen gik særdeles godt."

2.7.1855: "Besøg hos Directeuren, hjertelig Modtagelse overalt. Strax afgjort at Juliette Price skulde debutere den 12.e Juli som Helene i Robert le Diable"
4.7: "Prøve paa Robert [...] Componeret Juliettes Dands"
19.7: "Prøve paa Burgtheatret Kl. 8 Robert som gik fortreffeligt"
20.7: "Prøve paa B Theatret Kl. 8. Det gik udmærket"
21.7: "Kl. 8-11 Generalprøve paa Robert le diable. Juliette udførte Helenes Parti, det jik udmærket godt og Mange yttrede stor Tilfredshed dermed."
23.7: "Robert af Normandiet. Juliettes første Debuts. Hun præsterede ganske udmærket, men nød kun en kold Modtagelse. Det kunde ikke andet end nedslaae os Noget, men vi fattede dog snart Mod igjen, da vi fik Vished om at hun ikke havde mishaget, men kun frapperet ved det højst forskjellige i hendes hele Methode fremfor det, som man er vant til at see her. Vi haabe bedre Lykke for Fremtiden. Pigebarnet viste ved denne Leilighed en fortreffelig Characteer".

Page 14:
2.10.1872: "skrevet og studeret paa Dandsen til Robert"
3.10: "Componeret Dandsen til Robert"
7.10: "Prøve paa [...] Robert"
10.10: "Indstudering paa Dandsen til Robert"
1.11: "Costumemøde paa Robert"
10.12: "Prøve paa Robert"
13.12: "Eftermiddagsprøve paa 1.e og 3.e Akt af Robert"
14.12: "Prøve paa Dandsen til [...] Robert"
15.12. and 16.12: "Instructionsprøve paa Robert"
17.12: "Prøve paa 3.e Akt af Robert [...] skrevet, læst og componeret"
18.12: "Regieforretninger [...] Instructionsprøve paa Robert 4' og 5' Akt"
19.12: "Arrangement paa 1. ste og 2. Akt af Robert"
20.12: "Arrangementsprøve paa Robert 3.e og 4.e Akt (min Gravscene gik udmaerket smukt)"
30.12: "Prøve paa Gravscenen i Robert"
2.1.1873: "Prøve paa de to forste Akter af Robert [...] skrevet og componeret"
3.1: "Prøve paa Robert 3.e og 4.e Akt med Orchester [...] componeret"
4.1: "componeret og holdt Aftenprøve paa Robert"
5.1: "skrevet og componeret"
8.1: "Lille Prøve med Westberg"
9.1: "Prøve paa Robert 1.e - 2. og 4.e Akt"
10.1: "Prøve pa 3.de og 5.te Akt af Robert"
13.1: "Prøve paa hele Robert (Westberg dandsede overordentlig)"
15.1: "Prøve paa hele Robert"
17.1: "Generalprøve paa Robert, der gik særdeles smukt"
19.1: "I Theatret Robert af Normandiet, der gik udmærket godt, og for brilliant Huus (Westberg udførte sit Partie fortræffeligt)"
21.1: "overværet 2' Forestilling af Robert der gik meget smukt, for brilliant Huus men et dvask Publicum"

G. Meyerbeer's Notes in his Musical Drafts

The original of Meyerbeer's notes given in Appendix B:

[Bertram:] Nonnes m'entendez vous nonnes relevez vous
<u>Les Feux folets volent sur les tombeaux</u>
Les Tombeaux s'ouvrent. Procession des nonnes.
[...] (Le théâtre s'claire)
<u>Bachanale</u>
Les fem[m]es apercoivent Robert, & restent immobiles.

APPENDIX E 189

Les non[n]es voient de loin Robert & se cachent
Entrée de Robert qui ne voit pas les non[n]es = Recitatif: il veut cueillir le rameau, mais recule effrayé (dernier vers de Recitatif)
[...] Les Nonnes lui présentent des coupes, boivent alterna., & lui offrent à boire.
Robert refuse de boire: Lea reproche aux Nonnes leurs manières lestes: C'est ainsi qu'il faut s'y prendre semble-t-elle leur dire, en s'approchant de Robert qu'elle agaie [?] : Robert parait frappé de ses charmes, et la contemple avec ravissement.
Lea offre à boire à Robert
Robert boit: les non[n]es l'entourent en dansant & lui montrent le rameau (*) Si M.r Taglioni trouve ce morceau trop long, on peut couper ce qui est entre les deux (*)
(*) Silence
Robert s'approche lentement le rameau: les Nonnes rient à part entre elles Robert recule épouvanté
Les nonnes consultent entre elles[s]:
Lea et les Nonnes cherchent à entraîner Robert sur leurs pas, & le conduisent en dansant à l'endroit ou l'on joue
Les Nonnes jouent
Robert va lentement vers le rameau: les Nonnes rient à part.
Robert recule epouvanté
Lea dit à Robert: lâche Chevalier, est-ce la ton courage? - tu me fais [word illegible]! je vais ceuillir le rameau pour toi!: mais pas [?] après, car je te méprise
Robert semble répondre: Arrête: je me décide à le cueillir: c'était le souvenir de ma mère qui m'a épouvanté: mais laisse moi remettre de mon trouble: Lea fait assire Robert pre d'elle et appelle ses compagnes.
Lea et sa suite entourent Robert en formant continuellement des groupes autour de lui
M.lle Montesssu et sa suite s'emparent à leur tour de Robert, et l'entourent en dansant.
(M.lle Taglioni) (M.lle Montessu) (M.lle Taglioni) (M.lle Montessu)
(Robert) (M.lle Taglioni) Groupes autour de Robert & Lea pendant ce dialogue (M.lle Montessu) (M.lle Taglioni)
Entraîné peu à peu par les groupes Robert est arrivé au pied de la statue sans s'en apercevoir
Robert enflammé jusqu'au délire par les scènes précédentes fait signe qu'il va cueillir le rameau
Robert cueille le rameau Tonnere: Transformation
La Statue de la Sainte se brise.
<u>Choeur</u> (danse triomphale autour de Robert)
[...]
La toile tombe.
Si ce Morceau est trop long Mr. Taglioni peut couper ce que se trouve entre les deux signes #

Extract from L. Palianti's Manuscript Staging Manual

Page 23:
Les religieuses sont entrées silencieusement à très petits pas; plusieurs groupes même lissent sur des trappes à coulisses et arrivent ainsi en scène de tous les côtés du cloître; celles qui étaient couchées sur les tombes en descendent également st elles formant le <u>chartron</u> (sic) autour de <u>Bertram</u> dont elles attendent les ordres, et il se retire.

Alors elles rentrent dans les coulisses en un instant se dépouillent de leurs robes de religieuses, et paraissent en simples jupons et corsages de mousseline, jambes et bras couverts de maillots couleur de chair, chéveux en désordre et longs; elles se livrent à leurs jeux et à leurs passions profanes. Mais elles entendent que <u>Robert</u> s;approche et elles se cachent derrière les colonnes, les tombes. <u>Robert</u> arrive du fond et ne peut se défendre d'une secrète horreur; il parcout ce lieu silencieux, vient au tombeau de <u>S.te Rosalie</u>, veut fuir, et tout à coup il est entouré d'un essaim de femmes qui le contemplent avec admiration et veulent le séduire. Toutes lui tendent piège, deux entre autres et <u>l'abbesse</u> cherchent à le séduire, forment des pas voluptueux autour de lui; il les fuit, elles lui font horreur; d'autres l'entrainent près du premier tombeau, à droite du public, lui offrant de jouer aux dez; <u>l'abbesse</u> s'attache à lui, lui peint l'armour, ses voluptés, lui montre le tombeau de sa mère, le rameau vert, et après tant de séductions elle se baisse voluptueusement, il se laisse entraîner, l'embrasse au font et va s'empare du rameau.

Aussitôt les bruits de l'enfer se font entendre; les feux sillonnent le monastère; le bruit des grosses chaînes se fait entendre, les femmes dansent en rond autour de lui, elles parcourent ensuite la galerie, se tenant toutes par la main; il s'echappe alors par le fond.

<u>Les nonnes</u> se livrent un instant à de nouvelles folies. Mais les bruits de l'enfer se font entendre ainsi que celui des exorcismes - <u>Des démons apparaissent</u>, plusieurs nonnes sont saisies par ceux-ci qui secouent leurs torches ardentes, et toutes tombent mortes à l'instant.
Pendent cette dernière action un choeur infernal s'est fait entendre, et des diables ont parsouru les lieux - les plus reculés du monument.

APPENDIX F

Notes on Adjustments Made for the Reconstruction

The Ballet of the Nuns was originally part of a five-act opera. It must be assumed that Bournonville's notes recorded the ballet as it was in that context. Consequently, the first transcription of his notes into Labanotation was of this 'opera version'. However, because of the significance of this ballet as an entity in its own right, it was felt desirable to present and record it outside of the context of the opera, as a work that could presented on its own. To produce this independent 'dance version' some modifications obviously needed to be made. Reference to these changes is to be found in **The Task of Reconstruction**, page 15. Passages in the ballet for which Bournonville did not provide enough information have not been included; there being no reason to create new choreography or mime passages for inclusion in this book.

Bournonville's notes concentrated mainly on the step patterns and overall design; frequently no specific arm gestures were included. However, with the knowledge of his use of *ports de bras* in his own ballets which stem from the same period, appropriate arm gestures were added to make a more complete picture of the dance. Of course, for all the instances where Bournonville specified the arm positions or movements, these have been incorporated in the score. With the experience of three stage productions of this ballet I was able to make the necessary decisions as to which were the most appropriate arm gestures and upper body and head movements to include. It is the result of these collective staging experiences which have been recorded in Labanotation.

Knud Arne Jürgensen

APPENDIX G

The Piano Score

The complete piano score by A. Pixis for the Act III finale of *Robert le Diable*,
Berlin, Schlesinger (Rob. Lienau), pl. no. S. 6656.
(Royal Library of Copenhagen, call no. KTA 303 [Instruktørpartier]).

The six cuts made by Bournonville in the music
for the Act III ballet are here marked with deletions.

Nº 15. FINALE.
A. Beschwörungsscene.
Scène et évocation.

SCÈNE ET ÉVOCATION

194 ROBERT LE DIABLE - THE BALLET OF THE NUNS

Prozession der Nonnen.
Procession des Nonnes.

Andante sostenuto.

B. Bachanale.

Bertram's Wille hat den Instinkt der Leidenschaften den bis dahin unbeseelten Körpern wieder gegeben. Die Nonnen erkennen sich wieder und bezeugen sich ihre Freude darüber. Helena, die Oberin, ladet sie ein, die Augenblicke zu benutzen, und sich dem Vergnügen zu überlassen. Dieser Befehl wird auf der Stelle erfüllt. Die Nonnen nehmen Gegenstände ihrer profanen Neigungen aus den Grübern, Becher, Würfel und dergleichen. Einige von ihnen bringen einem Idole Opfer, andere schürzen ihre langen Gewänder und setzen sich Cypressen-Kränze auf, um leichter tanzen zu können. Bald artet das Ganze in ein rauschendes Bachanal aus.

La volonté de Bertram a rendu l'instinct des passions à ces corps naguère inanimés. Les Nonnes après s'être reconnues se témoignent le contentement de se revoir. Héléna, la supérieure les invite à profiter des instants et à se livrer au plaisir; cet ordre aussitôt est exécuté. Les Nonnes tirent des tombeaux les objets de leurs passions profanes; des amphores, des coupes, des dés sont retrouvés. Quelques unes font des offrandes à une idole: tandis que d'autres rattachent leurs longues robes et se parent la tête de couronnes de cyprès pour se livrer à la danse avec plus de légèreté. Bientôt elles n'écoutent plus que l'attrait du plaisir, et la danse devient une Bachanale ardente.

Erste Balletweise.
Verführung durch Trunkenheit.
Die Nonnen bieten Robert Becher an, indem sie ihn umtanzen und selbst begierig trinken.

1er Air de Ballet.
Séduction par l'ivresse.
Les Nonnes présentent des coupes à Robert en dansant autour de lui, et boivent elles-mêmes à longs traits.

(Robert weigert sich zu trinken.)
(Robert refuse de boire.)
502
(Helena wirft den Nonnen ihre zu freie Weise vor, nähert sich Robert und sucht ihn durch anmuthige Stellungen zu verführen.)
(Héléna, reprochant aux Nonnes leurs manières lestes, s'approche de Robert, et par ses poses gracieuses cherche à le séduire.)
Un poco meno mosso.
507
513
(Robert betrachtet Helena mit Bewunderung.)
(Robert contemple Héléna avec admiration.)
519
524
(Robert nimmt den Becher an, den ihm Helena beut und trinkt.)
(Robert accepte la coupe qu'Héléna lui offre et boit.)
528

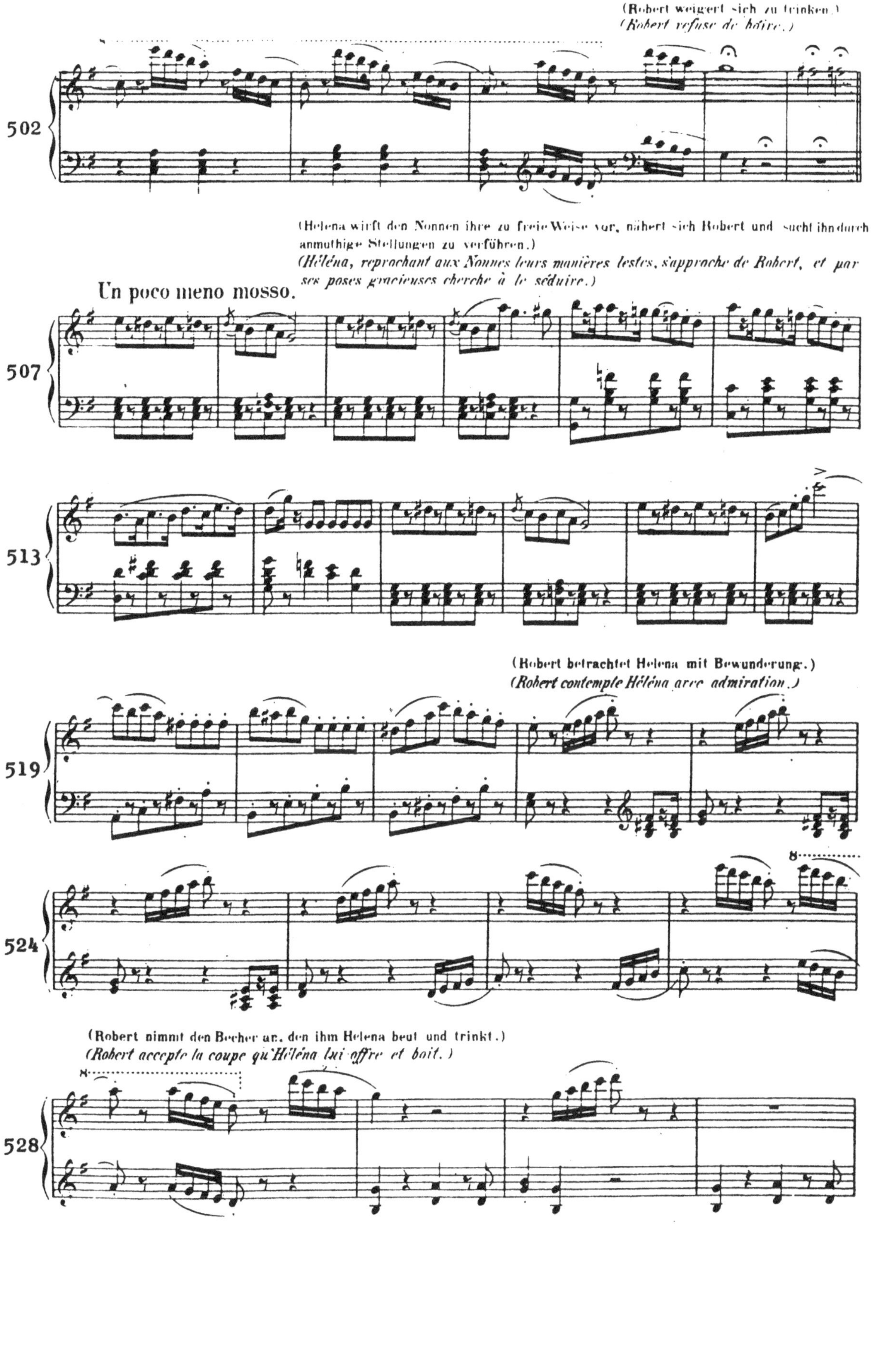

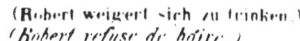

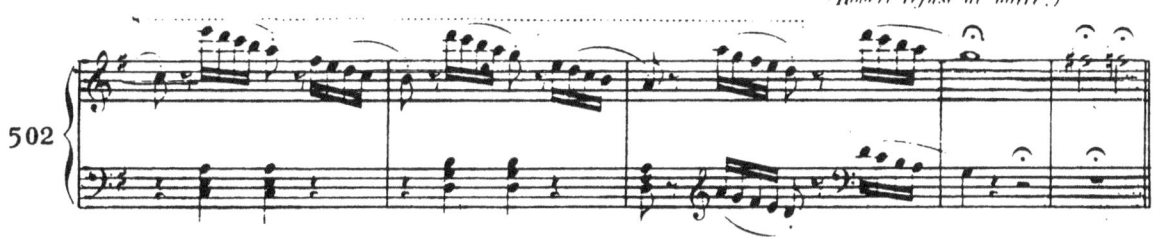

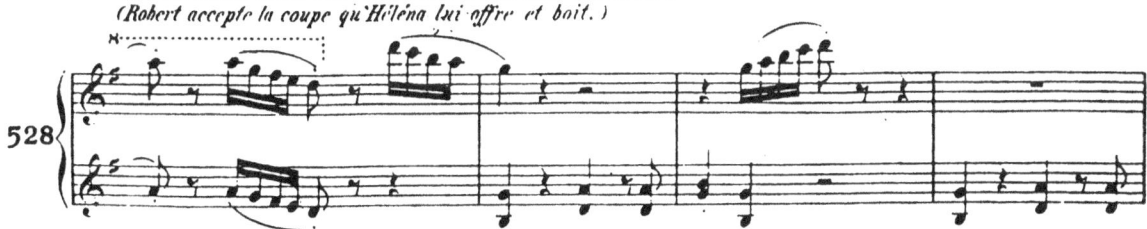

211

(E)

Zweite Balletweise.
Verführung durch Spiel.

Helena und die Nonnen suchen von neuem Robert's Leidenschaften zu erregen

2me Air de Ballet.
Séduction du jeu.

Hélèna et les Nonnes cherchent de nouveau à exciter les passions de Robert.

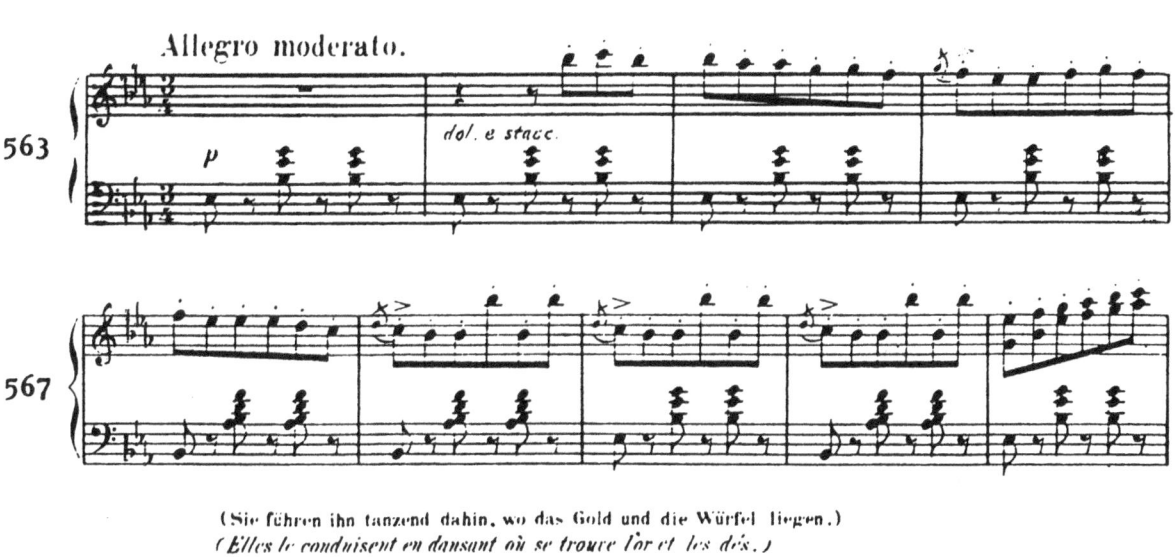

(Sie führen ihn tanzend dahin, wo das Gold und die Würfel liegen.)
(Elles le conduisent en dansant où se trouve l'or et les dés.)

2ᴹᴱ AIR DE BALLET

214

(F)

Dritte Balletweise.
Verführung durch Liebe.
Pas de seul der Helena.

3ᵐᵉ Air de Ballet.
Séduction de l'amour.
Pas de seul d'Héléna.

Andantino cantabile.

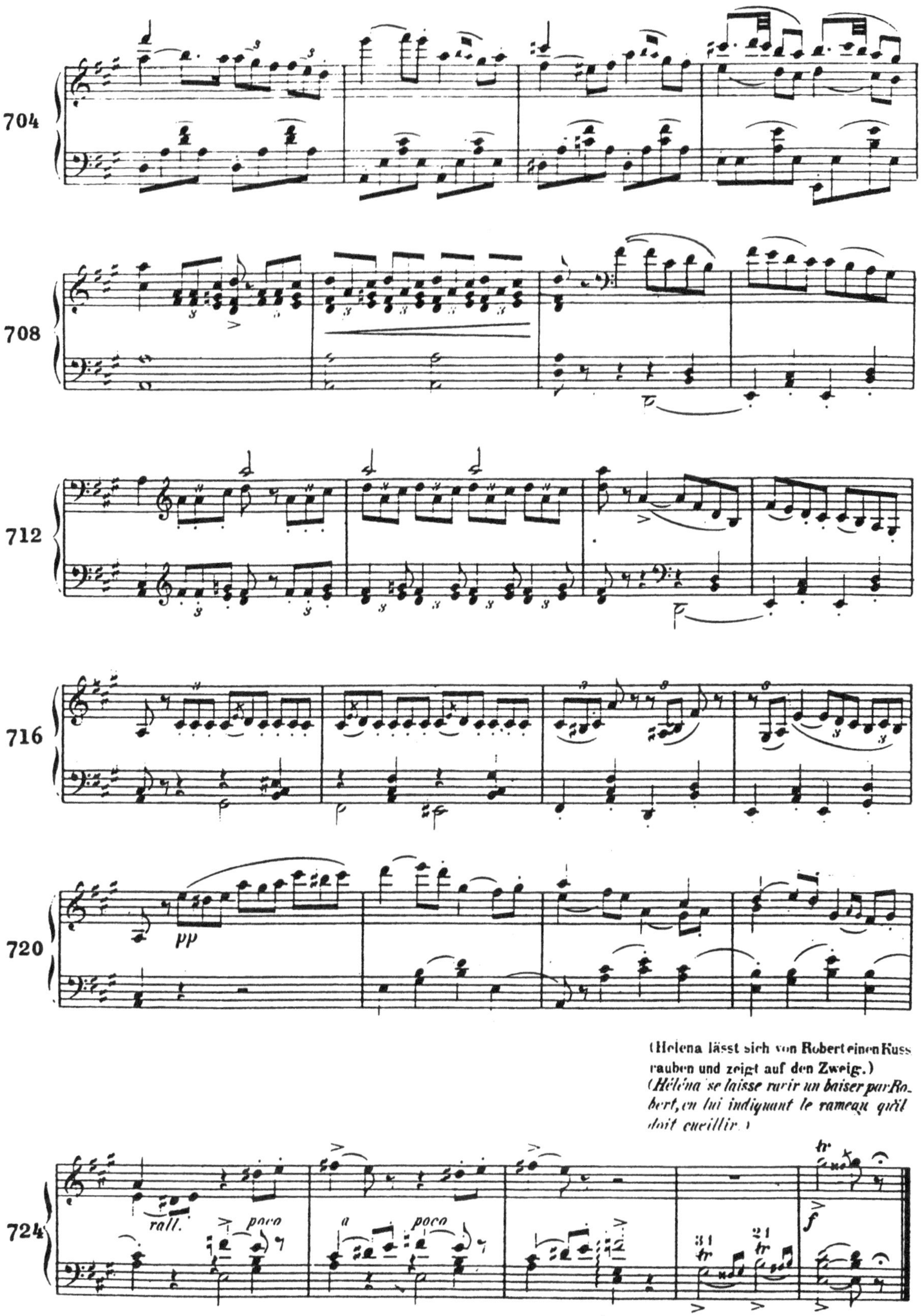

3ᴹᴱ AIR DE BALLET

(Helena lässt sich von Robert einen Kuss rauben und zeigt auf den Zweig.)
(Héléna se laisse ravir un baiser par Robert, en lui indiquant le rameau qu'il doit cueillir.)

216

(G)

Chor mit Tanz.   **Chœur dansé.**

Im Augenblick, wo Robert den Zweig bricht, ertönt der Donner, die Nonnen verwandeln sich in Gespenster, und Dämonen steigen aus der Erde herauf. Alles dreht sich um ihn in unregelmässigen Kreisen. Er bahnt sich mit seinem Zweige einen Weg durch die Gestalten.

Au moment où Robert cueille le rameau, le tonnerre éclate, les Nonnes se changent en spectres, et des démons sortent de dessous terre, tous forment autour de lui en dansant une chaîne désordonnée. Il se fraye un chemin parmi ces spectres en agitant son rameau.

www.ingramcontent.com/pod-product-compliance
Lightning Source LLC
Chambersburg PA
CBHW081107080526
44587CB00021B/3484